Feasting on the Word®

LENTEN COMPANION

ALSO AVAILABLE FROM
WESTMINSTER JOHN KNOX PRESS

Feasting on the Word Advent Companion

Feasting on the Word®
LENTEN COMPANION

A THEMATIC RESOURCE
FOR PREACHING AND WORSHIP

EDITED BY

David L. Bartlett

Barbara Brown Taylor

Kimberly Bracken Long

COMPILED BY

Jessica Miller Kelley

WJK WESTMINSTER
JOHN KNOX PRESS
LOUISVILLE · KENTUCKY

© 2014 Westminster John Knox Press

First edition
Published by Westminster John Knox Press
Louisville, Kentucky

14 15 16 17 18 19 20 21 22 23—10 9 8 7 6 5 4 3 2 1

Scripture quotations from the New Revised Standard Version of the Bible are copyright © 1989 by the Division of Christian Education of the National Council of the Churches of Christ in the U.S.A. and are used by permission.

Liturgical text herein originally appeared in Kimberly Bracken Long's *Feasting on the Word Worship Companion* (Louisville, KY: Westminster John Knox Press, 2012–2015). Permission is granted to churches to reprint individual prayers and liturgical texts for worship provided that the following notice is included: Reprinted by permission of Westminster John Knox Press from *Feasting on the Word® Lenten Companion*. Copyright 2014.

Devotional text herein originally appeared in David L. Bartlett and Barbara Brown Taylor's *Feasting on the Word, Complete 12-Volume Set* (Louisville, KY: Westminster John Knox Press, 2008–2011).

Book design by Drew Stevens
Cover design by Lisa Buckley and Dilu Nicholas

Library of Congress Cataloging-in-Publication Data

Feasting on the word Lenten companion : thematic resources for
preaching and worship / compiled by Jessica Miller Kelley.
— First edition.
   pages cm
   ISBN 978-0-664-25965-5 (alk. paper)
   1. Lent—Meditations. 2. Worship programs. 3. Common lectionary
(1992) I. Kelley, Jessica Miller, compiler.
   BV85.F385 2014
   263'.92—dc23

                                                          2014029782

PRINTED IN THE UNITED STATES OF AMERICA

∞ The paper used in this publication meets the minimum requirements
of the American National Standard for Information Sciences—Permanence of Paper
for Printed Library Materials, ANSI Z39.48-1992.

Westminster John Knox Press advocates the responsible use of our natural resources. The text paper of this book is made from 30% post-consumer waste.

Most Westminster John Knox Press books are available at special quantity discounts when purchased in bulk by corporations, organizations, and special-interest groups. For more information, please e-mail SpecialSales@wjkbooks.com.

Contents

TRIDUUM

Introduction

Easter is the highest holy day of the Christian faith, but to celebrate it in a vacuum, without immersion in all that comes before the resurrection—both chronologically and theologically—robs the day of its true significance. Lent can be a hard sell for many worshipers, with its intentional solemnity and encouragement toward self-denial. Others find it to be the most meaningful time of year—the most honest time of year, when we wrestle with the hard things of life and walk with Jesus through the darkest days of his life as well.

Feasting on the Word Lenten Companion offers an alternative and supplement to the Revised Common Lectionary for the Sundays and other significant days of Lent. In keeping with other *Feasting on the Word* resources, the *Lenten Companion* offers pastors focused resources for sermon preparation, ready-to-use liturgies for a complete order of worship, and hymn suggestions to support each day's scriptural and theological focus. Four essays provide exegetical, theological, homiletical, and pastoral perspectives on an Old Testament and a Gospel text for each Sunday. These essays are written by scholars, pastors, seminary professors, and denominational leaders, offering a bounty of starting points for the preacher to consider. The resources in this volume are a combination of material from existing *Feasting on the Word* volumes and newly written material.

The Gospel text for each Sunday features an encounter Jesus had during his public ministry and invites us into our own encounters with Jesus during the Lenten season. Complementary Old Testament passages enhance themes presented in the Gospel texts. A children's sermon is also included for each service to make the themes and texts of Lent accessible to all ages in the congregation, enriching the experience of worship with stories that respect both a child's intelligence and theological integrity. A liturgy for Holy Eucharist is included in the Holy Thursday service. This liturgy can also be incorporated where appropriate in Sunday services, depending on your congregation's worship patterns.

Holy Thursday, Good Friday, and Holy Saturday services provide the essential bridge between Palm Sunday and Easter and include liturgies and a sample homily based on traditional texts for those holy days.

Finally, to expand and enhance the congregation's experience of Lent, midweek services (beginning with Ash Wednesday and concluding with Wednesday of Holy Week) are also provided in this volume. These abbreviated liturgies and sample homilies are ideal for use in an existing midweek worship or Bible study gathering or a special series offered just for the weeks of Lent. These resources may also offer additional inspiration for planning Sunday worship.

Overview of Lent

Lent is a time of self-reflection and penitence, a time to acknowledge our sinfulness and need for God's mercy. From the church's earliest days, Lent was a time of preparation for baptism of new converts and penitence leading to the reconciliation of those estranged from the community.

Mirroring the forty days of Jesus' temptation in the wilderness (which itself mirrored forty-day periods of trial experienced by Noah, Moses, and Elijah), the season of Lent begins forty-six days before Easter Sunday. Because every Sunday was to be a celebration of the resurrection and therefore not a day of fasting, the Sundays of Lent are not included in the forty penitential days of Lent.

On Ash Wednesday, Christians are invited to enter a period of self-examination, repentance, prayer, fasting, and self-denial. We are called to use these forty days as a time of reflection on our sins, the ways that we separate ourselves from God and from one another. Thus it is easy to characterize Lent as the somber, solemn period of the church year, but there is also joy to be found in the journey. The juxtapositions of mortality and eternity, sin and grace, death and life, make the path to Jesus' cross and tomb a rugged, rewarding terrain.

Lent can be a dangerous time. People come to the church looking for discipline and a new way to live; they come to be challenged—prepared for the heartache and joy of the cross to come. The fallacy of Lent can occur when we contain the season to six weeks of intentionality and introspection rather than building a Lent that becomes a life.

It is dangerous to meet Jesus in the dark places, to ask the same questions of ourselves that Jesus asks of his disciples, to accept Jesus' radical touch. In these moments of utter truth and honesty, we find ourselves vulnerable enough to connect with the risen Christ as never before.

Weekly Texts and Themes

	Old Testament	Gospel	Theme
First Sunday of Lent	Num. 21:4–9 (the bronze serpent)	John 3:1–21 (Nicodemus comes to Jesus at night)	Jesus offers salvation; the value of seeking, questioning, and openness
Second Sunday of Lent	Exod. 17:1–7 (water from the rock)	John 4:1–42 (Samaritan woman at the well meets Jesus)	Jesus provides living water; God's provision
Third Sunday of Lent	Isa. 35:4–7a (phrophecy of a messiah who heals)	John 9:1–41 (a blind man is healed by Jesus)	Jesus brings healing; compassion is more important than rules
Fourth Sunday of Lent	Ezek. 37:1–14 (Ezekiel prophesies to dry bones)	John 11:1–46 (Lazarus is raised from the dead)	Jesus gives life even where there is death; hope in the midst of despair
Fifth Sunday of Lent	1 Kgs. 17:8–16 (Elijah and the widow's oil that does not run out)	John 12:1–11 (Mary of Bethany anoints Jesus' feet)	Jesus loves abundantly and invites us to love abundantly too
Sixth Sunday of Lent	1 Sam. 16:1–13 (anointing the boy David)	John 13:1–17, 34–35 (Jesus washes Peter's feet)	Jesus reverses expectations; God exalts the lowly and humbles the proud
Easter Sunday	Isa. 65:17–25 (a new heaven and a new earth)	John 20:1–18 (Mary Magdalene meets the risen Christ)	Jesus triumphs over death; the kingdom has come

Texts for Midweek Services

	Focus Texts	Theme
Week One (Ash Wednesday)	Isa. 58:1–12 (the fast God chooses)	Fasting for justice
Week Two	Matt. 6:1–6, 16–21 (beware of practicing piety before others)	Fasting in humility
Week Three	Josh. 5:2–12 (new food for the promised land)	Fasting as appreciation
Week Four	Luke 4:1–13 (Jesus' fasting and temptation in the wilderness)	Fasting in faith
Week Five	Joel 2:1–2, 12–17 (rend your hearts and not your clothing)	Fasting as repentance
Week Six	Acts 11:1–12 (Peter's vision of clean and unclean foods)	Fasting for reconciliation
Week Seven	Exod. 12:1–14 (Passover and its commemoration)	Fasting as redemption

Triduum Texts

	Old Testament	Gospel	Theme
Holy Thursday	Isa. 50:4–9	John 13:1–2, 20–32	Jesus is betrayed
Good Friday	Isa. 52:13–53:12	John 18:28–19:30	Jesus is killed
Holy Saturday	Job 14:1–14	John 19:38–42	Jesus is dead

First Sunday of Lent

Numbers 21:4–9

⁴From Mount Hor they set out by the way to the Red Sea, to go around the land of Edom; but the people became impatient on the way. ⁵The people spoke against God and against Moses, "Why have you brought us up out of Egypt to die in the wilderness? For there is no food and no water, and we detest this miserable food." ⁶Then the LORD sent poisonous serpents among the people, and they bit the people, so that many Israelites died. ⁷The people came to Moses and said, "We have sinned by speaking against the LORD and against you; pray to the LORD to take away the serpents from us." So Moses prayed for the people. ⁸And the LORD said to Moses, "Make a poisonous serpent, and set it on a pole; and everyone who is bitten shall look at it and live." ⁹So Moses made a serpent of bronze, and put it upon a pole; and whenever a serpent bit someone, that person would look at the serpent of bronze and live.

John 3:1–21

¹Now there was a Pharisee named Nicodemus, a leader of the Jews. ²He came to Jesus by night and said to him, "Rabbi, we know that you are a teacher who has come from God; for no one can do these signs that you do apart from the presence of God." ³Jesus answered him, "Very truly, I tell you, no one can see the kingdom of God without being born from above." ⁴Nicodemus said to him, "How can anyone be born after having grown old? Can one enter a second time into the mother's womb and be born?" ⁵Jesus answered, "Very truly, I tell you, no one can enter the kingdom of God without being born of water and Spirit. ⁶What is born of the flesh is flesh, and what is born of the Spirit is spirit. ⁷Do not be astonished that I said to you, 'You must be born from above.' ⁸The wind blows where it chooses, and you hear the sound of it, but you do not know where it comes from or where it goes. So it is with everyone who is born of the Spirit." ⁹Nicodemus said to him, "How can these things be?" ¹⁰Jesus answered him, "Are you a teacher of Israel, and yet you do not understand these things?

¹¹"Very truly, I tell you, we speak of what we know and testify to what we have seen; yet you do not receive our testimony. ¹²If I have told you about

earthly things and you do not believe, how can you believe if I tell you about heavenly things? [13]No one has ascended into heaven except the one who descended from heaven, the Son of Man. [14]And just as Moses lifted up the serpent in the wilderness, so must the Son of Man be lifted up, [15]that whoever believes in him may have eternal life.

[16]"For God so loved the world that he gave his only Son, so that everyone who believes in him may not perish but may have eternal life.

[17]"Indeed, God did not send the Son into the world to condemn the world, but in order that the world might be saved through him. [18]Those who believe in him are not condemned; but those who do not believe are condemned already, because they have not believed in the name of the only Son of God. [19]And this is the judgment, that the light has come into the world, and people loved darkness rather than light because their deeds were evil. [20]For all who do evil hate the light and do not come to the light, so that their deeds may not be exposed. [21]But those who do what is true come to the light, so that it may be clearly seen that their deeds have been done in God."

ORDER OF WORSHIP

OPENING WORDS / CALL TO WORSHIP
Come to the Lord with openness,   *John 3:1–2, 14–15*
seeking God's presence whatever it brings.
Bring doubt, bring belief.
Seek the Lord and live.

HYMN, SPIRITUAL, OR PSALM

CALL TO CONFESSION
We cannot earn God's grace or favor.
It comes to us, not as something owed,
but as a gift freely given.
Confident in God's love for us,
even when we are ungodly,
we confess our sins in faith.

PRAYER OF CONFESSION
Gracious God, we come before you
in need of forgiveness and grace.
You call us to trust in you completely,
but we do not.

We are timid and fearful as we follow your lead.
We justify our actions and words,
though we know they are not what you require.
We struggle to understand the new life Christ offers,
preferring old habits to risky change.
Forgive us, we pray.
Help us to be born again into the life of Christ,   *John 3:3*
trusting that you have included us by grace
in the family of faith.
In Christ's name we pray. Amen.

DECLARATION OF FORGIVENESS

Friends, God is for us and not against us!   *John 3:16–17*
For that very reason,
God sent the Son into the world
not to condemn the world,
but that the world might be saved through him.
Believe the good news,
in Jesus Christ we are forgiven!

PRAYER OF THE DAY

God of wilderness and nighttime,   *Num. 21:4–5; John 3:2*
as we devote these forty days to you,
shape us by your Holy Spirit
into the image of Christ our Lord,
so that we may be ready, by your grace,
to confront the power of death
with the promise of eternal life. **Amen.**

HYMN, SPIRITUAL, OR PSALM

PRAYER FOR ILLUMINATION

God of signs and wonders,   *John 3:1–15*
we come to your word again and again,
seeking understanding
and the new life it offers.
By the power of your Holy Spirit,
illumine our hearts and minds
so that we may believe this testimony
and have eternal life.

In the name of Jesus Christ,
our teacher and Savior, we pray. **Amen.**

SCRIPTURE READINGS

SERMON

HYMN, SPIRITUAL, OR PSALM

PRAYERS OF INTERCESSION
God our Helper,
we thank you for keeping our lives
always in your care and protection
and pray for any and all who are in harm's way.
For those walking in the midst of danger . . .
for those who are treading a slippery path . . .
for those exhausted and seeking relief . . .
for those who face a mountain of worry or debt
or any other obstacles. . . .
Be Guardian and Guide, we pray,
setting all our feet on your paths of righteousness and peace.

We pray for those who are struggling
with a new challenge or call . . .
with a major transition in life or livelihood . . .
with their faith and understanding . . .
with grief, ancient or new . . .
Keep in your tender care and mercy, O God,
those who are sick in mind, body, or spirit . . .
those weighed down by depression or pain . . .
those recuperating from surgery or accident. . . .

Protect not only us and those we love,
but also the whole wide world you so love.
In places of war, bring peace . . .
in places beset by natural disaster, bring calm and restoration . . .
where there is unrest and injustice, make justice our aim.
Where hope has grown tired and thin, lift our sights,
so that we may see hope beyond hope,
life beyond death,

and you, lifted up before us.
In the name of Christ,
who gave himself for our sake, we pray. **Amen.**

LORD'S PRAYER

INVITATION TO THE OFFERING
In plenty or in want, all that we have is a gift from God.   *Num. 21:5*
In faith and gratitude,
we return now a portion
of what we have so abundantly received,
as grateful heirs of the promises of God.

PRAYER OF THANKSGIVING/DEDICATION
Gracious God,
we dedicate to you not only these gifts,
but also ourselves, in deep gratitude—
for your call on our lives,
your guidance in the baptismal journey,
and for blessing us
that we may be a blessing to others.
Accept what we bring
for your own good purposes.
In Christ we pray. **Amen.**

HYMN, SPIRITUAL, OR PSALM

CHARGE
Go out in faith,
trusting in God's sense of direction.
Remember how much God loves this world   *John 3:16*
and so love the world in the name of Christ,
that your testimony becomes the good news   *John 3:11–12*
someone else has been waiting to receive.

BLESSING
You are free from condemnation, free to question
    and seek,
knowing God's love surrounds you in both the
    dark of night and light of day. Amen.

SONG SUGGESTIONS

Included are songbook numbers for the Chalice Hymnal *(CH), the Episcopal Church's* Hymnal 1982 *(EH),* Evangelical Lutheran Worship *(ELW),* the Gather Comprehensive, Second Edition *(GC),* Glory to God *(GTG),* The New Century Hymnal *(TNCH), and the* United Methodist Hymnal *(UMH).*

"Ah Lord, How Shall I Meet Thee?" (*ELW* 241, *GTG* 104, *TNCH* 102)
"As Moses Raised the Serpent Up" (*TNCH* 605)
"Come and Seek the Ways of Wisdom" (*GTG* 174)
"God Loved the World" (*ELW* 323, *TNCH* 208)
"I Heard the Voice of Jesus Say" (*EH* 692, *ELW* 332 and 611, *GC* 622, *GTG* 182, *TNCH* 489)
"Lord of the Dance" (*GC* 689, *GTG* 157, *UMH* 261)
"Lord, Who throughout These Forty Days" (*CH* 180, *EH* 142, *ELW* 319, *GC* 416, *GTG* 166, *TNCH* 211, *UMH* 269)
"What Wondrous Love Is This" (*EH* 439, *ELW* 666, *GC* 614, *GTG* 215, *TNCH* 223, *UMH* 292)

CHILDREN'S SERMON

Based on John 3:1–17

One night a visitor came looking for Jesus. This visitor was a man named Nicodemus. Nicodemus was a Jewish leader, a Pharisee. He knew a lot about God's law. When he found Jesus, Nicodemus asked, "Teacher, it is clear that you are a teacher sent by God because you have done many things that no one can do unless God is with that one." Nicodemus did not say what things Jesus had done, but apparently many Jewish people were talking about the wonderful things Jesus had done.

"Nicodemus, I assure you," said Jesus, "unless a person has been born a new person, it is not possible to see God's kingdom."

Nicodemus was puzzled. "What are you saying, Jesus? Once you are born as a baby, how can you be born again? That is impossible, isn't it?"

Jesus' answer sounded almost as if he did not hear Nicodemus's question.

"I tell you, Nicodemus, unless a person is born of water and the Spirit of God, that person cannot be a part of God's kingdom. This is a different birth. Do not be confused that I said you must be born a new person. God's Spirit blows wherever it wants to blow. You may hear its sound, but you do not know what direction it comes from or in what direction it goes."

If it had not been night and too dark to see Nicodemus's face, Jesus would have seen how confused Nicodemus looked.

"How can any of what you say be? Is this really possible?"

Gently, Jesus answered, "Nicodemus, you are a teacher of Israel. Do you not know these things? If I tell you about things on earth and you do not understand, how can you ever understand what I tell you about things of God not on earth? Yet God loved the world so much that God sent a son to the world, so everyone who believes in this son will be with God forever."

On his way home, Nicodemus surely thought about Jesus' words and what they meant for him.

SERMON HELPS

Numbers 21:4–9

THEOLOGICAL PERSPECTIVE

When Christian interpreters read this passage in Numbers, it is almost impossible not to jump immediately to the Gospel of John and Jesus' conversation with Nicodemus (John 3:1–21). In response to the Pharisee leader's questions about participation in the "kingdom of God," Jesus was remembered as saying, finally, "No one has ascended into heaven except the one who descended from heaven, the Son of Man. And just as Moses lifted up the serpent in the wilderness, so must the Son of Man be lifted up, that whoever believes in him may have eternal life" (John 3:13–15). For the writer of the Gospel this extended conversation with Jesus pointed forward to Jesus being "lifted up" on the cross, from the grave, and into the heavenly realm of God. Moses's experience in the wilderness was understood as a type pointing to a spiritual event in the future, namely, the redemptive work of Jesus.

The account in Numbers, however, has theological significance quite apart from Jesus. First, this story stands at the end of a series of "murmuring stories" that provide narrative structure for the wilderness traditions. From the beginning the people grumbled and complained about their condition in the desert (Exod. 16:2–3). Their complaints are noted at several different points along the way (e.g., Num. 11, 14, 16, 20) but come to a climax in Numbers 21. The failure to trust God (and God's intermediary, Moses) is the basic issue.

In the Bible, the concept of "faith" is regularly understood as "trust" rather than "belief." Moses did not challenge the people to "believe" in some doctrine about God. The aim of Moses was for the people to move forward trusting that God would keep the divine commitment to lead the people to a new land. In the immediately preceding verses (Num. 21:1–3) Israel had won a victory over the Canaanites after appealing for divine assistance. But then, as was regularly the case when one considers the long history of Israel's relationship with God, the people lapsed into their untrusting, unfaithful attitude and "spoke against God and against Moses" (21:5). Usually in the Bible, rebellion against God takes the form of faithlessness. And those who are "unfaithful" and "untrusting" are quite often unreliable toward one another as well as toward God.

There is a second important theological issue imbedded in this passage. What is the function of the bronze snake that Moses hoisted up before the people? For many, religious icons—indeed religion itself—are symbols connected with a belief in magic. The bronze snake to such folk was intended to assure people that divine, supernatural powers could be marshaled whenever needed to alleviate a human difficulty, namely a plague of venomous, hurtful reptiles. Such magical signs were believed to ward off evil and provide protection. All a sufferer had to do was look upon the magic icon, and relief was assured. In the course of Christian history some have considered the elements of the communion table in this way, but of course this is not a proper understanding.

Closely connected to such a magical approach was an even more dangerous possibility, at least from the Bible's point of view: idolatry. Deeply rooted in Israel's tradition was the prohibition against creating any image as a representative of the divine. The second commandment forbids all such representations (Exod. 20:4–6; Deut. 5:8–10). The worship or reverencing of any one or any thing other than God was a deadly error. It was utterly foolish to put trust in inert, unhearing, uncaring human creations. Such a perversion was a certain road to destruction (e.g., Exod. 32:1–10; Isa. 40:18–20; 41:21–28; 44:9–20; 46:1–7; Jer. 10:1–16; Pss. 115:3–8; 135:15–18). Paul, in his letter to the Romans, brought the biblical understanding of the connection of idolatry to sinful rebellion and death to forceful expression (Rom. 1:18–32). Idolatry has continued on the list of warnings that Jewish and Christians leaders regularly and rightly cite to their people.

Moses's bronze snake could easily have become an idol. In ancient Egypt and Mesopotamia, representations of snakes were often used as symbols for various deities, mostly dangerous ones, but sometimes the bringers of healing and fertility. Indeed, centuries later King Hezekiah, during a religious reform, removed from the temple "the bronze serpent that Moses had made, for until those days the people of Israel had made offerings to it; it was called Nehushtan" (2 Kgs. 18:4b). Thus we are reminded that things intended for one purpose can be turned to another. For some, the noblest of virtues can become twisted into icons of self-adulation. Nation, wealth, power, religion—we know the possibilities.

Finally, this passage prompts us to reflect once again, particularly in this Lenten season, about the relation between repentance and forgiveness. The first response of God to the clamorous, faithless griping of the Israelites was to send snakes among them as punishment (Num. 21:6). We do not like to consider that sin should receive judgment, but there is every reason it should. Certainly the continuing debate about the character and effectiveness of the atonement worked by Jesus suggests that judgment and punishment of sin is an important consideration.

More to the point of Lent, however, is that repentance is very much a possibility and a desire from God's point of view. When the Israelites recognized their transgression, they came to Moses and asked for his intercession to God on their behalf (Num. 21:7). Repentance is hardly ever a completely individual and private affair. Most of the time a candid admission of sin—unlike the generalized, one-size-fits-all kind often offered in corporate worship—requires the recognition of how one's individual (or a community's) behavior has harmed others. Each individual has to take responsibility for his or her behavior. Forgiveness and healing are readily available, but faithful repentance is necessary. As the apocryphal or deutrocanonical book Wisdom of Solomon notes, "For the one who turned toward it [the bronze serpent] was saved, not by the thing that was beheld, but by you, the Savior of all" (Wis. 16:7). This was not magic or idolatry, but faith, and no one could do it for another.

W. EUGENE MARCH

PASTORAL PERSPECTIVE

The Scripture passage from Numbers 21 describes a weird, mysterious, even gruesome, scene. The story should be read in the context of the church calendar and within the breadth of the scriptural narrative. The passage echoes the Lenten journey of repentance, drawing the reader into the drama of the suffering cross and the redemption of Easter. Today's pastoral message is this: The cross comes before the resurrection. Sometimes suffering is the only path to redemption, and often the road to healing and light runs straight through darkness and pain. It may not be a comforting message, but it is a truthful one.

Moses has led the Israelites out of slavery in Egypt. Day after day they have been tramping around in the desert, with God providing manna to eat and Moses at the helm. Because they are weary and frustrated, not at all sure where they are going or if their leader Moses knows what he is doing, and sure they are about to die, dissension has grown in the ranks. The "Let's go back to Egypt" committee gets wound up. "Let's go back to Egypt!" they whine. "Slavery in Egypt was bad, but it was better than freedom. With freedom comes too many choices," they cry. A pastor friend says that every church he has ever been a part of has had a "Let's go back to Egypt" committee, a group of people who are opposed to any sort of change and always want to go back to the way things used to be.

Eventually God has enough of their whining and sends a pack of poisonous serpents into their midst. Many in their number die before the "Let's go back to Egypt" committee convinces Moses to change God's mind. We have heard this story of a serpent getting the best of God's people before, back in the garden of Eden. No wonder the Israelites were terrified.

The drama turns when Moses crafts a poisonous serpent made of bronze and lifts it high on a pole. All the Israelites who had died were given new life, and every time an Israelite was bitten by a snake, all he or she had to do was look to the serpent and be healed. Anyone who has had surgery knows something about the terror and healing of snakes on a pole. The American Medical Association adopted the image of the ancient Greek god of healing, a snake twined on a staff. Sometimes, when you go to the hospital, they have to hurt you before they can heal you. Danger frequently paves the way to new life. Often an image of ugliness and death can be the means to wholeness. In this way, the Numbers story echoes the larger story of salvation. Jesus' violent death on the cross is the moment of God's redemption and the reconciliation between God and creation. Still, whether it is Moses raising up a dead serpent or Jesus bleeding on the cross, it is an odd way for God to show God's love and mercy to his people, granting healing through pain and lifting high an image of ugliness and death to bring about new life.

Pastorally, issues of pain, healing, and redemption are always important, particularly leading up to Easter. Thus the passion and resurrection of Jesus should be one of the primary hermeneutics for reading Scripture during Lent. As it is read in the context of Christian worship, the story of Moses lifting up the serpent in the wilderness foreshadows Good Friday and Easter morning. This is particularly true when this lesson is placed alongside the Gospel reading for the day, John 3:1–17. John tells us that just as Moses lifted up the serpent in the wilderness, so must the Son of Man be lifted up (v. 14). Seen through the eyes of the church, the image of death lifted high on a pole is not that of a serpent, but that of God in Christ lifted high on the cross.

When Jesus says, "God so loved the world," Jesus is asking us to see the God who created the world out of love as the same God who is lifted high on the cross in redeeming love. Sometimes it is hard to know whether love feels like dying or being lifted up, like the cross of Good Friday or the glory of Easter morning. Lent always journeys through Good Friday and all of us will eventually bear the sadness of the cross. Pastors know well that pain and love mingle together in our own stories, and in the lives of those whom we serve, as they do in the heart of God.

We are entering into Lent, that forty-day journey into the desert of our brokenness and the barrenness of our souls. The passage tells us that the answer to the Israelites wandering in the wilderness was lifting their eyes to see death on a pole. Only the serpent raised by Moses's arm gave new life to the dead Israelites and protected the rest. The church says the answer to our wandering in the wilderness of our sin is when the Son of Man is lifted high on the cross, the love of God given for the world. The tragedy of the story is that rather than receiving the heart of God, we tried to remake Jesus in our own image. When that did not work, we spit on him, whipped him, raised him up on a cross, and watched as the heart of God shattered into a million pieces.

The pastoral equation this Sunday is not complicated, though it is hard to get our minds around. The path to redemption is coated in suffering. The cure for a snake is a snake. The cure for human life is one man's life. The cure for death is death.

Lift up your eyes to the cross, and trust in the light of God's redeeming grace.

CRAIG KOCHER

EXEGETICAL PERSPECTIVE

Complaints, Complaints! From its beginning, the narrative of the wilderness wandering of the escaped Hebrews is rife with reports of trouble and suffering, accompanied by constant complaining (KJV: "murmuring") of the people against Moses and Aaron. The people did not like the bitter water of Marah (Exod. 15:22–25), so the Lord showed Moses how to sweeten it. They complained about the lack of food (Exod. 16:2–3), so the Lord gave them manna. They complained that they were thirsty (Exod. 17:3). Moses struck the rock at the Lord's command and water gushed forth (see also Num. 20:1–13). When the march resumed after Sinai, they were back at it again, asking for meat to eat (Num. 11:4–6). A wind from the Lord brought quails, but the birds were accompanied by a plague. In Numbers 14, the people rebelled at the prospect of invading Canaan. They were saved from extermination by an angry God through the intercession of Moses, but the Lord decreed that none of those who tested the Lord "ten times" (14:22), including Moses, should ever set foot in the promised land, except for Caleb, Joshua, and the innocent children (vv. 30–31).

Today's text records the final complaint of the people. It culminates the entire series because for the first time the people "spoke *against* God and against Moses." Whether or not the punishment by snakes is also climactic depends on how one views the pestilences and prohibition that precede it. Like other complaint stories in the series, this one too reports a gracious divine provision for survival. Does this one exceed the others? As we shall see, other biblical writers viewed God's merciful gift in this text as a prototype of God's ultimate provision for the survival and salvation of the people of God.

If It Does Not Kill You, It Will Make You Well. The final punishment inflicted by God upon the complainers is "poisonous serpents" (Num. 21:6; cf. Deut. 8:15) that bit and killed many people. The KJV translates this phrase "fiery serpents," which is understandable, considering that the Hebrew word in question (vv. 6, 8) is *serafim,* derived from the verbal root *saraf,* "to burn." Terrible as the wilderness critters must have been, however, it seems unlikely that the Hebrews encountered swarms of fire-breathing snakes or dragons (though Isaiah lists a "flying [fiery] serpent" among the animals of the Negeb, Isa. 30:6; see also Isa. 14:29). We are left to speculate that the fire of the "poisonous serpents" spoken of in most modern English translations may be the burning sensation in the vicinity of the snakebite.

In verses 8–9 we read of a bronze *saraf* that Moses is instructed to fashion and lift up on a pole. The very thing that killed people was graciously ordered by God, in replicated form, to ward off death and bring healing to the victims. The function is like that of the blood of the Passover lamb on the doorposts in Egypt (Exod. 12:1–13). The death of the lamb, symbolized by its blood, warded off the death of the firstborn in the households of Israelites.

Serpents rank high among cultic symbols around the world. As is the case in this passage, they play the ambiguous role of killer/healer. The serpent could stand for wisdom (think Gen. 3:1), fertility, and many other good things, as well as danger and death. Western culture, which is generally not fond of snakes (think of Medusa's hairdo), also draws from classical mythology a connection of serpents with healing. A prime example is Asclepius, the Greek healing deity. His staff, marked by a single twisted serpent, has been widely adopted in Europe and America as the symbol of the medical arts.

The Bronze Serpent as an Object of Worship. Nothing in this passage suggests the people immediately began to create a cult around the God-given source of their healing. By 2 Kings 18:4, however, we have evidence that such a thing did eventually happen. The first reform instituted by Hezekiah after he acceded to the throne of Judah in about 715 BCE was to destroy the idols and images that divided the absolute loyalty of the Judeans to YHWH. Among other things, "He broke in pieces the bronze serpent that Moses had made, for until those days the people of Israel had made offerings to it; it was called Nehushtan." From this we learn (a) that the serpent on a pole was still in Jerusalem centuries after the exodus period; (b) that people were worshiping it, because they were making offerings to it; and (c) it had a name that appears to be a play on the two Hebrew words *nahash,* "serpent," and *nehoshet,* "bronze or copper." Was this object located in the temple itself? Did it depict a lesser deity than YHWH? Does the explicit link to Numbers 21:4–9 suggest that that story began to be told in later years to explain an eighth-century-BCE object of worship? Were the people mistaking the magical agent of healing for the true and only Healer? We cannot answer any of these questions definitively, but the tentative answer to all of them is yes.

The Foreground of the Bronze Serpent. In front of the Franciscan friary that marks the traditional site of Mount Nebo, east of the Dead Sea, where Moses viewed the promised land that he would never enter, and where he died (Deut. 32:48–52; 34:1–8), stands a tall hammered metal sculpture by the Florentine artist Giovanni Fantoni. It depicts Moses's serpent on its pole, and it also evokes the cross of Christ. This work of art dramatizes the importance that Christians typically attach to the bronze serpent of Numbers 21:4–9. It is the prototype of the visible life-giving work of God manifested above all in its prime counterpart, the atoning death of Jesus. The Gospel of John makes the link specific: "Just as Moses lifted up the serpent in the wilderness, so must the Son of Man be lifted up, that whoever believes in him may have eternal life" (John 3:14–15). Exegete and homiletician alike must note this intrabiblical reimagining of the bronze serpent, because in the full canon of Scripture, the primitive image on the pole comes to mean more than it meant.

W. SIBLEY TOWNER

HOMILETICAL PERSPECTIVE

This odd passage from the book of Numbers owes its presence in the lectionary to the Gospel reading for the day. Without John's cryptic reference to the serpent in the wilderness as a simile for the Son of Man, preachers might never wrestle one of the most puzzling stories in Torah. Yet wrestle it they must, if they want to preach the gospel. In what sense is the lifting up of the Son of Man like Moses's lifting up of the serpent in the wilderness? What possible significance can this text have to a Christian congregation today?

The story is the last of five "murmuring" stories in the book of Numbers. Over and over, the people complain (or rail, or rebel, or speak against) their leaders in the wilderness. God moves to punish the people for their sedition. Moses intercedes on their behalf. In the present case, the people speak against God as well as Moses, which may be why this is the last mention of their murmuring. Complaining about Moses and Aaron is one thing. Complaining about God is something else altogether.

Their complaint is absurd as well as seditious. They have no food and water, they say, "and we detest this miserable food." What food? Are they hallucinating? At least they hope they are hallucinating when they see poisonous snakes crawling out of the rocks, heading straight for their feet. But no; these snakes are real. When they bite people, those people die, which brings the living abruptly to their senses. They repent of their sin, pleading with Moses to intercede for them with God.

The divine answer to their prayer is what makes this passage so odd. God tells Moses to make a fiery serpent and set it on a pole. Is this not an idol, and an Egyptian one at that? Didn't Pharaoh wear a headdress with a spitting cobra on it? Everyone who is bitten shall look upon it and live, God says. Is this not magic? Since when does a statue confer life? However problematic the answers to these questions are, the plan works. It works so well, in fact, that the people turn the snake sculpture into one of their ancestral treasures. Five hundred years later, it shows up in the temple in Jerusalem with a name (Nehushtan) and a popular following that leads King Hezekiah to destroy it (2 Kgs. 18:4).

As if all of this were not already a handful, the Hebrew word for the poisonous (literally, "fiery") serpent is *seraph*. Preachers will want to do their own word work here, paying special attention to the exegetical essay on this passage. If these fiery serpents are God-sent seraphim, then what does that say about the seraphim that show up elsewhere in Scripture? What can it mean that God's fiery ones both kill and save? Given the popular fascination with angels (manifest in a Web site that sells pink-cheeked seraphim named Emily and Abigail), this passage gives the preacher an opening to challenge the cultural captivity of God's messengers.

Preachers will also explore their associations with words such as "snake," "snakebite," and "fiery serpent." These are frightening words for many people. A recent Harris poll on "What We Are Afraid Of" discovered that 36 percent of all adults in the United States list snakes as their number one fear. Ophidiophobia is the clinical word for this fear, which affects 49 percent of women and 22 percent of men. The preacher's first impulse may be to calm this fear by intellectualizing the snake or (following John's lead) by allegorizing it. To do this will lessen the impact of the language, however, and the impact of the sermon along with it. The teller of today's story made full use of the human fear of snakes. The brave preacher will do no less.

While "venom" and "antivenom" do not appear in the passage, they are both alluded to. The bronze serpent is the medical antidote to the deadly bite of the fiery serpents. Once the people have recognized their sin and confessed it to Moses, their tormentor becomes their savior. Once Moses makes it possible for them to gaze fully upon what they are afraid of, they gain access to its healing power. Like the caduceus, this bronze serpent becomes a treasured sign of God's power to heal. It is not a living snake, however, nor is it in any sense sacrificed for the sins of the people. This precludes any easy interpretation of John's simile, especially for those preachers whose traditions stress substitutionary atonement. The passage from Numbers remains as mysterious as the passage from John. The preachers who honor the integrity of their composition will think twice before trying to clear their mysteries up.

In the context of Lent, there remains all kinds of room to think with the congregation about what humans are most afraid of and what that fear does to us, both as persons and as a people. What concrete things do we focus on that epitomize our fear? In what sense do these things become idols that keep our fear in place? What is God capable of doing with those idols, once they have been plucked out from under our feet and set up on a pole where we can see them clearly? How does God respond to our fear, both in the wilderness and at the foot of the cross?

There is also room for the preacher to consider the difference between faith in magic and faith in God. If the people believed that the bronze serpent was responsible for their cure, then that snake was an idol and Hezekiah was right to snap it in two. But if looking up at the serpent reminded the people to lift their hearts to God, then the snake was a sacrament. Looking up at it, they looked through it to their only Physician, who alone was their Health, their Salvation, and their Cure. Preachers who pursue this tack will connect the saving act of looking up to Christ with healing practices (actual or potential) in the life of the local congregation.

BARBARA BROWN TAYLOR

John 3:1–17

THEOLOGICAL PERSPECTIVE

This text is theologically rich and deeply provocative. Of the many themes that stir the imagination theologically, two are particularly important: the story's setting and what it suggests about discipleship, and its image of rebirth.

John begins the story somewhat abruptly. The reader is not told where the story takes place. We know only that Jesus is in Jerusalem during the Passover feast (2:23). John does little to introduce Nicodemus. We are told only that he is a Pharisee and a ruler, a member of the Sanhedrin. Readers familiar with the whole of John's story know that Nicodemus will reappear briefly, first interceding for Jesus with other Pharisees (7:50) and then in the story's conclusion (19:38–42), with Joseph of Arimathea, bringing spices to bury Jesus. Both in 3:1–21 and in 19:39 Nicodemus is identified as the one who first came to Jesus by night. He is the original night stalker.

Of the many images in John's Gospel, two major ones are light and darkness. Nicodemus emerges out of the night's darkness, seeking light from the teacher he believes to be sent from God. Just as suddenly as he appears, Nicodemus disappears back into the night from whence he came. Before he does so, Jesus tells him one must be born anew in order to see the kingdom of God, and the last we hear from Nicodemus is, "How can this be?" (v. 9). Jesus' last words are, "Those who do what is true come to the light, so that it may be clearly seen that their deeds have been done in God" (v. 21). It will take Nicodemus a long time—until 19:38–42—to come once and for all out of the night and into the light.

Nicodemus is the one who comes to Jesus by night. He hovers on the margins and in the shadows of John's story. He is neither the first in the church nor the last to follow Jesus from afar. No doubt it was difficult, perhaps even dangerous, for Nicodemus to follow Jesus publicly, during the bright light of the day. He was, after all, someone who was part of the Jewish establishment, for whom Jesus seemed to be at first only a nuisance but later a political problem and threat. Nicodemus had to be cautious and to exercise discretion. He was the forerunner of many of Jesus' disciples who have had to be careful about when and where they practiced their discipleship.

In his seven letters to the churches in Asia, John of Patmos warned them to beware of the Nicolaitans (Rev. 2:6, 15), Christians who were willing to offer worship to pagan and Roman gods in order to remain unnoticed, if not tolerated, in a non-Christian world.[1] In the sixteenth century John Calvin referred to those who sympathized with the movement for the reform of the church but were reluctant to be publicly identified with it as "Nicodemites." In the midst of National Socialism, Nicodemus's heirs, the German Christians, sought to accommodate the gospel to the racism and anti-Semitism of Nazi ideology. In response, the Confessing Church in May 1934 declared, in the second thesis of the Theological Declaration of Barmen, "As Jesus Christ is God's assurance of the forgiveness of all our sins, so in the same way and with the same seriousness he is also *God's mighty claim upon our whole life.*"[2]

Nicodemus admits that Jesus could not have performed his signs (2:23) unless God were with him. Jesus responds by answering a question Nicodemus did not ask. Not only is Jesus the presence of God, but those who are born from above—recreated in the water of baptism by the power of the Spirit—will see in these things Jesus has done the presence of the kingdom of God. Nicodemus does not understand what it means to be "born from above." Jesus tells him that to be born from above is to be born of the Spirit, and to be born of the Spirit is to believe in Jesus and in believing in him to have eternal life.

What does it mean to be born from above and to believe in Jesus? To be born from above by water and the Spirit, to believe in Jesus, is to leave the darkness and to come into the light (v. 19). What does it mean to live either in darkness or in light? Those who live in the darkness and hate the light do so because their evil deeds will be exposed (v. 20). To come into the light—to be born from above—is to do "what is true" (v. 21), to follow the one who is himself "the way, and the truth, and the life" (14:6).

For many Christians, the gospel is summarized by the words in John 3:16. Everyone who believes in Jesus will not perish but will have eternal life. Some Christians, however, understand faith or "believing in Jesus" to be simply what one does with one's mind. In John's Gospel, being born from above and believing in Jesus are clearly not so much about what one does with one's mind as about what one does with one's heart and one's life. "Those who do what is true come to the light, so that it may be clearly seen that their deeds have been done in God" (v. 21). In John's Gospel believing and doing are inseparable. Nicodemus lives in the darkness and the shadows

---

1. Richard Bauckham, *The Theology of the Book of Revelation* (Cambridge: Cambridge University Press, 1993), 123–25.
2. "The Theological Declaration of Barmen," in the *Book of Confessions: Study Edition of the Presbyterian Church (U.S.A.)* (Louisville, KY: Geneva Press, 1996), 311 (8.14). Italics added.

of this story until its conclusion, when he emerges publicly with Joseph of Arimathea, who is also a "secret disciple," to bury Jesus.

GEORGE W. STROUP

PASTORAL PERSPECTIVE

If any character from the Bible can be regarded as representative of twenty-first-century church members, it might be Nicodemus. In many ways he is a sympathetic character. A successful and self-confident man, he plays a leadership role in his community. He is spiritually open and curious, yet also rational. He approaches Jesus directly and tries to figure out Jesus' actions and social networks. He is committed and curious enough that he makes an appointment to talk with Jesus face to face. However, Nicodemus is not ready to go public with his interest in Jesus, so he makes the appointment in the middle of the night, when he can keep his faith secret, separated from the rest of his life. His imagination is caught by Jesus, but he wants to compartmentalize whatever faith he has. Nicodemus is not yet ready to declare his faith in the light of day, not prepared to let it change his life.

Like it or not, we look into the eyes of people like Nicodemus every Sunday morning. Being a mainline Protestant is not exactly trendy, and though people may come to church occasionally or even be active members, many believers with whom we interact are Nicodemuses in their wider life. They have faith, sometimes deep faith, and they are spiritually curious, but they keep faith in its own sphere.

Being a Nicodemus-like Christian is understandable in the twenty-first century. Believers, who have mixed marriages or pluralistic work settings, privilege tolerance and mutual respect over witnessing. Cultural norms push religion into the private sphere, positioning faith as appropriate for family and personal morality but inappropriate for public issues. For two centuries mainline Protestantism has encouraged such behavior and attitudes. Our brand of religion promotes self-restraint, tolerance, and personal morality, and all are worthy virtues. We support public morality and an engagement in social issues, too, of course, but that message has been muffled by the declining size and increasing marginalization of mainline Protestant denominations. If people in our pews are Christians like Nicodemus, it is not necessarily because they have somehow failed as individual believers. In some cases we have pushed our members into their compartmentalized faith.

In and of itself, there is much to praise about a faith that thrives in the dark. It is genuine, heartfelt, personal, and often deep. The point is not that this hidden faith is somehow faulty—as far as it goes; the point is that it is too small. In this text Jesus suggests that Nicodemus's kind of faith is incomplete, even immature. He likens his midnight encounter with Nicodemus to a child still safe in its mother's womb. You are still gestating, Jesus implies. You must be born again and declare this faith in the light of day.

Jesus seems impatient as he talks with Nicodemus. He is annoyed when Nicodemus does not immediately understand the metaphor of rebirth. He even mocks the Pharisee.

Jesus' impatience leads some people to read this text as a command: you must be born again. Many interpret rebirth as work that gestating Christians need to do. For these interpreters, the urgency of people making a decision to accept Christ as their Lord and Savior is paramount. However legitimate this interpretation might be, reading this text as a command is not the only option. In fact, it may be as legitimate—and certainly as pastoral—to read it as an invitation. When Jesus tells Nicodemus that he needs to be born again by water and Spirit, he is asking Nicodemus to let God work in his life.

In a wonderful sermon on this text, Debbie Blue observes that the metaphor of birth in this text is surprising and provocative.[3] It is surprising because it is so irrational, so beyond what will ever really happen to us physically, and Nicodemus gives voice to that. This invitation to rebirth is nonsensical; nobody can literally be born again.

The invitation is provocative too, because it invites us to open our imaginations and reconsider our relationship with God, which is the central focus of this text, and, indeed, of this Gospel. Jesus invites Nicodemus, as he invites each of us, to come into the light of day and become mature believers, full participants in the abundant life he offers. Jesus knows that neither Nicodemus nor contemporary believers can do this on their own. It is God who will give birth in water and Spirit. Rebirth is God's gift to give, God's work to accomplish, and it is God who labors to bring us new life.

God works hard for us and our faith. God conceives us as Christians and nurtures us in the wombs of our faith, safe and warm and secret. At some point, like any pregnant woman who is close to full term, God gets impatient with gestation and wants to get on with it; God wants to push that baby through the birth canal into greater maturity, into fullness of life, into a faith lived wholly in the world. That is what Jesus talks about in this text. Jesus thinks it is time Nicodemus came through that spiritual birth canal. Perhaps he thinks it is time for many others to be reborn too. God is ready to give us birth by water and Spirit.

---

3. Debbie Blue, "Laboring God," in *Sensual Orthodoxy* (St. Paul, MN: Cathedral Hill Press, 2004), 31–37.

How many of our church members (or preachers) might be Nicodemuses in twenty-first-century garb? How many of our congregations might be organizational versions of him—people and institutions with compartmentalized faiths that flourish behind the scenes, out of sight, away from the fray, essentially in private? How many of us are gestating Christians? Who among us has room to grow in our faith? The good news of this text is that God is prepared—even eager—to do the hard, messy, sweating labor that will bring us to maturity and new life.

DEBORAH J. KAPP

EXEGETICAL PERSPECTIVE

The story of Nicodemus is unique to John, and it epitomizes key themes for this Gospel. A recurring structural pattern for the Fourth Gospel is sign, dialogue, discourse. Jesus performs a sign that is followed by a dialogue between Jesus and those present and then a discourse by Jesus that interprets the sign. While Jesus does not perform a sign for Nicodemus, Nicodemus's reference to "signs" in verse 2 introduces the conversation with Jesus and sets up Jesus' discourse in verses 10–21. In verses 19–21, Jesus discloses a major theme for the Gospel of John, light and darkness. Light represents the realm of belief and darkness the realm of unbelief. When Jesus says to Nicodemus, "This is the judgment, that the light has come into the world, and people loved darkness rather than light" (v. 19), these words send the reader back to the beginning of chapter 3: Nicodemus comes to Jesus *by night*. The moment of judgment for Nicodemus is in this here-and-now encounter with Jesus.

It is because of Jesus' words in 3:18–21 that Nicodemus's meeting with Jesus is equivocal at best. The last words of Nicodemus to Jesus are "How can these things be?" (3:9), and in his conversation with Jesus he does not make much progress. Nicodemus interprets Jesus' words on a literal level, although (typical of Jesus in the Fourth Gospel) Jesus' words to him are deliberately ambiguous. "From above" (*anōthen*) can be translated three different ways—"again," "anew," or "from above" (3:3). Nicodemus hears only the first option. Whereas the Samaritan woman at the well (John 4) will be able to move to the next level of understanding, Nicodemus is not able to recognize what Jesus offers and, more importantly, who Jesus is.

For John's Gospel, an encounter with Jesus is the salvific moment. The dialogue with Nicodemus is not simply explanatory or conversational on Jesus' part. Rather, Jesus as the Word made flesh makes God known to Nicodemus (1:18). The question is whether or not Nicodemus will be able to see the truth about Jesus that Nicodemus himself confesses, that Jesus is the one who has come from God (3:2). So as to move Nicodemus along, Jesus' answer to Nicodemus's misunderstanding introduces the concept of being born of water and Spirit (v. 5).

While many commentators have interpreted these words through the lens of baptism, the whole of the Gospel narrative suggests other interpretive possibilities. In the next chapter, Jesus will offer himself as the source of living water (4:10) and will again connect water and Spirit, both of which he will provide (7:37–39). It is important, therefore, to situate interpretation of Jesus' words to Nicodemus within the context of Jesus' provision of water and this Gospel's unique understanding of the Spirit. The Spirit, the expressed gift from Jesus to the disciples when he reveals himself to them after the resurrection (20:22), is the Paraclete (Advocate, Comforter, Helper), the one who carries on the work and presence of Jesus when he returns to the Father. It should be this working out of water and Spirit that is brought forward to Jesus' words to Nicodemus.

After Nicodemus's incredulous question, "How can these things be?" (v. 9), he seems to disappear from the scene, and the reader is left with Jesus. All of a sudden, Jesus' words are directed specifically to the readers of the story. Verse 11 begins in the second person singular: "Very truly I tell you." Then the "you" in "yet you do not receive our testimony" switches to second person plural. This places the reader in the same position as Nicodemus: in an encounter with Jesus. God loves the world, and this Gospel intends to secure and sustain belief in Jesus as the Christ, the Son of God (20:30–31). Because of the death, resurrection, and ascension of Jesus—all of which are implied in "the Son of Man must be lifted up"—eternal life is possible, but the incarnation ensures that eternal life includes life now, abiding in Jesus.

As for Nicodemus, he appears two other times in the Gospel of John. In 7:50–52 he seems to come to Jesus' defense in the midst of the intense conflict between Jesus and the religious authorities that sets off chapters 7 and 8, but his question to the Pharisees gives the impression of lukewarm advocacy for Jesus. Nicodemus's last appearance in the Gospel is to help Joseph of Arimathea, a *secret* disciple of Jesus, with the burial of Jesus' body (19:38–42). The reader is thereby reminded that Nicodemus first came to Jesus by night (19:39).

Moreover, he brings an extraordinary quantity of burial spices for the preparation of the body. Does this last appearance of Nicodemus finally represent his coming to the light? Or is he still in the dark, weighing down Jesus' body with spices so there will be no doubt that Jesus will remain in the tomb? Given this complicated character and his ambiguous status in the Gospel of John, interpreting this passage should highlight these complications and not smooth them out. Nicodemus does not ask for or require his rescue. His encounter with Jesus and his recurring role in the narrative suggest that believing in Jesus is indeed an ambiguous effort. In the Gospel of John, "faith" is never a noun. Believing for the characters in the Fourth Gospel is a verb (3:15–16) and is subject to all of the ambiguity, uncertainty, and indecisiveness of being human. Having an incarnate God necessitates an incarnational faith: believing is just as complicated as being human.

KAROLINE M. LEWIS

HOMILETICAL PERSPECTIVE

Some texts are so familiar and so loaded with associations that the thought of preaching them *one more time* is almost exhausting. What, you wonder, can you possibly say that has not already been said? It reminds me of a violinist I know who gets a little depressed every November, as she contemplates another season of *The Nutcracker* performances. It is not that she does not love and appreciate the music. It is just that every year she plays the same part in the same way for six weeks straight, and there is only so much innovation one can bring to the third violin section. "I know it's an orchestra classic that comes with the territory, and I'm glad for the work," she says, "but I really wish people knew there was more to the repertoire than 'The Dance of the Sugar Plum Fairy.'"

John 3:1–21 is the preacher's equivalent of *The Nutcracker:* a pulpit classic that comes with the territory. Sooner or later we have to deal with its familiar prose, its theological elegance, its pride of place in our historical confessions. We also have a muddle of associations to manage, and that complicates things. The language of being "born again," and verse 16 in particular (instantly recognizable in its abbreviated form: "John 3:16"), is a staple of highway road signs and bumper stickers and football games. It is shorthand for a certain kind of religious fervor, as people everywhere, Christians and non-Christians alike, can tell you.

This means that before a preacher has any room to do her job, she has to muck out a lot of stalls. She has to name the stereotypes and bad press that this passage evokes so that there is space for us to hear the images afresh. John 3:1–21 may seem like the exclusive property of one brand of Christianity, but the wisdom it offers is for each of us and all of us. On our Lenten journey to the cross, we need it.

Three homiletical tasks in particular present themselves.

Name the Terms. Let us face it: this passage has been used in some pretty awful ways to sort us into groups. "Are you born again?" is code language for, "Are you saved, like us?" or "Are you crazy, like them?" In its insider mode, it functions as a way to determine a person's salvation as a believer in Jesus Christ. In its outsider mode, it serves as a convenient way to label religious fanatics. Neither version of the question is especially accurate or helpful, because both rely on stereotypes of what it means to be a card-carrying Christian.

So the first thing a preacher has to do is to name how the term "born again" functions in his community, for better or worse: Is this a phrase we use to describe ourselves? Is it a phrase we use to differentiate "us" from "them"? What do we mean by the phrase "born again," and how do our understandings play into stereotypes? How do we decide if a person is "born again"? Who has the power to make that decision? Do our practices bind us together and build up the body of Christ, or do they create separation and conflict? The point, here, is to name your terms and debunk the bunk so that the community can start a conversation.

Shed a Little Light in the Neighborhood. Some artists love the challenge of reinterpreting a tried-and-true classic. Think of the choreographer Mark Morris and his adaptation of *The Nutcracker* (entitled, appropriately, "The Hard Nut"), or the painter Jasper Johns's rendition of the American flag, or Jimi Hendrix's Woodstock performance of the "Star Spangled Banner." Classic texts (or symbols or songs or scores) are classic for a reason: they convey to us a truth that begs to be seen and heard in our own context. That is why actresses memorize Shakespeare and bands play Duke Ellington. You do not need to be brilliant and ahead of your time to do this work. The most important thing is to be *in* your time, right where you are; to be part of your community, rooted in your own context, in the season of Lent; to be a theo-logian in residence, someone who talks about God from the vantage point of truly *living* somewhere.

So what does "being born" look like where you live? Why would we want the chance to do it again? More accurately, since we cannot birth ourselves, why would we need someone to *bear* us again? Who bears us and bears with us today, and who has borne us in the past? Is this clean work or messy work? How are our bodies and spirits involved? There are hundreds of ques-tions and images to hold up to the light, again and again, to see how they grow in *your* neighborhood.

See the Humor. This text gives us a great foil in Nicodemus: he has already asked all the stupid questions. They are actually very funny questions. We can almost hear Jesus' amusement in verse 10: "Are you a teacher of Israel, and yet you do not understand these things?!" We could hear shame in those words—many have—but humor is often a better motivator than shame.

What if Jesus was exercising a little rabbinical irony instead of divine judgment? It changes our place in the story; suddenly, there is room for *our* ignorance too! Nicodemus reminds us that even the best educated and most authoritative among us are still searching. No sense in clucking over what we fail to understand (and will probably never grasp in its fullness until we see God face to face, as Paul says); better to laugh at our own efforts, and then get up and try again. Wisdom such as this passage offers is mysterious and paradoxical. It begs for a little space—both to be and to laugh.

ANNA CARTER FLORENCE

Second Sunday of Lent

Exodus 17:1–7

¹From the wilderness of Sin the whole congregation of the Israelites journeyed by stages, as the LORD commanded. They camped at Rephidim, but there was no water for the people to drink. ²The people quarreled with Moses, and said, "Give us water to drink." Moses said to them, "Why do you quarrel with me? Why do you test the LORD?" ³But the people thirsted there for water; and the people complained against Moses and said, "Why did you bring us out of Egypt, to kill us and our children and livestock with thirst?" ⁴So Moses cried out to the LORD, "What shall I do with this people? They are almost ready to stone me." ⁵The LORD said to Moses, "Go on ahead of the people, and take some of the elders of Israel with you; take in your hand the staff with which you struck the Nile, and go. ⁶I will be standing there in front of you on the rock at Horeb. Strike the rock, and water will come out of it, so that the people may drink." Moses did so, in the sight of the elders of Israel. ⁷He called the place Massah and Meribah, because the Israelites quarreled and tested the LORD, saying, "Is the LORD among us or not?"

John 4:1–42

¹Now when Jesus learned that the Pharisees had heard, "Jesus is making and baptizing more disciples than John" ²—although it was not Jesus himself but his disciples who baptized— ³he left Judea and started back to Galilee. ⁴But he had to go through Samaria. ⁵So he came to a Samaritan city called Sychar, near the plot of ground that Jacob had given to his son Joseph. ⁶Jacob's well was there, and Jesus, tired out by his journey, was sitting by the well. It was about noon.

⁷A Samaritan woman came to draw water, and Jesus said to her, "Give me a drink." ⁸(His disciples had gone to the city to buy food.) ⁹The Samaritan woman said to him, "How is it that you, a Jew, ask a drink of me, a woman of Samaria?" (Jews do not share things in common with Samaritans.) ¹⁰Jesus answered her, "If you knew the gift of God, and who it is that is saying to you, 'Give me a drink,' you would have asked him, and he would have given you living water." ¹¹The woman said to him, "Sir, you have no bucket, and the well is deep. Where do you get that living water? ¹²Are you greater than

our ancestor Jacob, who gave us the well, and with his sons and his flocks drank from it?" [13]Jesus said to her, "Everyone who drinks of this water will be thirsty again, [14]but those who drink of the water that I will give them will never be thirsty. The water that I will give will become in them a spring of water gushing up to eternal life." [15]The woman said to him, "Sir, give me this water, so that I may never be thirsty or have to keep coming here to draw water."

[16]Jesus said to her, "Go, call your husband, and come back." [17]The woman answered him, "I have no husband." Jesus said to her, "You are right in saying, 'I have no husband'; [18]for you have had five husbands, and the one you have now is not your husband. What you have said is true!" [19]The woman said to him, "Sir, I see that you are a prophet. [20]Our ancestors worshiped on this mountain, but you say that the place where people must worship is in Jerusalem." [21]Jesus said to her, "Woman, believe me, the hour is coming when you will worship the Father neither on this mountain nor in Jerusalem. [22]You worship what you do not know; we worship what we know, for salvation is from the Jews. [23]But the hour is coming, and is now here, when the true worshipers will worship the Father in spirit and truth, for the Father seeks such as these to worship him. [24]God is spirit, and those who worship him must worship in spirit and truth." [25]The woman said to him, "I know that Messiah is coming" (who is called Christ). "When he comes, he will proclaim all things to us." [26]Jesus said to her, "I am he, the one who is speaking to you."

[27]Just then his disciples came. They were astonished that he was speaking with a woman, but no one said, "What do you want?" or, "Why are you speaking with her?" [28]Then the woman left her water jar and went back to the city. She said to the people, [29]"Come and see a man who told me everything I have ever done! He cannot be the Messiah, can he?" [30]They left the city and were on their way to him.

[31]Meanwhile the disciples were urging him, "Rabbi, eat something." [32]But he said to them, "I have food to eat that you do not know about." [33]So the disciples said to one another, "Surely no one has brought him something to eat?" [34]Jesus said to them, "My food is to do the will of him who sent me and to complete his work. [35]Do you not say, 'Four months more, then comes the harvest'? But I tell you, look around you, and see how the fields are ripe for harvesting. [36]The reaper is already receiving wages and is gathering fruit for eternal life, so that sower and reaper may rejoice together. [37]For here the saying holds true, 'One sows and another reaps.' [38]I sent you to reap that for which you did not labor. Others have labored, and you have entered into their labor."

[39]Many Samaritans from that city believed in him because of the woman's testimony, "He told me everything I have ever done." [40]So when the Samaritans came to him, they asked him to stay with them; and he stayed there two days. [41]And many more believed because of his word. [42]They said to the woman, "It is no longer because of what you said that we believe, for we have heard for ourselves, and we know that this is truly the Savior of the world."

ORDER OF WORSHIP

OPENING WORDS / CALL TO WORSHIP
O come, let us worship and bow down; *John 4:23*
let us kneel before the Lord, our Maker.

The hour is coming and is now here.
In spirit and truth, let us worship God.

HYMN, SPIRITUAL, OR PSALM

CALL TO CONFESSION
[Water is poured into the baptismal font.]
In spite of our quarrels and distrust, *Exod. 17:5–7*
God provides grace to sustain us.
Trusting in God's abundant mercy,
let us confess our sin.

PRAYER OF CONFESSION
Lord, you know who we are. *John 4:5–24*
You know everything we have done.
We thirst for things that will never satisfy us.
We commit ourselves to things that will never last.
We worship things that will never bring salvation.

Still, you offer us the gift of living water.
Still, you offer us the gift of eternal life.
Forgive us, O Lord,
and give us this living water,
so that we may never thirst again. Amen.

DECLARATION OF FORGIVENESS

Christ the Lord speaks to us
words of grace.
Your sins are forgiven,
washed away and forgotten. Amen.

PRAYER OF THE DAY

Lord God, Great I Am,   *John 4:5–42*
you are living water.
As we worship you this day
show us who we are:
channels of your love
and vessels of your grace;
through Jesus Christ our Lord. **Amen.**

HYMN, SPIRITUAL, OR PSALM

PRAYER FOR ILLUMINATION

Living God, through the reading of the Scriptures   *John 4:41–42*
and by the power of your Spirit,
may we hear for ourselves the good news,
and believe, because of your Word,
that Jesus Christ is the Savior of the world. **Amen.**

SCRIPTURE READINGS

SERMON

HYMN, SPIRITUAL, OR PSALM

PRAYERS OF INTERCESSION

Let us pray for the needs of the world, saying,
Wellspring of mercy, hear our prayer.

Saving God,   *Exod. 17:6–7; John 4:14*
you are the giver of living water,
the source of deepest compassion,
the fountain of eternal life.
Therefore we pray to you:
Wellspring of mercy, **hear our prayer.**

For all who are thirsty—
thirsty for a life of meaning,   *John 4:5–42*
thirsty for a word of grace,
thirsty for a drink of water . . .
Wellspring of mercy, **hear our prayer.**

For all who are weary—
weary from life's long journey,   *Exod. 17:1–7*
weary from quarreling and testing,
weary from pain or grief . . .
Wellspring of mercy, **hear our prayer.**

For all who are broken—
broken by sin and suffering,   *John 4:16–18*
broken by shame and rejection,
broken by acts of violence . . .
Wellspring of mercy, **hear our prayer.**

Living God, through your Spirit,
pour your love into our hearts,
your grace into our lives,
your healing into our world,
until the earth is filled with your glory
as the waters cover the sea;
through Jesus Christ we pray. **Amen.**

LORD'S PRAYER

INVITATION TO THE OFFERING
See how the fields are ripe for harvest!   *John 4:35–36*
Already, God is gathering fruit for eternal life.
With rejoicing, let us offer our lives to the Lord.

PRAYER OF THANKSGIVING/DEDICATION
O Lord, you are our God;   *John 4:34–38*
by your grace we reap an abundant harvest.
As you have fed us by your mercy,
may it be our daily bread to do your will;
through Jesus Christ our Lord. **Amen.**

CHARGE

The hour is coming and is now here.   *John 4:23*
Go forth to worship the Lord your God
in spirit and in truth,
in all that you say and do.

BLESSING

May the grace of the Lord Jesus Christ,   *John 4:14*
springing up like living water,
fill your heart, and flow through your life.

SONG SUGGESTIONS

"Come to Me, O Weary Traveler" (*CH* 353, *GC* 637, *GTG* 183)
"Forty Days and Forty Nights" (*CH* 179, *EH* 150, *GC* 411, *GTG* 167, *TNCH* 205)
"Take Me, Take Me as I Am" (*ELW* 814, *GC* 692, *GTG* 698)
"The Glory of These Forty Days" (*EH* 143, *ELW* 320, *GC* 397, *GTG* 165)
"There's a Wideness in God's Mercy" (*EH* 469 and 470, *ELW* 587 and 588, *GC* 603, *GTG* 435, *TNCH* 23, *UMH* 121)
"When Like the Woman at the Well" (*TNCH* 196)
"Woman in the Night" (*CH* 188, *GTG* 161, *UMH* 274)
"You Are Mine" (*ELW* 581, *GC* 627, *GTG* 177)

CHILDREN'S SERMON

Based on John 4:1–42

Jesus and his disciples had been walking for a long time. They were in a Samaritan town, the town where Jacob had dug a well that he gave to his son Joseph. The disciples had gone into the town to find food for lunch because it was about noon. But Jesus was tired, so he sat down by the well to wait for them to return.

A Samaritan woman came to the well to get water. Jesus said, "Please give me a drink of water."

The woman was startled. "You, a Jewish man, are asking me, a Samaritan woman, for a drink of water?"

No wonder she was surprised, because Jews and Samaritans did not get along at all. Most Jews would not even walk into the land of Samaria but would go around it to avoid meeting any Samaritans.

"If you knew who I am," said Jesus, "you would ask me for a drink of water because I can give you living water."

Chuckling to herself, the woman replied, "How can you give me water? You do not have anything to bring the water from the well. And the well is really deep. Do you think you are better than Jacob, who gave us this well?"

"When you drink this water, you get thirsty again," Jesus said. "But if you drink my living water, you will never be thirsty again."

"Well, I would certainly like some of that living water. I would never have to come here for water again." The woman was not sure what Jesus was talking about, but she continued the conversation.

"Go get your husband and come back here," Jesus told her.

"I do not have a husband," she answered.

"Right," said Jesus. "You do not have a husband now. But you have had five husbands."

Now the woman was shocked. "You must be a prophet to know that about me. I do not know many things, but I know that when the Messiah comes, all things will be taught to us."

"I am the one," Jesus said quietly.

At that moment, the disciples returned. The woman left so quickly, she forgot her water jar. She told her neighbors about Jesus. They went to the well to see and talk with him. Jesus taught the people in this Samaritan town for two more days.

SERMON HELPS

Exodus 17:1–7

THEOLOGICAL PERSPECTIVE

Like many other pieces of the long, complex narrative that tells of Israel's wilderness sojourn, this story of thirst and testing has at its center a critical question concerning God's presence. How can we know if God is with us, more literally, "in our midst"? What signs or evidence do we use for discerning the presence and providence of God?

The quarrelsome wilderness generation makes an assumption that seems quite natural and universal. When they have what they need and want, they believe God is with them. In times of hunger, thirst, and affliction, they deem themselves abandoned or betrayed. Worse, they wonder if God has ever traveled with them. Their venture toward freedom might prove a disastrous self-deceit.

Moses himself taught this theology of sufficiency, and God seemed to play along. In the previous chapter, the lack of food prompted complaints against Moses and Aaron. God responded by providing manna and quail, leading Moses and Aaron to assure the people that these things would prove that it was indeed the Lord who brought them out of Egypt (Exod. 16:6).

In addition to provisions, leaders like Moses also serve as surrogates for God or signs of God's presence. Thus, when the thirsty people bring suit against Moses, Moses replies (v. 2), "Why do you quarrel with me? Why do you test the Lord?" Any word hurled at Moses strikes God as well, or so Moses and the narrator assume.

This notion of Moses as the manifestation of God comes with divine authorization in Exodus. God tells Moses, "See, I have made you like God to Pharaoh, and your brother Aaron shall be your prophet" (7:1). Moses speaks for God, and the sight of Moses will prove the closest Pharaoh will come to seeing the God he engages in battle.

All through Exodus, Israel sees God mostly as Pharaoh had, while Moses himself enjoys direct access. Thus, in this story of thirst and testing at Rephidim, God promises that Moses will see God standing on the rock that will yield water when struck. However, the people will not see God, but only Moses, the one through whom God gives to Israel what Israel needs to live.

This theological theme reaches something of a crisis when Moses tarries too long on the mountain in Exodus 32. In response, Israel makes for itself a new sign of God's presence. Aaron fashions a cherub, a pair of which already sit atop the ark of the covenant constructed, as the story now reads, back in Exodus 25. Cherubim serve as signs of God's presence (see Exod. 25:18–22 and 1 Sam. 4:4). God and Moses argue over whether and how God should punish this presumed apostasy. At least one consequence is a new, seemingly permanent uncertainty over whether God will continue to travel with Israel. Exodus 33, a highly complex series of smaller narratives on the subject of discerning God's presence, concludes with even Moses no longer able to see God face to face. At best, Moses can see God's backside. Now Moses and Israel must look behind God, at the places where God has presumably stepped or visited, for signs of where God may dwell and what God might be doing in the world. All who have looked for God in the vagaries of history know the difficulties inherent in reading and understanding the ambiguities of "God's backside."

Besides providence and people, places have also served as signals of

God's presence. For Israel, as for many others, tradition designated temples and other assorted holy places where God dwelled more surely than in common, ordinary spaces. Shiloh, where the ark of the covenant resided in the days of the judges, and Solomon's temple, where God promised to make the divine name live in perpetuity, served in this manner. When the temple fell to the Babylonians, Israel asked, "Where is God now?" Priestly writers, among others, responded by fashioning the tabernacle tradition we now see in the Pentateuch wilderness story. Once again, Israel lived between times, in this case between exile and home, and the people needed assurance that the Lord did not perish in the temple's fall. Rather, God dwells in a moving, fragile home not made with stones.

In John's Gospel, Christian theologians find a link between the tabernacling God and the divine absence humankind knows amid terrible thirst. In its prologue, the Fourth Gospel speaks of the "word made flesh" that dwelled (literally, "tabernacled") among us as a moving, fragile embodiment of God's glory (John 1:14). At the end, this one cries out in the only word of abandonment we find in John's Gospel, "I am thirsty" (19:28).

Between those moments, in the story of this week's Gospel lesson (John 4:5–42), we hear this same Jesus ask for another drink at noonday, then offer "living water" to a Samaritan woman with whom he also discusses the theology of God's presence. Does God dwell only in Jerusalem or also in Samaria?

For Christians, John's Gospel teaches, God dwells, speaks, and acts in the fragile one who knows completely the absence of God and who abides even now in that absence, so long as the thirst for living water still lingers in this world. God dwells in the tabernacle of the crucified Christ and in the bride with whom he became one flesh on the cross, the same communal body he restored to life with his own breath when the beloved fainted with fear upon seeing his resurrected but ruined flesh (John 20:22).

Few have known the thirst of God's absence more profoundly than Mother Teresa, whose private writings tell of a long, terrible sense of abandonment that bordered on a living hell. Even in such darkness, however, that tiny, wizened woman of God clung to the belief that she bore in her body and soul "the love of an infinite thirsty God," and that her labors on behalf of Calcutta's hopeless ones helped to satiate the burning thirst of Jesus on the cross.[1]

FREDERICK NIEDNER

---

1. Mother Teresa, *Come Be My Light*, ed. Brian Kolodiejchuk, MC (New York: Doubleday, 2007), 154–57.

Clergy quote Moses quite often. It could well be that next to Jesus, Moses is the most frequently quoted person in Scripture! As a denominational executive I consulted with numerous congregations in the Congregational tradition, as well as several churches in other traditions. During those consultations, Moses was quoted too many times. The spiritual leader (either lay or ordained) was usually the one who murmured, "Lord! What shall I do with this people? They are almost ready to stone me!" The quote was not precise, but the sentiment was the same. "Lord, you called me here to lead this people with a new vision, which we all agreed upon—it went well for a while, but now the murmurings are out of control."

One can imagine the growing excitement as Moses began to call God's people together, gathering their consent to lead them out of the bondage of slavery into the promise of freedom and a land to call their own. Support for his vision must have been overwhelming. While in Egypt, the people followed his directives to preserve themselves through the plagues, hail, storms, and, finally, Passover. When Pharaoh had had enough, the people packed up what was most important and headed in a hurry toward freedom and promise, not even waiting for the yeast to rise. The yoke of the past had been lifted, and a vision of milk and honey drew them forward.

A vision, coupled with the freedom to reach for it, is a powerful motivator. Freedom is also a taskmaster. It bears the yoke of choice—choosing whom you will follow, where, when, and why. Understanding the responsibility of that choice is the issue here, for these sojourners in the desert and for the sojourners in our pews and pulpits. Both suffer from misplaced authority. Both will murmur.

Having just returned to pulpit ministry, I recently met with several new colleagues from various faith traditions. One of them told me that he once tried to introduce my predecessor as the pastor from Plymouth Congregational Church. He was quickly corrected, and instructed to use the title "minister" instead. Asked why it made such a difference, I suggested that we all fulfill the role of pastor and minister, depending on the task at hand. The preference of one title over the other is rooted in our primary leadership style and our relationship with the membership. Pastor comes from the pastoral setting, a vision of idyllic life in the country—shepherds feeding their sheep, exerting control over the flock as the sheep habitually follow the shepherd who leads them merrily into greener pastures. Most Congregationalists know little of this because our members love their freedoms so much. There are few sheep, if any, to be led in a Congregational church. Our work is more analogous to herding cats!

Moreover, a minister by definition is one who acts upon the authority of another. Ministers are servants of another authority. We act on what we perceive to be God's vision, God's direction, and God's means *after* we check our perception against that of the congregation, because each member has equal access to God's vision! As "creeping Congregationalism" has made its way into all denominations, even Catholicism, the act of confirming our vision (as pastor, minister, rector, or priest) with the congregation has become increasingly important, if not imperative. So why is Moses's lament so often sung by clergy, even those in Congregational churches? Misplaced authority.

Despite the congregation's affirmation of a new vision, when the going gets tough, memories shorten. Our sojourners in the desert had a legitimate concern. They were out of water, with none in sight. So they began to quarrel with Moses. With Moses! They forgot that it was the living God who wished to bring them out of slavery. They forgot that it was the living God who protected them during the plagues in Egypt. They forgot that it was the living God who opened the sea for them and then closed it on their enslavers. They forgot that the living God led them with a pillar of cloud and fire. They remembered idolatry. As surely as they poured molten gold to fashion a calf to worship, they tried to gold-leaf Moses with the paradox of praise and protest—the idolatry of leadership, the habit of misplaced authority.

Many in leadership succumb to being gold-leafed with accolades for a journey of vision well begun. When difficulties arise and those who once offered praise now protest, the gold-leafed self-image becomes tarnished. Too many respond out of their own misplaced sense of authority, forgetting the One they represent and the vision's path, turning aside to the immediacy of adulation.

Unlike many of us, Moses would have nothing to do with the misplaced authority of the people. In each of their three murmurings (Exod. 15:24; 16:2; 17:3), Moses turned toward God. In each, he redirected the people's emotions toward the source and fulfillment of the promise of a land flowing with milk and honey, saying: "Your complaining is not against us but against the Lord" (16:8). In each, he reminded God's people that he was the servant of another authority: "You shall know that it was the Lord who brought you out of the land of Egypt, and . . . you shall see the glory of the Lord. . . . For what are we, that you complain against us?" (16:6–7). In each instance, Moses deflected the people's gold-leafing of him by affirming his place as a follower among many who follow.

Fruitful church leadership requires one to have the ability to follow. First, we follow our best perception of God's leading, understanding that we see only as in a mirror dimly and we hear with imperfect ears. We may hear some truth, but only one thus far has heard the whole truth and nothing but the truth (so, help me, God! Please!). Secondly, we live amid a faith community of followers who also see dimly and hear only in part. As we gather in the presence of Christ, grace must abound: grace that is able to forgive our misplacement of authority and call us anew to journey together toward the vision promised by God.

DONALD P. OLSEN

EXEGETICAL PERSPECTIVE

This passage is one of several "murmuring stories" that occur in Exodus and Numbers in connection with the wilderness wanderings of the people of Israel between their leaving Egypt and their entering the land of Canaan. These stories cluster both before (Exod. 15–17) and after (Num. 11–20) the giving of the law at Sinai. In the stories that occur in Exodus, the emphasis is on God's provision for the anxious Israelites. In the stories that occur in Numbers, the emphasis is on God's anger and punishment of the people. What accounts for the difference? Apparently, it is the fact of the covenant at Sinai (Exod. 19–24). Before the covenant, the people are simply slaves who have been liberated from Egypt but who still bear the psychological marks of their slavery—and thus their lack of trust. God is patient. After entering into the covenant at Sinai, they should be capable of trust in God. So their lack of faith on the far side of Sinai is a sign of a more serious problem.

The parallel text to Exodus 17:1–7 is Numbers 20:1–13. In Numbers, the similar event is used for a quite different purpose: explaining (though somewhat enigmatically) why neither Moses nor Aaron crossed into the promised land. The narrative structure of the murmuring stories in Exodus and Numbers soberly suggests how hard it is to leave behind an oppression that one has internalized. Sometimes only the second generation (Num. 14:20–23, 31–33) can carry to fruition the promise of liberation.

This short narrative has a simple structure: (1) need (v. 1); (2) complaint (vv. 2–3); (3) response by Moses (v. 4); and (4) miraculous intervention by God (vv. 5–6). The final verse (v. 7) provides an etiology (i.e., explanation) of the name of the place where the events occurred.

The first verse is part of the Priestly writer's itinerary list by which the stages of the wilderness journey are organized. The location of Rephidim is uncertain, but it is not germane to the significance of the story, which is primarily about the relationship between Israel and its God. It is not difficult to sympathize with the plight of the anxious Israelites. Although they have experienced miraculous deliverance from Egypt (Exod. 14–15), the trek through the wilderness is a daily struggle for survival. The resources needed for continual support are different from those needed for the defeat of Pharaoh's army. That the people have no water is a dire condition, and so they "quarrel" (Heb. *rib*) with Moses. This is the first of two key thematic words. Moses's response introduces the other, as he interprets their "quarrel" with him as a "test" (Heb. *nasa*) of God.

Previously God has "tested" the people (15:25; 16:4), by giving them ordinances to obey in connection with God's provision of food for the people. God has reason to wonder if the people are ready to enter into covenant partnership, but the people have no rational grounds to wonder about their God, who has acted reliably toward them in bringing them out of slavery. So for the people to "test" God by challenging Moses, after having already experienced the miraculous provision of water (15:22–25) and food (16:1–36), is to sound a warning note about the readiness of this generation for full liberation. The people are weighing their oppressed but viable lives as slaves against the unknown dangers of the wilderness, which may mean death by thirst (v. 3; cf. 16:3).

Moses's honest protest to God is the first of his distressed pleas concerning the burden of his leadership (see Exod. 18:17–18; Num. 11:11–15). Whereas the people and—especially—Moses have construed the issue as one of Moses's inadequate leadership, God ignores the terms of the quarrel as they have been presented and instead addresses the underlying problem, the provision of water.

As is often the course of delicate negotiations between long-estranged parties, God engages in "trust building" with the people by a miraculous action to provide water. The event will not happen out of sight. Moses will first publicly "pass before the people" and will take with him "elders" who can attest to the event (v. 5). Moreover, the same staff that Moses had instructed Aaron to use to turn the Nile and the other waters of Egypt undrinkable (7:19–24) is now used to bring drinkable water from dry rock (v. 5). Thus continuity is established between the wonders previously experienced and the provision in the wilderness. Just as God had been present in leading the people by a pillar of cloud and a pillar of fire (13:21), so God will be present (whether visibly or invisibly) at the rock (v. 6).

The place names given to this location, Massah ("place of testing") and Meribah ("place of quarreling"), commemorate the episode as they pick up on the key verbs used in verse 2. The events of Massah and Meribah were often recalled in later tradition (Deut. 6:16; 9:22; 32:51; 33:8; Pss. 78:15–16,

41, 56; 81:7; 95:8; 106:32). Although occasionally it was the divine provision that was remembered (Ps. 78:15–16), mostly the event conjured up Israel's fatal lack of trust. Indeed, that this is the burden of the story is suggested by the concluding line of the passage, quoting the question of the Israelites: "Is the LORD among us or not?"

Although the narrator clearly views the situation from the perspective of God's and Moses's irritation with the people, the people's own anguished expression of anxiety in verse 3, which encompasses not only themselves but the fate of their dependent children and animals, opens up the episode to more complex points of view and ways in which to evaluate the emotional as well as religious anxieties of the people who had undertaken this hopeful but deeply risky undertaking.

CAROL A. NEWSOM

HOMILETICAL PERSPECTIVE

What preacher has not wanted to identify with Moses in this passage? You have led the people out of the wilderness of sin, you have proclaimed the message of the Lord each and every week, you have moved in stages through a meticulous long-range planning process. By all accounts you have done everything right, and yet they grumble. The sanctuary is too warm, the floor is too cold, the organist only plays Buxtehude. What preacher, what pastor, has not spent a good many days roasting in the parched land of Massah and Meribah? How does this experience translate into preaching?

If homiletics begins at home, Exodus 17:1–7 calls the exegete to begin by wrestling with his or her own frustrations. The person preparing to proclaim this text does so in a mobile place, jostled back and forth somewhere between the curves of the sublime and the potholes of the ridiculous. All leaders of God's people spend days wandering in the desert of personal and corporate complaints, some of which may well date back to Moses. We wonder, "What is the matter with these people?" or, "What is the matter with me?" and, "Where is my staff?"

How profound it is when a preacher departs from attempts at profundity and speaks from the heart about his or her frustrations. While a steady diet of such speech would upset the stomach of even the staunchest churchgoer, this passage, coming as it does during the season of Lent, sets the table for bits of honest confession. What makes this preacher grumble? What makes his or her family grumble? What deeper reasons lurk beneath the grumbling? Could it be that the preacher and the congregation together are thirsting for spiritual waters they have not yet found?

The passage then calls the exegete, after some careful self-examination, to hear the grumblings of the congregation. As every preacher has complaints about a congregation, every congregation has its own gripes, often about the preacher. Perhaps the exegesis for this sermon begins not in the pastor's study, but in the board or session room. While the people of Israel may have been impatient, they were legitimately thirsty. What thirsts are left unquenched in the church? What complaints are bubbling large? Are these issues widespread among the people or confined to one or two? This is the stuff of church life. To address these complaints with a prophetic voice, one must listen and then prayerfully discern whether the people of God are grumbling from a legitimate thirst or because their bellies are full yet their mouths are still open. This is dangerous preaching, balancing across the thin edge between honesty and arrogance.

In a sermon, humor is the baptismal bathwater for those who mistake their own complaints for gospel. Surely even the most Moses-like preacher has tripped over his or her own ego when demonstrating how to beat water out of a rock. Surely pastors who endure the grumbling masses must have provided at least some of the grumble fodder. Rather than a rant about the congregation's failings, a sermon on this passage would invite the preacher to confess a few of his or her more embarrassing moments. Unlike Moses, when we cry, "Lord, what am I to do with these people?" the Lord may answer, "That's funny. I wonder the same thing about you." Likewise, a congregation's history is bound to have a few occasions where trivialities appeared to be signs of the apocalypse. Did we really argue about carpet for three years? Are handbells more biblical than electric guitars? Lifting these issues to the light of Scripture will test our quarreling against the true Rock of our salvation.

While trivialities do kidnap our attention, legitimate life-and-death issues may also be facing a congregation. A church might be clinging to life, doing what it can to minister to a declining membership. A church might be facing budget shortfalls that will impact its mission for years to come. The community around a church, or church members themselves, may literally need food and drink. A poignant turn in an artful sermon could juxtapose laughter at our own absurdities with the heartfelt cries of a world in peril. The Israelites had the benefit of journeying out of the Wilderness of Sin; our pastors and our pastorates languish in the wilderness of our own sin. What is God to do with us? What are we to do as those who have heard the voice of Jesus Christ as well as the voice of Moses? Where will we find water in the rocky soil of this troubled life?

In this sermon the homiletical leap may be a leap backward. If the preacher begins by illuminating the proximity of silliness and seriousness in church life, the remaining step may be an investigation of how Moses solved his problems. First, Moses prayed (v. 4). Moses prayed a brief, humble, and frightened prayer in plain words. Rather than contorting in theological or psychological gymnastics, the role of the homiletician ultimately may be prophetically to call the people to prayer.

Second, God reminded Moses that he possessed the tools to solve his own problems. "Take in your hand the staff with which you struck the Nile, and go" (v. 5). It may be that those who grumble in frustration and wail in trembling simply need to shut up and go do what they already know will work. Congregations and their pastors can spend so much time reinventing the wheels of methodology that they fail to accomplish the goals of the gospel.

Third, Moses worked the miracle of producing water from a rock not in the sight of the whole congregation but in the company of the elders (v. 6). If the exegesis of this sermon begins in the session or board room, its execution concludes in the same place. This is a passage that calls the proclaimer to be a listener, a prophet, and finally a coach. The sermon may be presented from a pulpit, but it is put to life through the leadership of the people, by the people.

JAMES MCTYRE

John 4:1–42

THEOLOGICAL PERSPECTIVE

Repeatedly in John's Gospel (and throughout the New Testament) people misunderstand Jesus in their first encounter with him. The unnamed woman at Jacob's well in Sychar and all of Jesus' disciples find themselves initially in this number. Some never come to know who he is. In her conversation with Jesus, the Samaritan woman slowly moves from unbelief to belief, from darkness to light, from blindness to sight, from ignorance to knowledge, from misunderstanding to understanding. Unlike Nicodemus in 3:2–10, she has seen nothing of Jesus' signs previously and has not heard he is a teacher "who has come from God" (3:2). The Jesus she first encounters at Jacob's well is only a thirsty Jewish stranger who dares to ask her for a drink. Jesus' request is daring because by speaking to her he crosses significant social boundaries of religion, ethnicity, and gender. Jesus speaks first to her, however, not only because of social convention, but because "the true light, which enlightens everyone" (1:9), was coming into her world. Light has entered her dark world, even though she is not yet able to see it. Truth is spoken to her, even though she is not yet able to discern it.

Irony abounds in this story, as it does in so many of the stories in John's Gospel. Those who view and understand the world literally do not always fare well with an ironical Jesus and an ironical Gospel. Irony presupposes a distinction between appearance and reality. What appears to be true is indeed true, but it is only a partial truth and not the full truth. Because of this distinction between appearance and reality, irony often takes the form of either humor or tragedy—or both.[2]

The Samaritan woman thinks Jesus is the petitioner and fails to understand that it is not he who needs what only she can provide (water from Jacob's well), but she who needs what only he can give (living water) (vv. 7–15). She tells Jesus the half-truth that she has no husband and Jesus reveals the full truth that she has had five husbands and the man currently living with her is not her husband (vv. 16–18). She then assumes Jesus is a prophet because he knows the truth about her marital situation, but she does not realize that he is a very different kind of prophet, one who not only knows the truth about her life but is himself the way, the truth, and the life (vv. 19–24). She believes in a coming Messiah but does not realize that in the person of this Jew from Galilee the Messiah is standing in front of her (vv. 25–26). Only when the woman leaves her water jar, returns to the city, and invites her neighbors to "come and see" Jesus does she begin to discern a deeper, larger reality beyond the initial appearance. "He cannot be the Messiah, can he?" (vv. 28–29).

No less than the Samaritan woman, Jesus' disciples are caught up in the irony of the moment. They encourage Jesus to eat and are puzzled when he tells them he has food they do not know about. Common sense leads them to ask, "Surely no one has brought him something to eat?" (vv. 31–33). They have no idea what kind of "food" Jesus is talking about. They anticipate a seasonal harvest in four months, but Jesus sees something they do not— fields that are already ripe for the harvesting. Just as the Samaritan woman did not begin to understand until she became a witness to Jesus, so the disciples will not begin to understand that Jesus is the bread of life (6:35) until they too invite others to "come and see" (1:46).

Irony (in this story and in many others from John's Gospel) is a literary device the writer uses to describe how Jesus, the Word become flesh (1:14),

---

2. For a splendid discussion of irony in John's Gospel, see R. Alan Culpepper, *Anatomy of the Fourth Gospel: A Study in Literary Design* (Philadelphia: Fortress Press, 1983).

was "in the world . . . yet the world did not know him" (1:10). The world did not know him because it did not understand what it was seeing. When Philip tells Nathaniel that Jesus son of Joseph from Nazareth is the Messiah, Nathaniel responds on behalf of the rest of the world, "Can anything good come out of Nazareth?" (1:46). When Jesus says "I am the bread that came down from heaven," the Jews complain because appearance suggests otherwise. Because they cannot see beyond the apparent, they do not understand. "Is not this Jesus, the son of Joseph, whose father and mother we know?" (6:41–42.) They see only what is apparent, not what the Spirit enables John the Baptist to see, "the Lamb of God who takes away the sin of the world!" (1:29). Only when Nathaniel responds to Philip's invitation, "Come and see" (1:46), does he begin to understand who Jesus truly is (1:49–51).

Irony is not simply a convenient genre for the particular story that John tells. John cannot tell his story about Jesus without using irony, because Jesus is himself an ironical Christ. Irony is not one possibility among others for how John will tell his story. Here content dictates form. Substance determines genre. Jesus is indeed the "son of Joseph, whose father and mother we know." The appearance is not deceiving, but that is not the full truth about Jesus. He is at the same time "the Word" that "was with God" and "was God" (1:1). It is no accident that John's Gospel dominates the early church's understanding of Jesus and figures prominently in the formula of Chalcedon. Jesus is both "fully human and fully God," but the mystery of his identity is that he cannot be the Word that was God without also being the son of Joseph. From "the beginning" the son of Joseph was the Word made flesh. John tells his Gospel the way he does not because he is fond of irony. The story that he tells demands irony.

GEORGE W. STROUP

PASTORAL PERSPECTIVE

At first glance, the woman whom Jesus meets at the well in Sychar could not be more different from Nicodemus. She is an uneducated woman, a learner; Nicodemus is an educated man whom Jesus describes as a teacher of Israel. She is a Samaritan; he is a Jew. She has a shameful past; he is a respected moral leader in his community. She meets Jesus at noontime; he comes at midnight. At a literary level the woman stands as a foil to Nicodemus, but in her own right she plays an important role in the Gospel narrative.[3]

---

3. Culpepper, *Anatomy of the Fourth Gospel*, 91.

One characteristic of the woman is that she is almost totally an outsider. A woman in a man's world, she is a stranger to Judaism, the practices and geography of faith, conventional morality, and the gospel (she remains unnamed to centuries of readers). Is she so much of an outsider that she is considered socially deviant by her community? Is she ostracized by them, stigmatized for her status or behavior? We cannot determine this from the text, and so to go that far is to exaggerate the woman's outsider status.

We may be able to say, however, that in the eyes of the Gospel writer this woman is a nobody. She does not even merit a name, and her gender, religious orientation, social standing, and personal habits distance her from Jesus and her community. We expect that people will try to avoid this woman and ignore her whenever possible.

Being a nobody is not an easy mantle to wear, except maybe for Emily Dickinson, who appeared to relish the role in her poem "I'm Nobody! Who Are You?"[4] For Dickinson the idea of being a public somebody was a gloomy prospect, but she may have been the exception. Most people want to avoid the pain of being nobodies; they want to be recognized and cherished as somebodies who matter.

This text is good news for anyone who has ever felt the humiliation of stigmatization or the pain of being a nobody, because Jesus does not turn away from this woman. On the contrary, he engages her in conversation, takes her seriously, and spends several days in her village. This woman, her community, and their welfare matter to Jesus, whether nobodies or not. That is good news.

It is also challenging news, because it reminds churches and their members that people who are nobodies to them may be somebodies in the eyes of Jesus. Who are those nobodies? They are the people we ignore. Maybe they are a congregation's neighbors, or the strangers who walk through the door, or a potential group to be evangelized and welcomed into the household of faith. This text reminds faithful readers that sometimes our attempts to draw the boundaries of the faith community are too narrow. We often prefer to leave out the nobodies, but Jesus does not do that. He welcomes outsiders, as well as insiders, into discipleship.

He also welcomes people who are just starting the journey of faith. The second characteristic of the woman is that she is a newcomer to faith, and during this conversation with Jesus she takes baby steps. Jesus is so patient with her! His willingness to explain his metaphors and stay with the conversation is in stark contrast to his impatient discussion with Nicodemus.

4. For the full text of this poem, do an Internet search using its title.

Jesus does not make fun of this woman, as he does of Nicodemus, and he does not chastise her for her left-brain response to his right-brain language. Instead, he nurtures her, nudges her along, like a parent teaching a young child. Though he is hard on Nicodemus, Jesus is kind to this woman.

I had a pastor once who liked to preach about what he called "the toughness and tenderness of Jesus." We see those paradoxical characteristics in Jesus as we put these texts side by side. Jesus can be confrontational, and he can be compassionate. He can be unyielding, and he can be generous.

We see his tenderness as he encourages the woman's growth in faith. Any believer who feels like a newcomer to faith and who is also taking baby steps can take heart in this. Jesus supports us as we move toward him and grow in understanding. He wants us to deepen and extend our faith, to recognize and acknowledge him for who he is.

Jesus can be tough too, and the woman gets a taste of that. In the course of her conversation with him, he uncovers her life story. The exposure comes as Jesus talks with her about her husband and looks beneath her self-presentation. She says of Jesus that he "told me everything I have ever done" (v. 29). There is an honesty in the woman's encounter with Jesus that lays open her past, yet she does not appear to be shamed by this conversation and confession.

Instead, her encounter with Jesus emboldens the woman to go and tell all her friends and neighbors about this man. Like the prophet Isaiah, who is liberated for service when he confesses his sin in the temple (Isa. 6:1–8), the woman is freed for discipleship after Jesus exposes her needs and failings. She becomes his witness.

This story narrates the dramatic transformation of the woman. She begins the story as an outsider and becomes a witness; from her status as a beginner in faith she becomes an apostle sent by Jesus himself to testify on his behalf.[5] As such she is a model for other women, for people who feel like nobodies, for newcomers to the faith, and for people with a past. Jesus encounters and welcomes many into the household of faith—even the least likely and maybe, even, you and me.

DEBORAH J. KAPP

EXEGETICAL PERSPECTIVE

The Second and Third Sundays in Lent juxtapose two characters unique to the Gospel of John. Nicodemus comes to Jesus by night and lasts all of

---

5. Culpepper, *Anatomy of the Fourth Gospel,* 137.

nine verses in his conversation with Jesus before fading into the night from whence he came. John 4 narrates the encounter with Jesus of another character, the Samaritan woman at the well. The contrast between Nicodemus and the Samaritan woman is striking. Given the fact that they appear one right after the other in the Gospel, we are meant to notice this contrast in all of its detail.

Nicodemus is a Pharisee—an insider, a leader of the Jews. He is a man, he has a name, but he comes to Jesus *by night*. The character to whom we are introduced in John 4 is a Samaritan—a religious, social, and political outsider. She is a woman, she has no name, but she meets Jesus at noon, in full daylight. The contrast between the conversations these two characters have with Jesus is even more extraordinary. Whereas Nicodemus is unable to move beyond the confines of his religious system, the Samaritan moves outside of her religious expectations to engage Jesus in theological debate (v. 20). Whereas Nicodemus cannot hear that Jesus is sent by God (3:17), the woman at the well hears the actual name of God, "I AM" (v. 26; "he" in the NRSV is not in the Greek text). While Nicodemus's last questioning words to Jesus expose his disbelief ("How can these things be?" 3:9), the last words of the woman at the well ("He cannot be the Christ, can he?" 4:29) lead her to witness to her whole town.

While Jesus' encounter with the woman begins at verse 7, one should not gloss over the beginning of the chapter. Verse 3 provides the setting for the scene, as Jesus leaves Judea for Galilee. The phrase "but he had to go through Samaria" (v. 4) is geographically true, but more importantly, it sets up the theological necessity of this journey. Jesus' stop in Sychar will result in a new witness to his revelation who becomes the narrative agent in the fulfillment of the claim, "For God so loved the *world*." Indeed, it is necessary for Jesus to pass through Samaria to find this witness to God's revelation in the world.

The Samaritan woman at the well is not a passive recipient of Jesus' offer. She immediately recognizes the societal barriers and boundaries that keep her in her place (v. 9); but at the same time she challenges Jesus' authority over and against the ancestors of the faith (v. 12). Like Nicodemus, she first interprets Jesus' words on a literal level. However, she also recognizes that Jesus has something that she needs and is able to ask for what Jesus has to offer, rather than question the possibility (v. 15).

While many commentators are preoccupied with the woman's "sin" and Jesus' offer of forgiveness as illustrated by verses 16–18, the text itself says nothing of any sin she has committed, nor does Jesus ever forgive her. Rather, like Nicodemus, his words are meant to move her to the next level of understanding of who Jesus is, and the conversation is successful. She sees that Jesus is a prophet (4:19). Moreover, sin in this Gospel is not a moral category related to behavior. Sin is unbelief—the inability or unwillingness to acknowledge Jesus as Lord and God.

When the woman successfully moves to a new level of understanding of who Jesus is, she then presses forward in a theological dialogue with Jesus regarding the acceptable place of worship, Mount Gerazim or Jerusalem, over which the Jews and the Samaritans have disagreed for centuries. In essence, her question about the place of worship is also a question about the dwelling of God and represents a fundamental issue for this Gospel. In Jesus, the Word made flesh, God has chosen to dwell, to tabernacle among us (1:14). As a result, Jesus reveals that very truth to the woman. "I AM," he says (4:26), the very presence of God before her. This is the first absolute "I AM" statement in the Gospel of John (cf. 6:20; 8:24, 28, 58; 13:19; 18:5, 7). The last absolute "I AM" statements will cause 600 Roman soldiers to fall to the ground (18:5–7).

Jesus makes God known to this woman at the well and, as a result, makes her a cowitness to his work in the world, one whose labor helps bring in the harvest (vv. 34–38). While she is not absolutely certain that Jesus is the Christ (in 4:29 the syntax of the Greek expects a negative answer), she does not let that stop her from leaving behind her water jar, which represents anything that might hold her back. Going into the city, she invites her fellow townspeople to their own encounter with Jesus. She responds to Jesus in a way that leads Jesus to reveal his true identity to her; in doing so, she sees her own identity evolve. We learn from the Samaritan woman that in our own encounters with Jesus, we are not only changed, but what God reveals to us changes as well.

When the woman returns to her village, she invokes the very words that Jesus says to his first disciples, "Come and see" (1:39). Through her invitation and the sharing of her experience, many believe in him (v. 39). The scene that follows replicates Jesus' calling of the first disciples. Jesus "stays" with the Samaritans, as did the first disciples (1:39), which is a fundamental category of relationship for the Fourth Gospel. The verb "stay" is *menō*— "abide" or "remain." It is because of this abiding with Jesus that the Samaritans are able to confess, "We know that this is truly the Savior of the world" (v. 42), the only time that the title "Savior" is ever used in John's Gospel. In this unexpected witness, this Samaritan village is the narrative fulfillment of 3:16, "For God so loved the world that he gave his only Son, so that everyone who believes in him may not perish but may have eternal life."

KAROLINE M. LEWIS

HOMILETICAL PERSPECTIVE

If I were asked to pick one story that shows us the most about who Jesus is, it would be this one. Here is a passage for a preaching life and a lifetime of preaching. Here too is a text with its own bucket, ready for the filling. Let it down again and again, and each time it comes up with another sermon of living water, another deep drink from the well that will not go dry.

Thirsty preachers need this text. We need the well and the water in it, and the bucket to draw it up, and the man sitting beside us, telling us everything we have ever done. The story gives us so many places to stand, so many moments of recognition, that maybe the first homiletical task is simply to feel our emptiness, and drink. Feel ourselves coming late to the well and meeting the stranger—is there not always another stranger?—who asks us for a drink. Feel ourselves muttering about messiahs with no buckets, so that we have to do all the work. Feel ourselves dry and empty and sermon-less to boot.

Then, as our buckets go down into the well and the stranger continues to talk, feel ourselves drawn into his words, just as surely as if they were a well of water themselves, until their coolness splashes over our faces and suddenly, we know who he is! Is that not the work of a sermon, pulling until the water comes? Day after day at the well: there is the preacher, waiting. Here is a passage for a preaching life and a lifetime of preaching.

There are so many ways to let down your bucket into this text. Here are some to try.

Notice That Jesus Initiates. There are always good reasons for Jesus not to talk with us. This time, it is because the person at the well is a woman and a Samaritan: double jeopardy. We could add a few more reasons to steer clear, based on textual inferences: a shady past, a low-down reputation, a scorching verbal dexterity. Jesus breaks rules to talk with her; his friends are shocked. As preachers and pastors we are conditioned to imagine ourselves in Jesus' role—the ones who break the rules to speak with outsiders. What if we imagine it the other way around?

What rules is Jesus breaking to talk with us? What social conventions is he disregarding? What lines is he stepping across, in order to speak about what truly matters, and what may save our life? Human beings are, by definition, rooted in social contexts and ordered by those realities. Sometimes we let "the way it is" determine what we can or are willing to see. Jesus has a distinct fondness for overstepping boundaries. What traditions or customs or conventions might Jesus have to cross in order to speak to you, the preacher? Before we have a word for the folk, we have to feel that word ourselves.

Notice That It Is Jesus Who Is Thirsty. The walk through Samaria is long and tiring. Jesus sits down by the well while his disciples go to buy food in the village; this is where he and the woman meet. It ought to be easy for a thirsty man to get a drink at a well, but notice that Jesus cannot do this by himself. He asks the woman to give him a drink, gives *her* the chance to recognize the face of Christ in a stranger.

There is something beautifully simple in the staging of this scene as well as its premise: Jesus is thirsty at the well, and we are the ones with the bucket. The deeper metaphorical conversation that follows makes no sense until we really take this in. Can a little thing like a cup of cool water, offered in love, be the beginning of a salvation journey? Yes; and we will never know until we meet the stranger and tend to the human need first.

Notice the Order of Recognition: Prophet, Then Messiah. It is always the flashy bits that get our attention: a healing, an exorcism, a reading of someone else's mind. Jesus pulls a few details about the woman's life out of thin air, and she is greatly impressed: "Sir, I see that you are a prophet" (v. 19). Maybe she needed to confront the supernatural power of the man before she could see the messianic truth. Maybe we all do.

The mighty acts of God are wondrous to behold and difficult to ignore; the Lamb of God who takes away the sins of the world is something else entirely. It requires another look before we can begin to get our heads around it. Maybe the prophet is like the cup of cool water: the visible manifestation of a deeper reality. Here is the first step on a journey to provide water for the soul as well as the body.

Notice What Is Said as Well as Not Said. When the woman comes to the startling recognition that she has been talking to the Messiah, she leaves her bucket and runs to the village with the news: "Come and see a man who told me everything I have ever done!" (v. 29) she cries. Notice the unfinished nature of that sentence, especially given what we know about the woman's history: Come see a man who told me everything I ever did . . . and loved me anyway! She does not say the last four words, but they are implicit in her action, and in the joy with which she runs.

"Everything she ever did" is a long list of sins, and common knowledge besides; it is always before her, in the judgmental expressions of her neighbors. For Jesus to have intimate knowledge of that list is not as singular as it might be; but for him to know her past and still love and forgive her— well, that is as unbelievably new and fresh as anything she has ever heard! The man who told her everything she ever did . . . *and loved her anyway* . . . is what saves her life.

In that moment, she sees God. She receives Christ—and leaps up to tell.

ANNA CARTER FLORENCE

Third Sunday of Lent

Isaiah 35:4–7a

⁴Say to those who are of a fearful heart,
  "Be strong, do not fear!
  Here is your God.
  He will come with vengeance,
  with terrible recompense.
  He will come and save you."

⁵Then the eyes of the blind shall be opened,
  and the ears of the deaf unstopped;
⁶then the lame shall leap like a deer,
  and the tongue of the speechless sing for joy.
  For waters shall break forth in the wilderness,
  and streams in the desert;
⁷the burning sand shall become a pool,
  and the thirsty ground springs of water.

John 9:1–41

¹As he walked along, he saw a man blind from birth. ²His disciples asked him, "Rabbi, who sinned, this man or his parents, that he was born blind?" ³Jesus answered, "Neither this man nor his parents sinned; he was born blind so that God's works might be revealed in him. ⁴We must work the works of him who sent me while it is day; night is coming when no one can work. ⁵As long as I am in the world, I am the light of the world." ⁶When he had said this, he spat on the ground and made mud with the saliva and spread the mud on the man's eyes, ⁷saying to him, "Go, wash in the pool of Siloam" (which means Sent). Then he went and washed and came back able to see. ⁸The neighbors and those who had seen him before as a beggar began to ask, "Is this not the man who used to sit and beg?" ⁹Some were saying, "It is he." Others were saying, "No, but it is someone like him." He kept saying, "I am the man." ¹⁰But they kept asking him, "Then how were your eyes opened?" ¹¹He answered, "The man called Jesus made mud, spread it on my eyes, and

said to me, 'Go to Siloam and wash.' Then I went and washed and received my sight." ¹²They said to him, "Where is he?" He said, "I do not know."

¹³They brought to the Pharisees the man who had formerly been blind. ¹⁴Now it was a sabbath day when Jesus made the mud and opened his eyes. ¹⁵Then the Pharisees also began to ask him how he had received his sight. He said to them, "He put mud on my eyes. Then I washed, and now I see." ¹⁶Some of the Pharisees said, "This man is not from God, for he does not observe the sabbath." But others said, "How can a man who is a sinner perform such signs?" And they were divided. ¹⁷So they said again to the blind man, "What do you say about him? It was your eyes he opened." He said, "He is a prophet."

¹⁸The Jews did not believe that he had been blind and had received his sight until they called the parents of the man who had received his sight ¹⁹and asked them, "Is this your son, who you say was born blind? How then does he now see?" ²⁰His parents answered, "We know that this is our son, and that he was born blind; ²¹but we do not know how it is that now he sees, nor do we know who opened his eyes. Ask him; he is of age. He will speak for himself." ²²His parents said this because they were afraid of the Jews; for the Jews had already agreed that anyone who confessed Jesus to be the Messiah would be put out of the synagogue. ²³Therefore his parents said, "He is of age; ask him."

²⁴So for the second time they called the man who had been blind, and they said to him, "Give glory to God! We know that this man is a sinner." ²⁵He answered, "I do not know whether he is a sinner. One thing I do know, that though I was blind, now I see." ²⁶They said to him, "What did he do to you? How did he open your eyes?" ²⁷He answered them, "I have told you already, and you would not listen. Why do you want to hear it again? Do you also want to become his disciples?" ²⁸Then they reviled him, saying, "You are his disciple, but we are disciples of Moses. ²⁹We know that God has spoken to Moses, but as for this man, we do not know where he comes from." ³⁰The man answered, "Here is an astonishing thing! You do not know where he comes from, and yet he opened my eyes. ³¹We know that God does not listen to sinners, but he does listen to one who worships him and obeys his will. ³²Never since the world began has it been heard that anyone opened the eyes of a person born blind. ³³If this man were not from God, he could do nothing." ³⁴They answered him, "You were born entirely in sins, and are you trying to teach us?" And they drove him out.

³⁵Jesus heard that they had driven him out, and when he found him, he said, "Do you believe in the Son of Man?" ³⁶He answered, "And who is he,

sir? Tell me, so that I may believe in him." [37]Jesus said to him, "You have seen him, and the one speaking with you is he." [38]He said, "Lord, I believe." And he worshiped him. [39]Jesus said, "I came into this world for judgment so that those who do not see may see, and those who do see may become blind." [40]Some of the Pharisees near him heard this and said to him, "Surely we are not blind, are we?" [41]Jesus said to them, "If you were blind, you would not have sin. But now that you say, 'We see,' your sin remains."

ORDER OF WORSHIP

OPENING WORDS / CALL TO WORSHIP

Jesus, Light of the World, *John 9:5*
give us eyes to see as you see!
Once we lived in darkness, but now—
as children of light, we are called
to what is good and right and true.
Jesus, Light of the World,
give us eyes to see as you see!

HYMN, SPIRITUAL, OR PSALM

CALL TO CONFESSION

As children of God's light,
we are called to do what is pleasing to the Lord:
to participate in what is good and right and true,
and expose what is unfruitful and evil.
God does not punish our sin with trials *John 9:2–3*
But desires our genuine contrition.
And so, we bring our confession to God,
so that what is hidden in us becomes visible,
and the shadows of our hearts may be illumined
by grace.

PRAYER OF CONFESSION

Healing God of majesty and glory, *John 9:6–7; Isa. 35:1–10*
we are thirsty for your grace.
You made a way for us in the wilderness,
and still, in our foolishness, we go astray.
We hide our eyes from your presence.

We do not listen to your word.
We are lifeless when we ought to dance
and speechless when we ought to sing.
Forgive us, O Lord.
Speak peace to our fearful hearts,
strengthen our weak hands,
and make firm our feeble knees
as we seek to follow in your holy way. Amen.

DECLARATION OF FORGIVENESS

Now return to the Lord with joy and gladness.   *Isa. 35:10*
Sing a song of redemption!
Let sorrow and sighing be no more.
In Jesus Christ we are forgiven.
Thanks be to God.

PRAYER OF THE DAY

Holy God,
why is it that we look but do not see?
Bring us again and again into your light
until your ways become visible to us,
and bear fruit in us.
Touch us so that we are utterly changed,   *John 9:6*
a "before" and "after,"
a "now" and "then";
that we may also say,
"One thing I do know,   *John 9:25*
that though I was blind, now I see."
Lord, we believe;   *John 9:38*
help our unbelief.
In Christ's light, we pray. **Amen.**

HYMN, SPIRITUAL, OR PSALM

PRAYER FOR ILLUMINATION

Gracious God,
illumine our hearts and minds
as the Scriptures are read and proclaimed,
so that by the power of your Holy Spirit
we may see what is good and right and true.

And seeing, help us to do what is pleasing to you,
so that your glory becomes visible
in our words and deeds.
In Christ's name, we pray. **Amen.**

SCRIPTURE READINGS

SERMON

HYMN, SPIRITUAL, OR PSALM

PRAYERS OF INTERCESSION
Remember your mercy, O Lord, and help us,   *Isa. 35:4–7*
for you are strong and trustworthy.
Let all generations see your blessing,
for your name is holy and your mercy is great.
Show the strength of your hand,
quiet our fears.
Comfort those of us who are afflicted,
with your mighty, healing hands.

Afflict those of us who are comfortable,
to feel the pain of all who suffer.
Then we will sing out with joy and glorify you forever;
for your mercy shows no bounds. Amen.

LORD'S PRAYER

INVITATION TO THE OFFERING
Our lives overflow with the goodness of God.
Sharing what we have so abundantly received,
we bring now our tithes and offerings to God,
with gladness and gratitude.

PRAYER OF THANKSGIVING/DEDICATION
In gratitude, O God, we come to your table,
into your presence, into your house.
For all that you have done for us,
most especially, for the gift of your gracious son,
we offer our thanks and praise.

We long to live as children of light,
doing what is pleasing to you
and bearing the fruit of the light
through Jesus Christ,
who opens the eyes of the blind
    and makes the lame to leap.
In his name we pray. **Amen.**

HYMN, SPIRITUAL, OR PSALM

CHARGE

Go peaceably,
looking upon the hearts of others
    with the same compassion Christ has shown you.
Trust that he is able to open your eyes,   *John 9:6*
enabling you to walk by faith
in his name.

BLESSING

May the love of God pursue you,
the light of Christ enfold you,
and the Holy Spirit keep you;
as you dwell in the house of the Lord
your whole life long.

SONG SUGGESTIONS

"Blest Are They, the Poor in Spirit" (*ELW* 728, *GC* 636, *GTG* 172)
"Breathe on Me, Breath of God" (*EH* 508, *GC* 800, *GTG* 286, *TNCH* 292,
    UMH 420)
"Come Ye Sinners, Poor and Needy" (*GTG* 415, *UMH* 340)
"O for a Thousand Tongues to Sing" (*CH* 5, *EH* 493, *ELW* 886, *GTG* 610,
    TNCH 42, *UMH* 56 and 57)
"Our Help Is in the Name of God the Lord" (*GTG* 330)
"Where Cross the Crowded Ways of Life" (*CH* 665, *EH* 609, *ELW* 719, *GTG*
    343, *TNCH* 543, *UMH* 427)
"Within Your Shelter, Loving God" (*GTG* 168)
"Woman Hiding in the Crowd" (*GTG* 178)

CHILDREN'S SERMON

Inspired by John 9:1–41

(Note: This children's message uses a modern allegory for Jesus' healing of the blind man and the Pharisees' outrage at Jesus healing on the Sabbath. In the Feasting on the Word Guide to Children's Sermons, authors David and Carol Bartlett advise not using healing stories in the children's sermon, due to the complexity of addressing healing stories with young children, who may wonder why Jesus does not heal them or their loved ones as he did in the Gospels.)

Let me tell you a story about a group of kids a lot like you. They went to school every day and did their work and tried to do what their teacher told them to. One day, their teacher, Mrs. Jones, told them, "Students, I have to go to the office for a few minutes. While I'm gone, I want you to stay in your seats and work quietly on the worksheet I gave you. There should be no talking and no getting up and moving around the room."

So Mrs. Jones left the classroom. The students heard the clip-clop, clip-clop of her shoes going down the hallway toward the office. They liked Mrs. Jones and wanted her to be proud of them, so they all focused on their worksheets and resisted the urge to talk with their friends.

The classroom was quiet, except for the sound of everyone's pencils writing the answers on their worksheets. Suddenly, the silence was broken by a loud cough. It was Brandon, the new kid in the class. He kept coughing and coughing until his face turned red. Everyone looked up from their worksheets and stared at him. Was Brandon OK? What was wrong with him? Did he need help? Everybody at the class looked at Brandon and looked at each other. No one wanted to disobey Mrs. Jones by getting out of their seats or calling the teacher next door for help.

One girl in the class, Anna, finally spoke up. "Brandon, are you OK?" Brandon did not answer. He was coughing so hard that he could not catch his breath enough to answer Anna. "We have to help him!" Anna said. "SHHH-HHH!" the other kids said. "Be quiet! Do you want to get in trouble?"

Anna jumped out of her seat and went over to Brandon. "Sit back down, Anna!" the other kids said. But Anna did not listen. She patted Brandon firmly on the back a few times, the way her mom did when somebody was coughing really hard. That did not seem to help, so she ran to the classroom sink to get a cup of water for Brandon. Brandon took a few sips of water and his cough died down. "Thanks, Anna," he said.

Just then, the class heard the clip-clop, clip-clop of Mrs. Jones walking back toward their classroom. As Mrs. Jones came in the door, several kids shouted to her, "Mrs. Jones! Anna was talking and got out of her seat while you were gone!" They could not wait to tattle on Anna, even though Anna had talked and gotten out of her seat only to help Brandon.

Before Mrs. Jones could scold Anna, Brandon spoke up. "Mrs. Jones," Brandon said. "I got a bad cough while you were gone, and Anna was helping me. She was not being bad. She was being a good friend."

SERMON HELPS

Isaiah 35:4–7a

THEOLOGICAL PERSPECTIVE

All language for God is metaphorical, and when metaphorical language for God hangs around too long, it begins to look literal—as if my finger could actually point directly into God. The metaphor "God the Father" is an example of metaphor that for many people has gone stale to the point of being uninformative and even abusive. The metaphor of God as Father often suggests qualities associated with an authoritarian, tough-love male parent, and it has become so sedimented that the metaphor has lost its power to challenge and inspire and, most importantly, to change. Because we refuse to let go of old metaphors, new ones, of which there are many in Scripture, are ignored or underused and thus sound awkward when spoken. (For example, "Mother Bear," from Hos. 13:8, "Like a bear robbed of her cubs," comes to mind.) If our understanding of God continues to change and grow, then our language for God should change and grow as well.

However, when preachers, teachers, and other theologians fool around with God-talk, people get nervous, and frequently they get angry. When we show the inherent and *necessary* instability of our finite words for the infinite mystery of God, we appear to take away the familiar God people have known from childhood. These emotional reactions occur because human language *for* God has *become* God. As we are well aware, substituting anything earthly for the Divine, like continuing to use certain metaphors as if they were gods themselves, is idolatry.

Metaphorical language for persons can become sedimented, literalized, and abusive, as well. Consider the language of physical disability as the metaphor for spiritual disability in today's reading. The language used in this passage intends to show the extreme nature of Israel's brokenness and, with that, God's power to change what appeared to the Israelites to be intractable human "problems." Our spiritual ancestors, for whom these metaphors had resonance, saw literal deafness, blindness, and other physical limitations as beyond human ability to heal. Biblical commentaries on this passage in Isaiah disagree on whether or not the healing of the people who are blind, deaf, mute, and lame is literal or metaphorical. It may be that the prophet is describing an eschatological reality wherein all physical (and spiritual) limitations are no more. However, whether the healing preached in Isaiah is literal, physical healing or a metaphor for spiritual disease and remedy, unexamined use of this language represents scholarly and pastoral negligence.

If the healing described in this passage continues to be understood literally, and we believe that at the eschaton, all physical ailments will be healed by God, we are suggesting that physical differences are "problems" to be "fixed." We expect that the body transformed at the eschaton will be "perfect." Even using Paul's notion of a transformed "spiritual body" (1 Cor. 15), we simply cannot imagine that bodies will retain the marks or characteristics of their earthly physical reality. (Medieval theologians spent a great deal of time debating the age and condition of the body assumed into heaven. "Will I look like I did in my twenties, even if I died dismembered in my forties?")

Disability theorists point out that what we call "disabilities" are simply failures of imagination in architecture and infrastructure. Human bodies are not the "wrong" shape, nor are they incomplete; rather, the physical environment in which we live is what is wrong or incomplete. For instance, when arthritis changes how high I can reach, and I am unable to grasp items on the upper grocery-store shelves, the remedy should not have to be that I stop going to the store alone, but rather that products be relocated on the shelves for easier access or that tools be created to help me reach up without pain.

We simply fail to see the environment as malleable and assume that "fault" for inability lies with the individual. In this case, the specter of the perfect, transformed body *imposes* the concept of disability on the naturally aging body. We usually live with the unspoken assumption that human bodies should be changed to fit an ideal, and we refuse to consider instead that the environment should change to fit human differences. We can all count on being "disabled" at some point in our lives.

If the labels "deaf," "blind," and "lame" function metaphorically as tropes for spiritual dysfunction, we perpetuate an age-old but faulty connection between "disability," sin, and the divine will. Historically, theologians have attributed any form of embodied difference (having a womb, having black skin, or being gay, blind, or paralyzed) to an ontological category that ranges from simply inferior and needing human mastery to sinful and needing divine mastery.

The theologically unspecified but functionally perfect human body, the body we imagine God created pre-fall, hovers in the background in these metaphors. This body, when explicated, usually resembles a twenty-year-old, Anglo-European, heterosexual athlete or model. Conformity in appearance exemplifies the perfection of Eden, while diversity of embodiment becomes a function of the imperfect realm outside of Eden. The historical pairing of different or diseased bodies with fallen spiritual states serves to contain our desperate human fear that pain and suffering are randomly distributed. With the tidy theological equation wherein socially stigmatized people are such because of the divine displeasure with us, we can guarantee our own physical safety (until such time as we cannot).

Many members of our congregations can tell stories, if we ask, about the shadows that cross the faces of well-intentioned Christians when they are introduced to a deaf daughter, a spouse with multiple sclerosis, or a brother in a wheelchair. Fear that "we" could be "they" causes the faithful, well-intentioned person to refer by default to the still-preached equation of physical disability and spiritual brokenness. When language for disability functions as a trope for spiritual disease and sin, even beloved hymns like "Amazing Grace" ("was blind but now I see") can isolate and stigmatize some children of God.

EMILY ASKEW

PASTORAL PERSPECTIVE

A story from the Sufi tradition of Islam tells of a stream that finds itself butting heads with the edge of the desert, trying to make its way across the burning sand. It soon realizes that it cannot flow through the sands and that its futile efforts will result only in its becoming a stagnant quagmire. It hears the sand whispering that the way across the desert is to surrender itself to the wind in evaporation. As it becomes a mist, the wind will carry it across the desert to the mountains. In the cooler temperatures of high altitude, it will become rain falling on the mountainside and will find itself a stream again. The act of surrender and trust is foreign to the stream, who has forged its path tumbling down to the desert's edge, growing bigger and stronger as it moves though gentle rolling hills and rocky gorges. After much debate with the sand and with itself, the stream finally lifts its arms to the wind and surrenders. The stream allows itself to be changed as it is carried aloft. It discovers that its essence remains intact despite its transformation. When it rains down upon a new mountainside, the stream remembers that it has undergone this transformation time and again in its eternal quest to BE the essence of stream.[1]

There is scientific, factual basis for this ancient Sufi tale. No doubt the original tellers observed and experienced the transformation of the water cycle many times in the arid terrain in which they lived. Obviously they also considered, imagined, and lived the spiritual transformation the process implies. In Isaiah 35 waters spring up in the midst of the desert, defying the laws of nature. The image illuminates the transformative power of God. What is the connection between the ancient practical, yet mystical, story and the words of the ancient prophet? Can this ancient tale from a sister faith help us understand the workings of God in our time as well as in the prophet's?

Isaiah's oracles in chapters 34 and 35 most likely date to the exilic period rather than the period of kingship in the other chapters of First Isaiah. Their context and their audience are people in exile and captivity, people who may believe that God has abandoned them to their enemies. They may believe that this is God's justice, punishment for their sins of moral lapse and abandoning the ways of God. They are people enduring in the midst of despair. How unfathomable it must be to hear the prophet's words of God's strong protection, comfort, and deliverance! They long to have their sight restored and see the future with hope, to have their ears unstopped and hear good news, to be healed so they can leap for joy and sing God's praises. They long for liberation! They yearn for abundance in the barren landscapes of their lives, abundance that flows miraculously like a stream in the desert. Can they trust these words?

Most likely the readers of commentaries such as these have never been literally forced into exile and captivity. The metaphors of these words may still strike a deep emotional chord within us as twenty-first century people. The prophet's vivid language of liberation may spark light in our souls for reasons not fully known to our conscious minds. Individually, people know the pain of exile and isolation of captivity in broken relationships, in disillusionment with daily work and routine, in unexpected illness or joblessness, in choices we have made that lead to addictions. "Where is God in the midst of the pain of life?" is the perennial question. Where is God when we feel akin to the stream in the story, butting heads with burning desert sands and becoming a stagnant wasteland?

Faith communities feel the metaphor of exile as they watch membership

---

1. Indries Shah, "The Tale of the Sands," in *Tales of the Dervishes* (New York: E. P. Dutton and Co., 1970), 23–24.

and pledge numbers dwindle. In twenty-first-century culture they are not in the center of people's lives as they once were, particularly if they are in the mainline tradition. People choose to practice their spirituality in private, alternative ways. There are a wide variety of institutions outside the church to which people give their resources and in which they volunteer to serve their neighbor. Where is God in the midst of what may seem like a quagmire to the institutional church? Does God not want God's communities of faith to survive, to thrive? Communities and individuals long to hear the life-giving words, "Be strong, do not fear! Here is your God," in the midst of death-dealing situations.

Here is where the words of the prophet meet the Sufi tale. God is always present with God's saving power. The decision of the stream to trust the wind is the secret to transformation such as the prophet foretells. Transformation and liberation come through trust in the willingness to allow God to do the shaping, especially when this reshaping requires radical change of form. God knows the true essence of any because it is God who creates it. God comes to save the true essence of individuals and communities as they give themselves wholeheartedly to the healing and renewing work of God. Surrendering to transformation in trust allows eyes to be opened, ears to be unstopped.

Here is where the words of both ancient story and prophet meet the meditation of a pastor's heart. Who in the community is in a quagmire, refusing to allow transformation? Where are the quagmires in the life of the community together? How can the community be of service to the quagmires in the world, bringing the good news of God's transforming power even in the midst of its own transformation?

Full trust brings joy. It brings singing and dancing in the heart as people become cocreators with God, living water for others who are in the parched, desert places of life. The ancient prophet and storyteller call twenty-first-century people to be miraculous streams of God's mercy, love, and grace. They are called through firsthand experience of the liberating miracle of trust and transformation.

JANE ANNE FERGUSON

EXEGETICAL PERSPECTIVE

Our text in chapter 35 is a preview and an anticipation of the fuller visioning poetry of chapters 40 and following. Already here, ahead of the ominous narratives of chapters 36–39, the tradition of Isaiah anticipates and promises restoration that depends upon the powerful, reliable resolve of God. Our verses, 4–7a, are sandwiched between two vivid images. In verses 1–2, the poetry bespeaks the revivification and restoration of fruitful creation, which will exhibit the glory of the creator God who is at the same time "our God," the God of Israel (v. 2). In verses 8–10, the poetry describes a coming homecoming on the "Holy Way" (= the new highway) that will be safe and joyous. Thus the preceding verses on creation (vv. 1–2) and the following verses on historical return (vv. 8–10) bring together the spheres of "nature" and "history" to affirm that every imaginable sphere of reality is subject to the restorative power of YHWH's rule. The outcome of such a display of transformative power assures the enhancement of YHWH and permits joy among those who benefit from the reassertion of divine governance.

The focal point of our verses is the divine declaration (given in prophetic oracle) in verse 4, a typical "oracle of salvation" that features the entry of YHWH, via such speech, into a context of despair. The declaration purports to transform such a situation of despair. At the center of the oracle is the exclamation "Behold your God" (NRSV "Here is your God"). Those addressed see and notice the arrival of God in a situation from which God has been thought to be expelled. In context this is an announcement that God is now present in the midst of exilic despair in the Babylonian imperial world that had thought that YHWH had been eliminated as player in imperial history and politics. The rhetoric is parallel to Isaiah 40:9 and 52:7–8; in both cases the declaration of God's transformative presence is said to be the "gospel," the news that YHWH is back in play in a way that will change everything.

The consequence of this divine coming, effected in and through prophetic speech, is that YHWH is one who will punish and repay the ruthless imperial overlords and give back to them what they have enacted against the vulnerable . . . including Israel. As a result, the subjugated people Israel will be delivered ("saved"). This declaration asserts that the historical process is not just an interface of imperial power and vulnerable subjects, as these two parties are wont to think. YHWH is a third agent, who transforms the entire context of power and powerlessness. Thus the coming of God is always disruptive, revolutionary, and emancipatory. The terms of engagement are shifted so that established power is placed in jeopardy and the vulnerable have new historical possibility because of this third agent.

Here that "news" is addressed to those without energy or courage, the ones who have given in to imperial absolutism and so ended in despair. The "weak hands" and "feeble knees" of verse 3 do not refer to physical disability but to hopeless resignation that has concluded that Israel is forever caught in imperial deathliness and brutality from which there could be no exit (see Isa.

40:27 and 49:14). When YHWH is absent or disinterested or defeated, Israel is exposed to the unchallenged power of despair, and so is left passive and without possibility. Thus the oracular assertion of verse 4 is exactly a direct contradiction to the mood of those in verse 3. The coming of God contradicts that "world without God" in which the vulnerable have no possibility.

The ones who have "weak hands" and "feeble knees" in verse 3 are in verses 5–6 identified as the blind, the deaf, the lame, and the dumb, the ones with diminished human capacity who are narcoticized to the rule of the empire, who in resignation accept the absolutism of the empire, who expect nothing outside the empire, and who submit without energy or courage to the world given by the empire.

Now, in this moment of prophetic utterance, all of that is changed. They are wrenched out of their narcoticized state. They are summoned beyond their resignation. They are empowered to new possibility:

The blind now see!
The deaf now hear!
The lame now leap!
The dumb now sing!

They notice in their new wakefulness; they recognize in the utterance their new freedom. They may again become active agents in their own history. They are now, again, ready to turn toward some new future possibility. (That rhetoric of course is reiterated in the summary statement of Jesus' transformative ministry in Luke 7:22.) It is the reentry of the gospel God that reopens human possibility and that culminates in the joy of departing empire. Such joy constitutes restless defiance and new venturesomeness in this world opened by utterance.

The imagery of "like a deer" in verse 6 provides a segue from revived human history (vv. 5–6a) to revived "nature" (vv. 6b–7). God not only makes Israel's new life possible; God also makes available the new life of all creation. Thus the promise of transformed human life is matched by the transformation and "return" from arid failure to the waters of life, for creation, since Genesis 2:10–14, has depended upon water to make flourishing possible. Thus in rapid succession there is witness to water, streams, pools, springs, swamps, all a contradiction of the lethal environment of wilderness, desert, burning sand, and thirsty ground. The waters make possible grass, reeds, and rushes that will sustain the entire ecosystem of "return." We may imagine a thousand species, along with jackals, swimming in delighted abandonment at the gift of rain and the abundance of sprouting life.

All—the most vulnerable, the most resigned, those most in the grip of despair and death—are summoned to newness. Those who leap and sing and dance may do so along with blooming crocuses (v. 1) and with sated jackals (v. 7)!

WALTER BRUEGGEMANN

HOMILETICAL PERSPECTIVE

The nations have assaulted Israel, pummeled her until beaten down. In the calculus of geopolitics, it would be hard to imagine that she would be able to survive the onslaughts of greater powers, and yet the prophet declares that Israel's God "will come and save you." What will that salvation look like? Anticipating Israel's liberation from the disgrace of exile, the prophet hands on divine promises that visualize the people's future in a way that contrasts sharply with the misery of strength lost and hope dried up. The prophet's word addresses a people whose losses have dimmed any vision of a salvageable future, and they can no longer hear God's voice. God will open eyes and ears, remove the burdens of servitude that weigh the people down, and restore their voices, long suppressed. With sight, hearing, strength, and voices recovered, it will be as though the natural world itself will join in celebrating relief from Israel's time of diminishment and spiritual drought.

No doubt an oppressed people's interest lies in the immediate future. Isaiah uses dramatic language to open the people's eyes and ears to the promise that God has not abandoned them and will have the last word. The exile ending—it must have seemed at the moment that God's dominion was being made manifest, reversing their despair, and it was. But only for a moment, because such a grandly drawn vision of a healed humanity and a repaired creation can never be entirely realized in human history.

This text can be preached without reference to the New Testament, of course, and when it is, the focus might be on the ways that God is always at work to free people from afflictions that diminish joy and disrupt communities. One might fairly say that God can lead a community of faith from its season of sterility—even a kind of death—to new life. There are different ways, both literal and metaphorical, of losing sight, hearing, and voice and of being so weighed down that it is impossible to stand straight and strong. The need for healing is always contemporary—for Israel, for the church, and for the whole human race—and we pray it will be granted us and all who have need of it, sooner rather than later.

While the text certainly has to do with hope for the immediate future, at the same time and on another level it also points to the ultimate future, the eschatological moment of universal redemption, a new creation. A new creation is God's business, in which we may be called to assist, but it is not the natural, organic outgrowth of historical processes. When we pray, as Jesus taught his disciples, "Your kingdom come," we are praying for this new creation, a pure gift of God.

While Christians can read Isaiah without reference to Jesus Christ, we can also quite legitimately read Isaiah through the lenses of the New Testament. However the people of Isaiah's time may have heard his prophecy, by the time Matthew's Gospel was composed, Isaiah's promise of the restoration of the people's sight, hearing, strength, and voice would be heard eschatologically, as a sign of the advent of the transforming presence of the Messiah (see Matt. 11:2–6). Where Jesus is, the kingdom (reign) of God becomes manifest, exhibiting the characteristics of Isaiah's images of redemption. Jesus' healing of Gentiles projects an eschatological vision of the kingdom that is bigger than the healing/restoration of Israel alone.

It is all too easy to hear the Gospel stories of Jesus' healings interpreted as merely ornaments designed to heighten his reputation, but they are central to the church's faith. One may not be prepared to decide exactly what was a "miracle" and what might be explained differently in order to perceive that these "mighty acts," taken together, make a profound theological statement. For example, the Gospels portray opening the eyes of the blind sometimes literally and sometimes mystically. (Cf. John 9:14; Luke 24:31; Acts 9:17.) There is more than one way of losing sight, hearing, strength, or voice. The contemporary church, ideologically polarized, diminished in influence and culturally marginalized, may find itself suffering a kind of exilic experience not entirely unlike Israel's in Babylon. In its own crisis of faith, not seeing things too clearly, hearing impaired, limping along, it appears to have lost its voice. Yet there is cause for hope, for the Lord of the church is One who heals and restores. The "mighty acts" point as well to the ultimate healing of the whole creation.

Waters in the wilderness and "streams in the desert" portray an abundance of water as a redemptive image. Humanity's need for clean, fresh, and reliable sources of water elevates the everyday need for water to near-redemptive status. Although Isaiah knew nothing of Christian baptism, Christians may hear his water images in baptismal terms, trusting that the "living water" of the Holy Spirit is at work redemptively in the sacrament that forms the church, both relieving spiritual thirst and preparing our dry ground to bear fruit.

Even though we still live in historical time, it is possible to witness signs of the kingdom among us, now here, now there. The church is that community of baptized people that transcends race and tribe and ethnicity (i.e., it is "catholic"), and its work is, along with Israel, to become a blessing to "all the families of the earth" (Gen. 12:3). While the church itself looks for and trusts in God's healing for itself, it understands that the calling of all the baptized is to share with Christ the work of healing persons, whole communities, and a stressed creation. Needy as we are ourselves, it is nevertheless our privilege to be invited by God to participate in the divine work of new creation, even though, in historical time, the new creation will become manifest in the world only now and then, here and there, as we await the coming of the divine reign.

RONALD P. BYARS

John 9:1–41

THEOLOGICAL PERSPECTIVE

Attempts to quantify either sin or evil are difficult, if not impossible. Even more difficult are attempts to assign blame or responsibility. Is one person more sinful than another? How should we measure sinfulness? Has one person suffered more or greater evil than another? Has the twentieth century, for example, been the occasion for more evil than previous centuries? For Jews and Christians the experience of evil, both personally and collectively, has long raised two large theological questions. First, how can God's goodness and sovereignty be defended (or "justified") in light of the reality of evil? Second, does the reality of evil negate human faith in God's covenant faithfulness?

Abraham obeyed God's command and took Isaac, his "only son," the bearer of God's promises to Abraham, to a mountain in Moriah to sacrifice him. An angel intervened and a ram was miraculously provided for the sacrifice. "So Abraham called that place 'The LORD will provide'" (Gen. 22:8, 14). Furthermore, God promised Israel that if it kept God's commandments, "I will place my dwelling in your midst, and I shall not abhor you. And I will walk among you, and will be your God, and you shall be my people" (Lev. 26:11–12). Not even the devastating experience of exile seemed to shake Israel's belief that in God's own time and way "the Lord will provide." Similarly, Christians have been drawn to Jesus' words, "Are not two sparrows sold for a penny? Yet not one of them will fall to the ground apart from your Father. And even the hairs of your head are all counted. So do not be afraid; you are of more value than many sparrows" (Matt. 10:29–31).

Classical Christian theology sometimes draws a distinction between general and special providence. The former affirms, in the words of John Calvin, that God "watches over the order of nature set by himself." The latter, special providence, affirms that "God so attends to the regulation of individual events, and they all so proceed from his set plan, that nothing takes place by chance."[2] That conviction is reflected in the answer of the Heidelberg Catechism (1563) to the question concerning the meaning of the first line of the Apostles' Creed, "I believe in God the Father Almighty, Maker of heaven and earth." It means that "whatever evil he [God] sends upon me in this troubled life he will turn to my good, for he is able to do it, being almighty God, and is determined to do it, being a faithful Father."[3]

However, the horrors of the twentieth century—the unimaginable slaughter in the trenches of the First World War, the genocide of six million Jews in the Holocaust, the use of the atomic bomb on Hiroshima, the killing fields of Cambodia and Rwanda—have made it difficult, if not impossible, for many to affirm that all events proceed from God's set plan. Do the horrors of the twentieth century mean that Christians must relinquish the Bible's claim that "the Lord will provide"?

The story of Jesus' healing of the man born blind in John 9 may help us think through some of these perplexing questions. It may provide some clues for a contemporary Christian understanding of providence. First, John 9 may suggest that a contemporary doctrine of providence should be chastened, more modest, and less grandiose than its classical predecessors. John 9 does not say that all events reveal God's works, only that in this specific individual, this particular man, God's work—God's providence—is revealed. Neither this story nor any other story should be used to explain the Holocaust.

Second, just as Jesus never explains why this individual was born blind, so a contemporary doctrine of providence might hew more closely to the language of confession than that of explanation. Jesus' disciples do not know the distinction theologians sometimes draw between natural and moral evil, but they assume that this natural evil—the man's blindness—must in some way be due to (and therefore explainable by) someone's sin, either that of the man himself or that of his parents. Jesus, however, rejects all attempts to explain this man's blindness by means of the category of sin. The man's healing serves a different purpose than that of explanation: "he was born blind so that God's works might be revealed in him" (v. 3). A contemporary doctrine of providence—one that takes its clues from this story—might eschew grand theories that try to explain all events, and focus instead on what particular events reveal about God.

2. John Calvin, *Institutes of the Christian Religion*, ed. John T. McNeill, trans. Ford Lewis Battles, LCC (Philadelphia: Westminster Press, 1960), 202–3 (1.16.4).
3. The Heidelberg Catechism, in *Book of Confessions: Study Edition* (Louisville, KY: Geneva Press, 1996), 62 (4.026).

Third, God's presence and activity in the healing of the blind man cannot be explained because it is not publicly accessible. It is not so much perceived as it is revealed, and it is revealed only to those who are given the gift of faith. The irony in John's story, of course, is that the blind man receives his sight, but everyone else in the story loses theirs—not their physical vision, but their capacity to believe and understand what they have witnessed. Without exception, neighbors, Pharisees, and parents are unable to see in this event that "God does provide." Not even the man who has been healed understands what has happened to him. Only after Jesus seeks him out and calls him to faith in the Son of Man does he truly "see." Only after he first believes does he worship the one who is truly from God (v. 38) and who has healed far more than just his blindness.

Providence is not a Christian explanation of history, nor is it a compelling rational answer to and explanation of the horrors of the twentieth century. Providence is a confession by those who are given the eyes of faith that in particular events God works in, around, through those things that oppose God, to accomplish God's purposes.

GEORGE W. STROUP

PASTORAL PERSPECTIVE

Over the past few decades several cultural observers have voiced concern about the erosion of social capital in the United States: the breakdown of neighborhoods, lower rates of participation in organizations like the PTA and churches, and fewer bowling leagues. People are *Bowling Alone*, as the title of a famous book described it, and that is troubling to many people.[4] Even more troubling to others are reports about the breakdown of a more basic American institution—the family. Many people are understandably concerned about high rates of divorce, the scattering of extended families, and pressures to embrace new family configurations.

This loss of social capital is troubling not just to those who are directly involved in those institutions but also to social observers, because the latter are aware of the side effects that social isolation can have for communities and individuals. Communities with more isolation tend to feel (and maybe are) less safe; people often have less stability when they are isolated from friends and loved ones; and a recent study suggests that they may be less happy too. Happiness, it seems, is contagious, and we are more likely to catch it if we are hooked up with happy family members, friends, or neighbors.

---

4. Robert D. Putnam, *Bowling Alone: The Collapse and Revival of American Community* (New York: Simon & Schuster, 2000).

In light of these concerns, some people look nostalgically to the communities of the past, in which people were more connected, attentive to one another, and supportive. That was when people knew how to take care of each other—or did they?

Reading John 9 through the lens of anxiety about collapsing social capital is interesting, because it is so counterintuitive. All our presuppositions about the strength and health of earlier communities and family systems collapse when we read this text, because each of the supports, which we assume are in place, fails to deliver. The text narrates the story of Jesus healing a man who had been blind from birth and the reactions of his community, the religious authorities, and his family. Nothing plays out the way we might expect it to.

The first surprise is the community's reaction; they do not recognize the man who was born blind. This is so odd. The man has lived in their midst all his life; his neighbors have interacted with him, perhaps helped him cross the street or draw water; they have worshiped with him. Why do they fail to recognize him after he is healed? Is it because the only marker of his identity was his blindness? Has the fact that he was differently abled been the only thing they could ever see in him?

This raises a pastoral issue for any of us who interact with persons who are differently abled. How do we identify and come to know people who are different from us? Do we allow disability to be a defining marker, or are we able to look beyond that and recognize the humanity of people? How limited or keen is our sight when we are with people who are differently abled?

A second pastoral issue surrounds the actions of the religious community, in which leaders seem to want to control the narrative. The Pharisees do not want to hear or believe the man's story, because it opposes the story they want to tell. They want Jesus to be the sinner, not the hero of the story; they want another explanation, one that leaves them in control of all the religious goods and services.

Perhaps it is reassuring to realize that even in the first century religious authorities fought over ecclesiastical authority. The privileges of defining sin or dispensing grace are powerful ones, and it is no surprise that religious authorities covet them. In one form or another we have fought over these privileges, this power, for centuries, and we continue to do so. This text convicts the religious antagonists who battle over definitions of sin or the gifts of grace and who allow those battles to obscure God's presence in our midst. How do we get caught up in battles like this? What issues or preoccupations divert our attention from God's presence and action and passions?

Almost everybody fails the man born blind. Even his family backs away from him, and his parents put their own safety before his welfare. Maybe we can understand an older couple being reluctant to sacrifice their home, work, and community for their son, but would we not expect them to celebrate with him, to be joyful over his healing? There is nothing of that in this text. The parents' fear overwhelms their joy, and they abandon their son to the authorities.

The community fails. The religious authorities fail. The family fails. The only trustworthy figures in this story are the man born blind and Jesus. The man tells the truth, and even in the face of threats, the abandonment of his community and family, and expulsion, he sticks to his guns. I was blind, but now I see. Again and again and again, the man witnesses to the saving grace he has experienced in Jesus Christ.

Jesus is the only one the man can trust, and he is the only one we can trust in this story. Although the Pharisees lay claim to dispensing grace, it is Jesus who transforms. It is Jesus who heals. It is Jesus who stands with the man in his final isolation. He stands with us too.

Sometimes when the sun is really bright, or when an artificial light is intense, we need to squint or shut our eyes. The brightness seems dangerous to us, and the reflex is automatic. Metaphorically we see this human reaction unfolding in John 9: the light of the world shines bright, and the community, the Pharisees, and the man's family shut their eyes in self-defense. That is the intuitive thing to do, right?

Wrong. In this text, everything is counterintuitive. The light of the world is in our midst, and we need not shut our eyes. In fact, the best thing to do is to open our eyes, wide. We will not be blinded by the light. We will be saved.

DEBORAH J. KAPP

EXEGETICAL PERSPECTIVE

In the history of scholarship, John 9:1–41 has taken on a life of its own that has effectively detached its content from, and significance for, the Johannine narrative as a whole. Commentaries have neatly divided the chapter into an isolated drama of seven scenes narrating the aftermath of Jesus' healing of the man born blind, who never asked to be healed in the first place. While interpreters have been content to let the meaning of the story reside in the miracle itself, Jesus himself comments on and provides the interpretation of the healing in 10:1–21. Jesus does not stop talking in 9:41, and Jesus' words in 10:1–21 function as the discourse that interprets the meaning of the healing of the blind man. This is a recurring structural pattern in the Gospel of John.

Jesus performs a sign (*sēmeion* in the Fourth Gospel, not *miracle*), which is followed by dialogue and then commentary from Jesus that provides the theological framework through which to interpret the meaning of the sign. The actual healing itself is narrated very succinctly, because it is not the miracle that is the critical point. Rather, as sign, it points to something beyond itself, to what an encounter with Jesus signifies. The narrative weight is given to the dialogue and discourse that follow.

When the discourse on the healing of the blind man is ignored in the interpretation of John 9, the events in chapter 9 are not allowed their full meaning and impact. Only after the healing do we learn that the work (9:14) occurred on the Sabbath (cf. 5:9). Much like the Samaritan woman at the well, the blind man grows in his understanding of who Jesus is, yet this time not through direct dialogue with Jesus but through witness to his encounter with Jesus. In his interrogation by the Pharisees, the blind man repeatedly tells his story and comes to know that Jesus is from God (v. 33). This confession is the impetus for the man's expulsion from the synagogue. It is important to note that Jesus has been gone from the narrative since the healing itself and does not reappear until verse 35 when he finds the man who has been cast out of the synagogue (*aposynagōgos*). The truth of who Jesus is, set out immediately in the prologue, is what the blind man is able to see.

Interpreting 9:1–10:21 as a unit yields a number of exegetical insights for the interpretation of the healing of the man blind from birth. While a first interpretation of this story may focus on the importance of seeing, or "spiritual sight," in recognizing who Jesus is, the importance of hearing is revealed in the discourse of the story. In fact, the blind man first responds to Jesus' voice. Jesus tells him, "Go, wash in the pool of Siloam" (v. 7), which the blind man does. He hears Jesus before he sees Jesus.

Like the woman at the well, the blind man recognizes Jesus gradually. He goes from seeing "the man called Jesus" (v. 11), to calling Jesus a prophet (v. 17), to recognizing that he must be from God (v. 33), to addressing him as "Lord" and worshiping him (v. 38). In fact, in verse 37 Jesus himself reveals the importance of both sight and hearing when it comes to belief. "You have seen him," he says, "and the one speaking with you is he."

The importance of hearing and seeing comes into full relief when Jesus' words in 10:1–21 are heard along with the healing of the blind man. In the discourse Jesus integrates seeing and hearing with believing. Jesus reiterates that those who *know* him, his sheep, hear his voice and follow him. In the Gospel of John, such "knowing" articulates relationship. In the figurative language of the sheep and the shepherd, Jesus recasts the importance of seeing and hearing by creating new images for what has already occurred in chapter 9 between the blind man and Jesus.

The blind man is more than one whom Jesus heals; he is one of Jesus' sheep, a member of the fold, a disciple. Like the sheep, the blind man hears Jesus' voice. Like the shepherd, Jesus finds the blind man when he has been cast out (v. 35). Jesus provides for the man born blind much more than sight. He provides for him what he, as the good shepherd, gives all of his sheep: the protection of his fold (10:16; cf. also 21:15–19), the blessing of needed pasture (10:9), and the gift of abundant life (10:10). As a result, hearing and seeing are much more than ways by which one recognizes or believes in Jesus. They are, in fact, expressions of relationship with Jesus, and relationship with Jesus means also relationship with the Father (10:14–15).

Moreover, relationship with Jesus reimagined as the relationship between shepherd and sheep becomes representative of discipleship. Jesus the good shepherd will protect his sheep, his disciples, leaving them safely in the "fold" by coming out of the garden (the Greek verb is *exerchomai*—"came out," not NRSV "came forward") to meet Judas and the soldiers and Jewish police (18:4). In chapter 21, Jesus will ask Peter to take on the role of shepherding the sheep.

Sight and hearing are both critical in this story, as Jesus makes God known in the healing of the blind man. Without both chapters together, one sense is afforded greater significance than the other, and the blind man's "sight" is reduced to mere example or miracle. In fact, he embodies that of which Jesus speaks in 10:1–18.

KAROLINE M. LEWIS

HOMILETICAL PERSPECTIVE

A preacher can talk and talk about this story, but it is not a story about talking. It is a story about time: before and after, then and now, years ago and today, always and then suddenly.

In between is what happened, but a preacher cannot really talk about that, either—at least, not in a way that makes sense. There was a moment, you say. There was a thing that happened. There was a man you met. He touched you, with mud and light. The rest is a song.

Amazing grace, how sweet the sound, that saved a wretch like me!
I once was lost, but now am found; was blind, but now I see.

The inquisition comes next; you might as well expect it. People notice. Amazing grace does not pass over the body without leaving indelible marks. What happened, they ask? What did you do? What did he do? How do you explain your new body, your new self, your new life, your new sight?

How do you *explain* what we know cannot be and what therefore cannot be explained?!

A preacher can talk and talk about this passage and what happened to the man born blind, but be clear: it is not explanatory talk. Some things, some miracles, can never be explained. We can only describe them, tell what we know, say what happened and what we believe about it. Proof and explanation have their place, but not in this passage. *This* passage is about time: before and after, then and now, who we were for years and years and who we are today. The moment of conversion itself is not as important as the difference it made: *I once was lost, but now am found; was blind, but now I see.* This, a preacher can talk about. This, a preacher can describe.

As we do, here are a few homiletical strategies to keep in mind.

Set the context for blindness as a place to be rather than an ethical shortfall. I have a friend who was born blind. She has taught me the folly of pity: she neither wants nor deserves mine. Her life is rich and full and she lives and moves in that life. To be sure, she has had to learn a measure of adaptation; to be blind in a world structured for sighted people means that she has to find ways to understand and cope with our ways. She also has to teach us, constantly, how to live with (not "help") her, because that is *our* blindness: even if we were to walk around with kerchiefs over our eyes or develop cataracts, we would never know what it is like to be *born blind.*

This is a delicate point, but essential if we are going to enter this passage: we are talking about *different worlds* more than *different ethics.* Many preachers get fascinated by the historical details in this text (for example, the key fact that in Jesus' day, blindness was interpreted as a punishment for human sin) and become preoccupied with how far we have evolved in our theological interpretations of illness; in many cases, thankfully, we have. The text does not ask us to enter its ethical world as much as it asks us to enter the state of blindness itself.

What is it like to be born into one experience of the world that will *never change?* What is it like to live and move among others whose experience of the world is so radically different? What is it like to try to understand their world and describe yours to them? Blindness is first a state of being rather than a metaphor for unbelief. Before we can enter this text, we have to try to place ourselves there—in a world that is radically different from the one we know now.

Let the moment of conversion simply be a turning point in the plot rather than something to explain and defend. Let us be frank: conversions are messy. They can even be downright revolting, as John 9 illustrates ("He spit in the dirt, made mud with his saliva, and put it on my eyes!"), and most important of all, they never sound convincing. Just because *you* had a holy moment with mud does not mean that the rest of us will stop scraping it off our boots, right?

A preacher has to remember this: one person's ecstatic moment with mud usually looks, to the rest of us, like a classic case of self-delusion. Try to describe it, as the man born blind did, and others will question your sanity, doubt your word, and write you off. The muddy details of John 9 remind us of how carefully we have to tune our ears (and possibly our stomachs) before we can listen to one another's stories. Obsessing about our own discomfort ruins our ability to hear.

Focus on what we can actually describe: the difference between before and after. Notice that the man born blind cannot describe his conversion moment to anyone's satisfaction, but he *can* tell the difference it makes. "All I know," he tells the authorities, "is that I was blind, and now I see!" This is a better tactic, because now he is talking about things others can see and hear for themselves. They knew him before; they can see him now, and clearly, he is no longer blind!

So let description of the before and after be the thing. Once I saw the world like this; now I see it like this. Once I believed this; now I believe this. Once I lived in a place that I now see was blind to certain things. Now my eyes are opened, and here is what I see and know! These are the stories the church needs to hear.

Confess Jesus; do not explain him. In the end, all we can say is that we believe Jesus healed this man. We cannot tell how or why or offer any proof that will be convincing. Our confession is everything, in the new world of faith. It is everything he asks.

ANNA CARTER FLORENCE

Fourth Sunday of Lent

Ezekiel 37:1–14

¹The hand of the LORD came upon me, and he brought me out by the spirit of the LORD and set me down in the middle of a valley; it was full of bones. ²He led me all around them; there were very many lying in the valley, and they were very dry. ³He said to me, "Mortal, can these bones live?" I answered, "O Lord GOD, you know." ⁴Then he said to me, "Prophesy to these bones, and say to them: O dry bones, hear the word of the LORD. ⁵Thus says the Lord GOD to these bones: I will cause breath to enter you, and you shall live. ⁶I will lay sinews on you, and will cause flesh to come upon you, and cover you with skin, and put breath in you, and you shall live; and you shall know that I am the LORD."

⁷So I prophesied as I had been commanded; and as I prophesied, suddenly there was a noise, a rattling, and the bones came together, bone to its bone. ⁸I looked, and there were sinews on them, and flesh had come upon them, and skin had covered them; but there was no breath in them. ⁹Then he said to me, "Prophesy to the breath, prophesy, mortal, and say to the breath: Thus says the Lord GOD: Come from the four winds, O breath, and breathe upon these slain, that they may live." ¹⁰I prophesied as he commanded me, and the breath came into them, and they lived, and stood on their feet, a vast multitude.

¹¹Then he said to me, "Mortal, these bones are the whole house of Israel. They say, 'Our bones are dried up, and our hope is lost; we are cut off completely.' ¹²Therefore prophesy, and say to them, Thus says the Lord GOD: I am going to open your graves, and bring you up from your graves, O my people; and I will bring you back to the land of Israel. ¹³And you shall know that I am the LORD, when I open your graves, and bring you up from your graves, O my people. ¹⁴I will put my spirit within you, and you shall live, and I will place you on your own soil; then you shall know that I, the LORD, have spoken and will act, says the LORD."

John 11:1–46

¹Now a certain man was ill, Lazarus of Bethany, the village of Mary and her sister Martha. ²Mary was the one who anointed the Lord with perfume and

wiped his feet with her hair; her brother Lazarus was ill. ³So the sisters sent a message to Jesus, "Lord, he whom you love is ill." ⁴But when Jesus heard it, he said, "This illness does not lead to death; rather it is for God's glory, so that the Son of God may be glorified through it." ⁵Accordingly, though Jesus loved Martha and her sister and Lazarus, ⁶after having heard that Lazarus was ill, he stayed two days longer in the place where he was.

⁷Then after this he said to the disciples, "Let us go to Judea again." ⁸The disciples said to him, "Rabbi, the Jews were just now trying to stone you, and are you going there again?" ⁹Jesus answered, "Are there not twelve hours of daylight? Those who walk during the day do not stumble, because they see the light of this world. ¹⁰But those who walk at night stumble, because the light is not in them." ¹¹After saying this, he told them, "Our friend Lazarus has fallen asleep, but I am going there to awaken him." ¹²The disciples said to him, "Lord, if he has fallen asleep, he will be all right." ¹³Jesus, however, had been speaking about his death, but they thought that he was referring merely to sleep. ¹⁴Then Jesus told them plainly, "Lazarus is dead. ¹⁵For your sake I am glad I was not there, so that you may believe. But let us go to him." ¹⁶Thomas, who was called the Twin, said to his fellow disciples, "Let us also go, that we may die with him."

¹⁷When Jesus arrived, he found that Lazarus had already been in the tomb four days. ¹⁸Now Bethany was near Jerusalem, some two miles away, ¹⁹and many of the Jews had come to Martha and Mary to console them about their brother. ²⁰When Martha heard that Jesus was coming, she went and met him, while Mary stayed at home. ²¹Martha said to Jesus, "Lord, if you had been here, my brother would not have died. ²²But even now I know that God will give you whatever you ask of him." ²³Jesus said to her, "Your brother will rise again." ²⁴Martha said to him, "I know that he will rise again in the resurrection on the last day." ²⁵Jesus said to her, "I am the resurrection and the life. Those who believe in me, even though they die, will live, ²⁶and everyone who lives and believes in me will never die. Do you believe this?" ²⁷She said to him, "Yes, Lord, I believe that you are the Messiah, the Son of God, the one coming into the world."

²⁸When she had said this, she went back and called her sister Mary, and told her privately, "The Teacher is here and is calling for you." ²⁹And when she heard it, she got up quickly and went to him. ³⁰Now Jesus had not yet come to the village, but was still at the place where Martha had met him. ³¹The Jews who were with her in the house, consoling her, saw Mary get up quickly and go out. They followed her because they thought that she was going to the tomb to weep there. ³²When Mary came where Jesus was and saw him, she knelt at his feet and said to him, "Lord, if you had been here,

my brother would not have died." ³³When Jesus saw her weeping, and the Jews who came with her also weeping, he was greatly disturbed in spirit and deeply moved. ³⁴He said, "Where have you laid him?" They said to him, "Lord, come and see." ³⁵Jesus began to weep. ³⁶So the Jews said, "See how he loved him!" ³⁷But some of them said, "Could not he who opened the eyes of the blind man have kept this man from dying?"

³⁸Then Jesus, again greatly disturbed, came to the tomb. It was a cave, and a stone was lying against it. ³⁹Jesus said, "Take away the stone." Martha, the sister of the dead man, said to him, "Lord, already there is a stench because he has been dead four days." ⁴⁰Jesus said to her, "Did I not tell you that if you believed, you would see the glory of God?" ⁴¹So they took away the stone. And Jesus looked upward and said, "Father, I thank you for having heard me. ⁴²I knew that you always hear me, but I have said this for the sake of the crowd standing here, so that they may believe that you sent me." ⁴³When he had said this, he cried with a loud voice, "Lazarus, come out!" ⁴⁴The dead man came out, his hands and feet bound with strips of cloth, and his face wrapped in a cloth. Jesus said to them, "Unbind him, and let him go."

⁴⁵Many of the Jews therefore, who had come with Mary and had seen what Jesus did, believed in him. ⁴⁶But some of them went to the Pharisees and told them what Jesus had done.

ORDER OF WORSHIP

OPENING WORDS / CALL TO WORSHIP
O mortal, can these bones live? *Ezek. 37:3*
Only the Lord God knows.

O people, hope in the Lord.
With the Lord there is steadfast love
and great power to redeem.

HYMN, SPIRITUAL, OR PSALM

CALL TO CONFESSION
To set the mind on the flesh is death,
but to set the mind on the Spirit is life and peace.
Trusting in the Spirit of God,
let us confess our sin.

PRAYER OF CONFESSION

O Lord, if you held our sin against us,
who could live, who could stand?
We seem to have more faith in death
than hope in your promise of life.
We seek peace through war
and find security in weapons.
We abandon the hungry, sick, and dying,
and pursue wealth by making others poor.

And even so, you love us;
still there is forgiveness with you!
Therefore we worship you;
for you alone, O Lord,
can save us from death
and redeem us from our sin. Amen.

DECLARATION OF FORGIVENESS

O dry bones, hear the word of the Lord!   *Ezek. 37:4*
If Jesus Christ dwells in you,
the Spirit of God will be your life
and the grace of God will be your righteousness.
And if the Holy Spirit dwells in you,
then God, who raised Jesus from the dead,
will also give life to your mortal bodies.
Friends, this is the good news of the gospel:
In Jesus Christ we are forgiven.
Thanks be to God.

PRAYER OF THE DAY

Lord God, Great I Am,   *John 11:1–45*
you are resurrection and life.
As we worship you this day
show us who we are:
bearers of good news,
messengers of resurrection;
through Jesus Christ our Lord. **Amen.**

HYMN, SPIRITUAL, OR PSALM

PRAYER FOR ILLUMINATION

O Lord, we wait for you,
and in your Word we trust.
By the power of your Spirit,
set our hearts and minds
on the source of life and peace:
Jesus Christ our Savior. **Amen.**

SCRIPTURE READINGS

SERMON

HYMN, SPIRITUAL, OR PSALM

PRAYERS OF INTERCESSION

In desperation we cry to you, O Lord.
We know you hear. We know you care.

We pray for those whose hope is lost,   *Ezek. 37:11–12*
who feel dried up and cut off from you.
By your grace, open their graves;
bring them back to the land of the living.

We pray for those who are oppressed,   *John 11:44*
held captive by the power of death.
Release them from their chains;
unbind them and let them go!

We pray for those who weep,   *John 11:32–33*
lost and lifeless in fear and regret.
Grant them the peace of your presence;
show them what your love can do.

We pray for those who are dying,   *John 11:25–26*
the light of life fading in their eyes.
Help them to believe in you
so that they may live and never die.

We thank you, O Lord,   *John 11:40–41*
for having heard our prayers.
Enable us to trust in you,
and thus to see your glory;
through Jesus Christ,
the resurrection and the life. Amen.

LORD'S PRAYER

INVITATION TO THE OFFERING
Without the breath of God,   *Ezek. 37:9; John 11:43*
we are dry bones,
and without the Word of God,
we are dust.
With gratitude,
let us offer our lives
to the Lord of all life.

PRAYER OF THANKSGIVING/DEDICATION
Holy God, giver of life,   *Ezek. 37:11–14*
we thank you for raising us up
and joining us together
as one people, your people,
flesh and bone in the body of Christ.
As you have delivered us from death,
use our lives to proclaim the good news
of new life in Jesus Christ our Lord. **Amen.**

CHARGE
Arise, dry bones, and live!   *Ezek. 37:5; John 11:43*
Come out, Lazarus,
and give glory to God!

BLESSING
May the Lord Jesus Christ,   *John 11:25*
who is the resurrection and the life,
bless and keep you in this life
and the life to come.

SONG SUGGESTIONS

"Abide with Me" (*CH* 636, *EH* 662, *ELW* 629, *GTG* 836, *TNCH* 99, *UMH* 700)

"Come Live in the Light" (*ELW* 720, *GC* 710, *GTG* 749)

"God Weeps with Us Who Weep and Mourn" (*GTG* 787)

"Let Us Hope When Hope Seems Hopeless" (*TNCH* 461)

"O God, Our Help in Ages Past" (*CH* 67, *EH* 680, *ELW* 632, *GC* 614, *GTG* 687, *TNCH* 25, *UMH* 117)

"Our Hope, Our Life Are in the Lord" (*GTG* 847)

"Up from the Earth and Surging Like a Wave" (*GC* 452)

"When Jesus Wept" (*EH* 715, *GTG* 194, *TNCH* 192)

CHILDREN'S SERMON

Based on Ezekiel 37:1–14

Ezekiel was with the people of Israel who had been forced to leave their homes and go to Babylon because they had been captured by the king of Babylon. God gave Ezekiel many visions or dreams and messages so the people would have hope. This vision is the most famous one in the book of the Bible about Ezekiel.

Ezekiel reported that God's Spirit came over him, took him to a valley filled with bones, and plunked him down in the middle of all those bones. God's Spirit led him around among the bones. Ezekiel could see that there were many, many bones, and they were very old and dry.

"Human, can these bones become alive again?" asked God.

"Only you can answer that question, God!" said Ezekiel.

God told Ezekiel to say these words: "Listen, bones! The Lord God says to you, 'I am going to breathe life into you. You will be alive again! I will put muscles on you. I will cover them with flesh and skin. Then I will breathe life into you. When you come alive, you will know that I am God.'"

Ezekiel did as God told him. Immediately, he heard a great clatter, a great shaking, and he watched as the bones came together to form skeletons. Then the skeletons were covered with muscle, and suddenly the muscles were covered with flesh and skin. But they were not alive.

Then God told Ezekiel to tell the breath this message: "The Lord God says to you, 'Come from the four winds. Breathe life into these dead bodies!'"

Ezekiel did as God told him. And when the breath came into them, the bodies came alive and stood up. Ezekiel was surrounded by a big crowd of people.

Ezekiel was stunned. Then God explained this vision to him. "These bones are the people of Israel. In Babylon they feel dead, without any hope. They think they are finished. You tell the people this message from me: 'I am giving breath and life to them. I will take them to good land where they can plant and grow food. Then they will know that I am God. This is what the Lord says.'"

SERMON HELPS

Ezekiel 37:1–14

THEOLOGICAL PERSPECTIVE

This poignant description of dry bones strewn across a valley is one of the Bible's great gifts to the eschatological imagination of both Jews and Chris- · tians. Under Ezekiel's watchful eye, these bones suddenly reassemble them- selves in a great clatter, then are strapped with sinew and flesh and skin, and, finally, reanimated with a breath called forth from the four winds. Apart from this passage, the Hebrew Bible is largely silent regarding any blessed afterlife for the dead, and this *Grey's Anatomy* account may be the earliest appearance in the Bible of what became a central belief for both rabbinic Judaism and Christianity: the resurrection of the body.

Most commentaries stress that Ezekiel's intent was more metaphori- cal than physiological. That is, his vision was about the eventual return to the land of Israel of the descendants of those Jews who had been marched against their will to Babylon. The dry bones represent the dusty sense of hopelessness that the exiles would ever find their way home. "These bones are the whole house of Israel," Ezekiel is told (v. 11), and they will, one day, return to the land of Israel.

John Calvin granted as much. For Calvin, these verses are about arousing the despairing refugees to hope for a return, and it is essential to recognize how this image of the valley of revived dry bones works at this level. It is also worth appreciating the way in which Ezekiel based this political hope upon a more fundamental hope for the resurrection of the dead that is the source of all hope, "the chief model of all the deliverances that believers experience in this world." More than anything else human beings can hope for, Calvin claimed, the resurrection of the dead is so utterly dependent upon God that there can be no doubt that it lies outside of our powers. There are forms of immortality that one can recognize as intrinsic to existence in the normal course of things—the survival of one's heirs, influence, or reputation, for instance. For a body to be resuscitated long after it has begun to decompose, that is a miracle.[1]

In ways that we find baffling today, Christians of the early church were convinced that life after death required a body. This was a fundamental disagreement between proto-orthodox Christians and gnostic Christians. For the gnostics, nothing was more desirable than the eventual liberation of the soul from its physical encumbrance of a body. Church fathers like Irenaeus and Tertullian, however, were adamant that without flesh, there is no person to overcome death, because a human being, in this life and the next, is an intermingled soul and body. Indeed, for the miracle of resurrection to occur, there must be a corpse. A permanent separation of soul and body, for which the gnostics hoped, would not be immortality, but extinction.

This belief was put to the test in the early centuries when Christian martyrs were hacked to pieces by gladiators, or eaten by lions during waves of persecution. Was there a point at which a body was so mangled, or its parts so widely dispersed, that it could not be reconstituted—even by God? By the mid-second century, according to Eusebius, the Romans in Gaul began decapitating and burning the corpses of Christians executed in the amphitheaters, and then dumping the remains to float down the Rhine, to "rob the dead of their rebirth" and ruin the confidence of surviving Christians that martyrdom would be rewarded with resurrection. Does God have the power to recover and reassemble these particles that have been swept away by the current? To think in even more grisly terms, what becomes of the saintly martyr who is eaten by a lion, which is in turn sacrificed and eaten by pagans? Consumed and digested by two carnivores, whose flesh has the martyr's body become? In response, Tertullian suggested that bones and teeth, as the most enduring particles, even though crushed will sprout like blastulas. The view developed among the Fathers that just as God made Adam from dust, God can reconstitute a body from its smallest material bits, and thereby recover the person with identity intact, complete with her peculiar memories and even the precious scars of her martyrdom etched upon her resurrected body.[2] In the Talmud, one of the rabbis suggests that

1. John Calvin, *Institutes of the Christian Religion*, ed. John T. McNeill, trans. Ford Lewis Battles, LCC (Philadelphia: Westminster Press, 1960), 3.25.4.
2. Caroline Walker Bynum, *The Resurrection of the Body in Western Christianity, 200–1336* (New York: Columbia University Press, 1995).

our iniquities are engraved into our bones, an indelible, telltale moral record of how we conducted ourselves through the lives that were given to us.

The Talmud contains a curious mechanism for Ezekiel's vision of the opening of the graves that will enable the Jews to return to the land of Israel. For the righteous who die in exile, God will excavate underground chutes through which their bones will roll until they reach the promised land. As they arrive, God will restore to them their breath, and they will stand and live again.

This brings into the foreground a theme of Ezekiel's vision that is so deeply engrained in Jewish and Christian thought that it can be missed. At the core of biblical narrative is the story of displacement—of having wandered a long way from home, and longing to return. This is the underlying plot of being cast out of Eden, of being foreigners in Egypt, of the journey to the promised land, of the longing of exiles in Babylon to return to the land of their fathers.

While there are additional, and equally biblical, ways to understand the story of salvation—for example, vanquishing the forces of evil or being cleansed of sin and filled with divine purpose—this plot of exile and return is part of the deep structure of the Bible. According to it, we are separated from God and are seeking a way to return, though we may not know it. This is Augustine's confession of the restless heart that will find rest only when it returns to God. It is certainly the unrequited longing that is expressed in Ezekiel's vision of the valley of dry bones.

KELTON COBB

PASTORAL PERSPECTIVE

This passage has captured the imagination of readers of the Hebrew Bible for centuries. Proof of this can be found in visual art, ministerial proclamations, music, literature, and even pop culture. More than 80,000 references to this biblical passage can be found on Google, including drawings, paintings, and illustrations from as early as the third century.

Few parts of the Bible offer richer material for visualization and imagery than Ezekiel and the valley of the dry bones. As you read these Bible verses, it is virtually impossible not to envision a desert scene with bones and skulls lying in disarray as far as the eye can see. Ezekiel stands in the midst of the dry bones listening to the "words of the Lord." In some of the art depicting this passage, God is also present, standing above Ezekiel as a shadow or in a clearer representation. In one book illustration painted in 1372, the Lord is depicted as a young man leaning down from heaven directing Ezekiel's actions. Ezekiel is an old man preaching to bodies rising from wooden coffins and to the bones on the ground.[3]

As we progress through Lent, perhaps it would be valuable for us to consider what dry bones (and dry times) are represented in our own spiritual lives. What can we learn from the lonely and parched periods of our spiritual journeys? The "dark night of the soul" is familiar in literature and the human experience. Most of us can point to periods of time when doubts, hopelessness, depression, fear, and anxiety were prominent in our daily living. Certainly hopelessness and despair were a communal experience for the people of Israel at the time of Ezekiel's vision of dry bones. What could we possibly learn from these "dry" periods of life when we feel as disconnected and brittle as the bones in Ezekiel's vision? The following poem beautifully describes the conditions of these dry periods:

Bone

Bone lay scattered and artifactual
Wind-rowed like dead branches
Whose tree bodies repeat the desiccation
All hope bleached and lost
Living moisture evaporated

Calcified memories of what was
Or seeds of what could be
Wandering shards of vessels
That once thrummed with pure energy
Where honor and dishonor wrestled

Stripped of living water to walk the hills
Needing only gravity to line the valley

It was never about the bones anyway
Rather a glimpse of pure power
A reminder of who's in charge of restoration
Real hope lies in the Source

Dempsy R. Calhoun (unpublished)

---

3. Description of the illustration of "Ezekiel's Vision of the Valley of Dry Bones" (artist unknown), in Petras Comestor, *Bible Historiale,* France, 1372.

In many interpretations, proclamations, sermons, and other written materials on this passage in Ezekiel, the major theme is renewal, resuscitation, restoration, rest, rejuvenation, and resurrection. There is the temptation to move quickly in our consideration of Ezekiel's vision to the "good" part, the part about the joy of a new, vibrant life. We are drawn away from the lessons buried in the dry, barren landscape. Maybe God's question to us this Lent is, "What can your spiritual dry bones teach you? What can you learn about yourself and your relationship with the world from the painful, difficult paths you are called to walk?"

In *National Geographic*, an article entitled "Lost Tribes of the Green Sahara" describes how archaeologists unearthed some 200 graves near a vanished lake that indicated the Sahara was once a fertile area. The skeletons buried there disclosed amazing information about two groups of people who had lived at least a thousand years apart. The bones and teeth unearthed from the graves revealed the sex, age, general health, diet, diseases, injuries, and habits of the deceased. The size and condition of the bones gave clues to lifestyles, work, and living conditions of the inhabitants.

Based on the teeth of the Kiffian people, investigators could tell that their diet included coarse grain; they drank from a local water source and probably did not travel far from Gobero, where they lived. The bones of the Ternerian people disclosed that they were more lightly built and may have been herders, but they also likely depended on hunting and fishing.[4]

What would an analysis of our spiritual bones indicate this Lenten season? What would we find out about our spiritual maturity if we examined our spiritual bones? Would we show a deficiency of a substantial diet of study, reflection, prayer, and a meaningful relationship with God? What would this examination tell us about the richness of our spiritual practices? How sincerely do we long and pray for the gifts of the Spirit: love, joy, peace, patience, kindness, goodness, faithfulness, gentleness, and self-control? What would be our answer if the Lord spoke directly to us and questioned, "Can these bones live?"

Can we honestly give the humble Ezekiel's response, "O Lord GOD, you know" (v. 3), to God's great offer of love and mercy? Who is God telling to preach to our bones? What words do we need to hear for our life today? How do we open ourselves up to that living breath of the Spirit? God is so willing to breathe into us and fill us once more with the transformation that allows us to be a part of the kingdom of God. Can we envision our spiritual bones

4. Peter Gwin, "Lost Tribes of the Green Sahara," *National Geographic* (Sept. 2008), 136, 137, 142.

with new flesh and blood? Can we work with the Spirit to prepare ourselves for the resurrection of Jesus and our own resurrection?

The African American spiritual entitled "Dese Bones Gwine Rise Again" has the refrain "I know it, deed I know it, Dese bones gwine rise again."[5] This assurance can underlie all of our living. With the difficulty and joy of living, God continually challenges us to read the bones and then offer them up to God for the breath of restoration and resurrection.

KATHERINE E. AMOS

EXEGETICAL PERSPECTIVE

Ezekiel 37:1–14 has three sections, an introduction (vv. 1–4), a speech event (vv. 5–10), and an explanation (vv. 11–14). The metaphor "the hand of the LORD" (v. 1; cf. Exod. 9:3) describes divine action for the salvation of the Hebrews. The same phrase also occurs in Isaiah (Isa. 19:16; 25:10; 41:20; 59:1; 66:14) and elsewhere in Ezekiel (Ezek. 1:3; 3:22; and 40:1). As an expression of divine redemption beyond social and political trauma, it appears nearly 190 times in the Hebrew Bible.

The writer builds parallelism between the hand of the Lord and the spirit of the Lord. The parallelism of agency tracks with a parallelism of action. The verbs "brought me out" and "set me down" figure prominently in the recollection of the divine action of the exodus event. However, the current aspiration is not about coming to the promised land. The prophet does not see a land of milk and honey. The valley is a metaphor of opportunity as well as challenge. The writer sends an important descriptive and clarifying note: the valley is full of bones.

When the NRSV says "led me all around them" (v. 2), it has the sense of round and round and time and time again. This is no cursory observation on Ezekiel's part. Here the writer uses nouns to emphasize the capacity of the bones in the second and third measures. The Hebrew term "behold" goes untranslated in the NRSV before both "very many" and "very dry" (v. 2). The use of the word "dry" makes clear to the reader that death is in fact real, not illusory or temporary.

The use of the metaphor of "desiccated and disarticulated bones" occurs elsewhere in the Hebrew Bible (see Isa. 66:14; Job 21:24).[6] The language of "very dry" indicates that the death and the disarticulated bones are really dead. The "very dry" is also a cue that the bones are absent bone marrow

5. Leonidas A. Johnson, *Go Down, Moses! Daily Devotions Inspired by Old Negro Spirituals* (Valley Forge, PA: Judson Press, 2000), xx.
6. Joseph Blenkinsopp, *Ezekiel*, Interpretation series (Louisville, KY: John Knox Press, 1990), 171.

and very white. The NRSV "lying in the valley" (v. 2) can be translated "on the face of the valley." The dry white bones lie strewn on the valley floor. The valley beneath is likely a dry, rocky surface.

Imagine the first two verses transpiring in silence, a silence that is broken only in verse 3. The passage begins as a sign event but then quickly becomes a word event. The spirit of the Lord addresses the prophet with the title *ben-adam*, "mortal." The term can be found elsewhere in the Hebrew Bible (see Ps. 80:18; Jer. 49:18, 33; 50:40; 51:43; Dan. 8:17), but the preponderance of use of the term is in the book of Ezekiel. The book of Ezekiel describes one aspect of prophetic vocation as a sentinel (Ezek. 3:16–21; 33:1–9). The confluence of the sentinel language with the "mortal" language in chapter 33 illustrates how the writer fuses these two functions for the job description of the exilic prophet as a sentinel but also as a representative human being. The representative function includes the intercessory role for the people.

Typically the human reflects a significant amount of deference to the spirit of the Lord (see Isa. 7:10–12). Here the dialogue between the prophet and the spirit of the Lord is appropriately coy. When asked if the bones can live, the prophet retorts with a nod to divine omniscience, "O Lord GOD, you know" (v. 3). The question that frames the passage is embedded in this dialogue: "Can these bones live?" (v. 3).

The instructions coming from the spirit contain two elements. First, "prophesy to these bones" (v. 4). The second part of the instruction lays out for the prophet the message, "Dry bones, hear the word of the LORD" (v. 4). The prophet begins with the formula "thus says . . ." that introduces a prophetic/divine speech (v. 5). The key word in the passage is *ruach*. The term can mean "breath," "wind," or "spirit." Here the writer wants to play on the polyvalence of the term. The verbs of verse 5b build together: "I will cause breath to enter you, and you shall live." The resuscitation accompanies any new life. Verse 6 expands on the promise of verse 5. Still the breath/wind/spirit plays a central role. While life would have been enough for the bones, it is not enough for the Deity. The passage grafts life to the knowledge of God (v. 6b). The new creatures will know that YHWH is God.

The next section (vv. 7–8) describes the result of Ezekiel's compliance. The prophet prophesies as instructed. The bones come together; flesh and skin cover the package. However, the narrative tension continues. There is still no breath/spirit. So another command comes to the prophet to prophesy to the wind/spirit. The writer of Ezekiel 37 gives us one of the earliest examples in the Bible of the idea of the four winds (v. 9b) (see 1 Chr. 9:24; Jer. 49:36; Ezek. 42:20; Dan. 8:8; 11:4; Zech. 2:6). The language that describes the bones shifts slightly. At first, they are dry and dead, but in verse 9 they are the "murdered" or "killed" (NRSV "slain"). Verse 10 once again describes the prophet's compliance and its aftermath.

The final section (vv. 11–14) contains the interpretative summary. The bones are the "whole house of Israel." The phrase occurs in the Old Testament some twelve times, with half of the occurrences in the book of Ezekiel (Ezek. 3:7; 5:4; 20:40; 36:10; 39:25; see also Exod. 40:38; Lev. 10:6; Num. 20:29; 1 Sam. 7:2, 3; Jer. 13:11). This marks a return to the pan-Israelite sense of identity after the fall of Samaria (722 BCE) and especially after the fall of Jerusalem (587 BCE). God broke into the cemetery of the dead pan-Israelite community to inspire, bringing the Spirit in order to prompt a new life.

STEPHEN BRECK REID

HOMILETICAL PERSPECTIVE

As our journey through Lent draws near to Easter, we hear one of the most imaginatively dramatic readings in all Scripture: Ezekiel's vision of the valley of dry bones. This vision reminds every generation that God not only gives life but restores life, that death will not have the last word, even when all signs of life have been taken away. Our God is the Creator God of life, its origin and goal.

The reading opens with Ezekiel, a prophet raised up by God for Israel exiled in Babylon, being brought by the hand and spirit of God to a valley full of dry, human bones. After the prophet walks all around these bones, God asks: "Mortal, can these bones live?" (v. 3a). What could be more lifeless than dry bones?

I remember following a guide through a Franciscan church in Lima, Peru, to an ossuary where the bones of those long dead were stored—piles of skulls, leg and arm bones, in a room whose lighting cast a golden glow on the remains. As impressive as this space was, there was also an impersonal quality to it. These long-deceased persons were nameless to those who looked on them and saw only a room full of dry bones. They were not so once.

A scene in Kenneth Branagh's version of Shakespeare's *Hamlet* takes place in the graveyard just before the burial of Ophelia. While walking, Hamlet and his friend Horatio come upon a gravedigger who is preparing her grave. He has just dug up a skull. Hamlet asks whose skull it was; the man answers, "Yorick." Hamlet takes the skull, cradling it tenderly in his hands, and lifts it to his eyes, saying, "Alas, poor Yorick! I knew him, Horatio—a fellow of infinite jest, of most excellent fancy. He hath borne me on his back a thousand times. . . . Here hung those lips that I have kissed I know not how oft. Where be your gibes now? Your gambols? Your songs?"[7] As he ponders what remains of the former court jester, a flashback shows the young Hamlet laughing at Yorick, playfully throwing his arms around him and kissing him. Then, suddenly, we are jolted back to the graveyard and the lifeless skull.

"Can these bones live?" God asks Ezekiel, challenging the prophet and all who have ever looked into the face of death, calling for a response. Ezekiel answers, "O Lord GOD, you know" (v. 3b). God does know. It is the God of Israel, the God who created the world and all that is in it, who brought a people to birth from a childless couple in Haran, who freed their descendants from the living death of slavery in Egypt and entered into covenant with them, who raised up judges and kings and prophets, calling them to life again and again, while they continued to choose death.

Ezekiel's vision is given for a people who have lost heart, who are suffering a death of the spirit, a living death in exile in a foreign land. Their temple has been destroyed, their holy city plundered, their leaders maimed and put in chains, their soldiers put to the sword, their young men and women either killed or dragged off into a foreign land. Ezekiel witnesses the soul of his people gradually wither and die, becoming as lifeless as a valley of dry bones. Can these bones live? That is what God asks.

This vision is held up again today, when so many in the world have had their own experience of dry bones, literally and metaphorically. Our earth has been fashioned into massive graveyards of dry bones, transforming valleys into vales of desolation—from Darfur and the Congo and Zimbabwe to Myanmar and Syria and Iraq, from the gang slayings and the drug wars in our cities to all those places lacking food or drink or clothing or shelter or any respect for life. Not only is there the physical toll people continue to pay, but also the spiritual death that poverty, natural disasters, and genocide exact from people to reduce them to a state of dry bones. Can these bones live?

Today we hear a promise only God can give. God tells the prophet to speak to these bones, saying: "Thus says the Lord GOD: I will cause breath to enter you and you shall live" (v. 5). God promises not only sinews and flesh and skin, but, most importantly, God calls the breath to come from the four winds and breathe upon the slain. So it happens. This breath is the spirit of God, the life-giving *ruach* God breathed into the first human creature in the garden.

This breath moves forth in the Lazarus story. This same breath was

7. William Shakespeare, *Hamlet*, 5.1.201–9.

breathed into Jesus crucified, lifting him up to resurrection life, and touched us when the Spirit came upon us in baptism. This breath moves through the world, raising people into new life when all the odds are against it. We need to hear the vision of Ezekiel in the valley of dry bones. It is a scene meant to live in the imagination and the heart, when we find ourselves gasping for breath, struggling to stay alive. Preachers can ask themselves, where are the dry bones today, where is the valley of death that needs to hear the promise of the living God?

Lent will move quickly to the three great days of Holy Week. Can the bones of a crucified man live? Yes, just as we live in him, with him, through him, and for him. We live now in the power of that same Spirit given by Jesus and poured into our hearts. We are only three weeks away from that moment on Easter when we renew our baptismal promises: Do you believe in the God of life who created all that is? Do you believe in Jesus, the crucified and risen Lord, who died and rose for us that we might have abundant life? Do you believe in the Spirit of God, the divine breath that brings new life wherever it blows? "Mortal, can these bones live?" Yes, Lord, most definitely yes.

JAMES A. WALLACE

John 11:1–45

THEOLOGICAL PERSPECTIVE

This reading is commonly referred to as "the raising of Lazarus." The shorthand designation is by no means inappropriate. It is a story about Lazarus, whom Jesus loved—his illness, death, burial and decay, and emergence from his tomb, upon being recalled from death to life, with burial wrappings still dangling around him. Even so, its focus is not so much Lazarus the individual as it is wondrous deliverance from death to life itself (viz., the *sign*, in John's Gospel), the one who brings it about, and responses of others to it. These occasion the most lengthy, searching theological reflection within the narrative itself and among its commentators.

All three foci are bound up with striking, in certain respects singular, theological emphases of the Fourth Gospel. Although all four canonical Gospels are written from a vantage point of a post-Easter faith, John's surfaces that faith notably often and in high relief within his account of the ministry of Jesus itself. In so doing, the discourses of Jesus himself, as well as his exhibition of certain divine attributes, reinforce the Gospel's faith claim that Christ is "one" with God. Such traits lead some later theologians to praise (or fault) John for depicting the least truly human Christ and many others to rely on Johannine Christology as the most truly incarnational. Likewise, while in the Synoptics a fuller understanding of Christ's person and work emerges, despite initial misunderstandings, as later events unfold over time, in John's work the whole truth of the matter is revealed immediately, although in paradoxes, wordplays, and category confusions calling forth explanatory words by Christ the Word.

The wonder, marvel, or miracle of the raising of Lazarus is a case in point. "Did it really happen?" is one nearly irrepressible question. Debates over miracles raged in biblical and theological studies during the Enlightenment era and its aftermath. They have by no means disappeared. In certain respects John's account complicates the discussion. His is the only report of the raising of Lazarus. Given its narrative placement, it is manifestly a prefiguration of the death and resurrection of Jesus. How factual it is may be inconsequential. Even so, in all the Gospels, extraordinary events are associated with the ministry of Jesus and understood as indicative of workings of God's power. The question of whether or not to "believe in miracles" (in general, as it were) in light of what is subject to critical scientific investigation and confirmable by the physical sciences is a far cry from concerns of early Christians.

The Johannine contribution to the discussion is the view of wonders as "signs." The raising of Lazarus is in John's reckoning the climax of the series of signs Jesus performs. It extends the manifestations of the presence and power of God he exhibits to that of supremacy over death itself. Such signs are marvels indeed, displayed for eyewitness viewing, and as such are mighty attestations of God's glory, evoking in some the faith in the glorification of Jesus as well. For John, however, the terms "glory" and "glorification" ultimately have to do with being exalted, "lifted up" on the cross and from death to life, in oneness with God.

The raising of Lazarus, then, *signifies* that God's eschatological promises are here and now, already, being realized amid and despite the ordinariness of the course of life, which includes illnesses, deaths, and burials like those of Lazarus. This and the other such signs point to Jesus, the sign-maker, who in turn by his attitude of prayer points to God. His "oneness" with God is transparent. His life-giving action is not dependent on human faith, whether that of Mary, Martha, Lazarus, or the onlookers, but calls it forth. The incident thereby presents yet another of John's leitmotifs: the sheep recognize their shepherd's voice. Lazarus comes out of the tomb at Jesus' word, and "many" of those who see believe.

Preceding this climactic sign is a discourse by Jesus, the climax of the series of "I-sayings" in John's Gospel: "I am the resurrection and the life" (v.

25). Its context is a dialogue regarding the character of Martha's faith, and Mary's. Each is already a believer, and yet each, independent of the other, tells Jesus that had he been there, Lazarus would not have died. The others at the scene say the same thing shortly afterward. The record, earlier on, that Jesus deliberately delayed his response to the sisters' call gives such comments bite. Hence the stage is ready for a Johannine theological clarification. Those who live and believe in the one who is the resurrection and the life shall never die. This life is not a matter of belief in a "general resurrection" to come, but, as Martha's confession tells, a personalized faith: "You are the Christ, the Son of God" (v. 27). Then the raising of Lazarus comes about, in the end time that is already present.

The episode raises theological questions even as it seeks to clarify them. Consider, for example, whether metaphors or metaphysics could offer the most adequate account of "the resurrection and the life" of which Jesus speaks, and in any case what they might be. Consider as well the thrust of Martha's confession, which has as its object of belief not an object at all, but the person of Jesus. It is one of a series of differently worded Johannine confessions of faith, the climactic one that of Thomas, who confesses (20:28) the still-wounded but resurrected Christ as "my Lord and my God."

The confession of Thomas at the conclusion of the Gospel is a reminder that, as a sign, the raising of Lazarus calls for theological consideration of the Johannine signature theme of "seeing and believing." Having *seen* what Jesus has done, many of those who come with Mary believe, and the faith of Martha and Mary themselves becomes, shall we say, enlightened. For Thomas also, *seeing* Christ, crucified yet risen, evokes faith. The Gospel's summary word with regard to the seeing of all such signs, however, is another Jesus saying (20:29): "Blessed are those who have not seen and yet have come to believe." Faith, then, is not based on *seeing*. It is a provocative point for theologians and preachers to address.

JAMES O. DUKE

PASTORAL PERSPECTIVE

The tension between the hope of resurrection and the finality of death is palpable during this season of intense personal and communal reflection. Amid painful circumstance and death-dealing social realities, we yearn for resurrection and the *unbinding* that releases us to dream beyond the boundaries and experience life anew. To dream beyond the boundaries is to imagine a world in which wholeness, well-being, health, and prosperity are normative expressions of human existence and to partner with the God of life in making that dream a reality. It is to recognize that our world is not as it should be, while rejecting assertions that the socioreligious strictures that prevent persons from experiencing God's presence in their lives are impervious to change. Our narrative, on this Fourth Sunday in Lent, invites us to consider the possibility of resurrection in the lives of the many persons and communities who deeply need God's presence in the nowness of our existence.

One of the greatest hindrances to imagining possibilities is perceptual distortion. Obstacles appear larger and more ominous than they are, keeping us preoccupied with trying to avoid danger rather than discerning alternatives. This is evident in today's lesson. The disciples have been Jesus' constant companions throughout his ministry, traveling with him from one village, town, and mountainous region to the next, yet they often appear more concerned with situational limitation than with the restorative possibility of resurrection and life. Their interests are often at cross-purposes with Jesus' ministerial focus, as in their concern in last week's gospel text for the origin of the blind man's condition rather than in the curative potential of Jesus' encounter with the man.

Having received the news of Lazarus's illness and subsequent death, the disciples again struggle to come to terms with Jesus' decision to make the treacherous journey to Judea after a two-day delay. They question the wisdom of returning to Judea at all, recalling their narrow escape from stoning just a few days earlier. What is more, by Jesus' own admission, Lazarus is already dead. Nonetheless, Jesus insists that they make the journey, emphasizing the revelatory possibility that Lazarus's illness and subsequent death have occasioned and assuring the disciples that the journey will be stumble-free. Although Thomas and the others are not completely convinced—"Let us also go, that we may die with him" (v. 16)—these friends and companions make the journey with him, intrigued by the possibility of resurrection.

As Jesus and the disciples approach Mary and Martha's home, the tension between life and death intensifies and the immediacy of grief is overwhelming. Weeping and lament fill the air as family and friends gather to mourn Lazarus's demise and final sleep. It has been four days since Lazarus's death, marking the completion of the soul's journey from life to death. His soul no longer lingers near the body, indicating that Lazarus is truly dead.

The finality of death deepens the grief of Mary and Martha and their disappointment that Jesus has not arrived until now—"Lord, if you had been here, my brother would not have died" (v. 21). Martha and Mary consider Jesus a friend and believe that God would have honored his requests—if Jesus had arrived sooner. They trust him as a teacher, healer, miracle worker, and believe him to be the Messiah come from God. They unquestionably anticipate the resurrection of the dead *on the last day* and look forward to uniting with their brother Lazarus again. However, they have no experiential referent to support Jesus' self-identification as "the resurrection and life." Jesus is speaking of resurrection as a present reality—"I am"—leaving Martha, Mary, and their community skeptical, yet fascinated with the possibility of new life.

As we observe Mary, Martha, and their community from a distance, we too are intrigued by the possibility of resurrection and feel compelled to join them at the tomb. We listen as they wonder out loud if Jesus' tears are indicative of love or regret; we hear the strain in Jesus' voice as he instructs them to remove the stone that covers the tomb; we sense the anticipatory tension as profound faith and debilitating doubt converge in this single event. We know the conclusion yet breathlessly await Lazarus's emergence from the tomb. "Lazarus, come out!" (v. 43) reverberates throughout the tomb, awakening Lazarus's lifeless body to the revivifying call of life.

As Christians, we believe in the power of resurrection, having been formed in a liturgical tradition in which birth, life, death, and resurrection are cyclical occurrences. Resurrection and life are central to the meaning that we make for our lives, informing our sense of Christian vocation. In this respect, resurrection confronts us as an urgent call, beckoning us to consider the possibility that those whom our world deems socially, physically, spiritually, and emotionally dead might live into a new reality. We pray for the power of resurrection in the lives of persons and communities bound by the graveclothes of war, genocide, poverty, disease, dis-ease, systematic abuse, and systemic oppression.

Releasing persons and communities from the clutches of death also demands something of us, as did Lazarus's resurrection of his community. Though Jesus called Lazarus from the tomb, he urged those who were alive and well, "Unbind him, and let him go." Resurrected women, men, and children today also require caring communities that are willing to nurture and strengthen them until they are able to walk alone; to remove the graveclothes of self-doubt, social isolation, marginalization, and oppression; to tear away the wrappings of fear, anxiety, loss, and grief, so that unbound women, men, and children might walk in dignity and become creative agents in the world.

A few years ago, a friend gave me a poster with the slogan, "Consider the possibilities . . ."—ellipsis marks indicating that there is more to be said, this slogan provocatively reminds us to dream beyond the boundaries, to consider the possibility of resurrection, anticipating it so profoundly that we stand at the tomb of suffering and pain, listening for the voice of Jesus, ready to unbind those whom God delivers, even now.

VERONICE MILES

EXEGETICAL PERSPECTIVE

As the last in a series of seven narrated "signs" (see John 12:18), the raising of Lazarus marks a turning point in the narrative concerning the one
who is the resurrection and the life (v. 25). Appearing only in John, the episode functions as a narrative bridge connecting Jesus' public ministry with
the events (and extended discourse) related to the final Passover and Jesus'
death and resurrection. Like much of the rest of this Gospel, the passage
points repeatedly to the importance of the act of believing (always a verb in
John, never the noun "belief") in the identity of Jesus and in his power to
bring life out of death. At the level of the story, the result of this seventh sign
is twofold: it leads people to "believe in him" (v. 45), and it accelerates the
conflict between Jesus and the religious authorities (vv. 47–53).

Although the episode could stand on its own as a narrative depiction
of the one who brings life out of death, a number of verbal threads tie the
passage to the prologue of John: the glory of God/Jesus (v. 4; cf. 1:14;); light
(v. 9; cf. 1:4–9); life (v. 25; cf. 1:4); believing (vv. 15, 26–27, 40, 42, 45; cf.
1:12); Jesus as "the one coming into the world" (v. 27; cf. 1:9). Several additional words and phrases are similarly Johannine: "I am . . ." (v. 25); love
(*agapē; phileō*, vv. 3, 5); resurrection on "the last day" (v. 24); came . . . saw
. . . believed (v. 45). In addition, the events taking place at Lazarus's tomb
mirror many of those that will occur at the tomb of Jesus. By pointing simul-
taneously forward and back in the narrative, the raising of Lazarus embodies
many of the fundamental themes of the Gospel.

Two distinct reactions to Jesus—belief and conflict—appear together in
an inclusio that frames the story. In the first part of the frame, before receiving the news about Lazarus's illness, Jesus is in Jerusalem for the feast of
the Dedication, where the Judeans (NRSV "the Jews") push him to reveal
whether he is the Christ. Offended by his response, they take up stones
to kill him, charging that "you, though only a human being, are making
yourself God" (10:22–33). Jesus and his disciples escape, retreating across
the Jordan, where "many believed in him there" (10:42). The same two
responses—believing Jesus and threatening him—occur again, at the end of
our pericope in the other part of the frame, after Jesus calls Lazarus out of
the tomb. "Many of the Jews . . . believed in him," but others of them go to
the Pharisees, who worry that Jesus is a threat to the nation. They confer to
determine how they might put him to death (11:45–53).

Lazarus, for his part, ends up the target of threats as well, even though he
had nothing to do with his own resurrection. His return to life adds fuel to

the fire of Jesus' enormous popularity, so that a short while later, at a dinner party held in Bethany, a crowd has gathered to see this one whom Jesus had raised from the dead (12:1–9). This crowd, as well as those who continue to talk about Lazarus and Jesus at the time of Jesus' entry into Jerusalem, cause considerable concern to the chief priests and the Pharisees, respectively, who seem to be getting increasingly nervous about the number of people flocking after the doer of signs. The religious authorities, determined to undo the life-giving nature of Jesus' miraculous work, conspire to kill Lazarus as well, since it was on his account that people believed in Jesus (12:10–11, 17). Apparently, being brought to life by the one who is the resurrection and the life can get a person killed.

A good deal of ink is given over to the identity of the people involved in Lazarus's return to life, with emphasis on the two sisters. Could it be that they are known to the original community for which this Gospel was written? Lazarus is introduced by way of his relationship to these women, and not, as we might expect, the other way around; he is a man from Bethany, "the village of Mary and her sister Martha" (11:1). Fine tuning the identity of the characters, the writer says that Lazarus is the brother of Mary (v. 2) and that Jesus "loved Martha and her sister and Lazarus" (v. 5). Perhaps reflecting later redaction, Mary receives special attention with reference to her act of anointing Jesus and wiping his feet with her hair (v. 2). That event has not yet happened at the level of the narrative, but its occurrence will reemphasize the importance of Jesus' seventh sign as an opportunity to believe in him or not (12:1–11).

Mary and Martha interact with Jesus individually, but they say the same thing: "Lord, if you had been here, my brother would not have died" (vv. 21, 32). Whether their statement is a confession of faith or an accusation is difficult to determine, but their charge echoes repeated assertions that Jesus is the one who brings life (e.g., 1:4; 5:24; 8:12; 10:10). Moved by Mary's weeping, Jesus asks, "Where have you laid him"? (v. 34). Ordering the stone to be taken away from the tomb (v. 39), he cries out in a loud voice, "Lazarus, come out!" (v. 43), and the man who has been dead for four days comes forth from the darkness. In a sign of God's glory (v. 40), death is overcome. However, the burial cloths that bind Lazarus's hands and feet and cover his face are a vivid reminder that death still clings to him.

On another day, another Mary, weeping at another tomb, asks the same question: "Tell me where have you laid him" (20:15). On that day, the burial cloths will be left behind in the tomb—the face cloth rolled up in a place by itself—no longer required for the one whom God has raised. On that day, the disciples will see a sign even greater than the raising of Lazarus. Here, at the tomb of Lazarus, death is denied for a time. There, at the tomb of Jesus, death is overcome for good.

AUDREY WEST

HOMILETICAL PERSPECTIVE

Today's Gospel reading includes what some of us memorized as the shortest verse in the Bible: "Jesus wept" (v. 35). The terseness of the older RSV and AV translations is certainly not improved upon rhetorically in the NRSV's wooden and unnecessary doubling of the word count to "Jesus began to weep."

This verse serves as a truly authenticating mark of Jesus' humanity in John's Gospel, which, despite its unrivalled witness to the Word become flesh, in contrast to the Synoptics tends to picture Jesus as being not quite "grounded" in this world. Helping to counter this is the scene of Jesus' weeping at the sight of his friend Lazarus's corpse. This is an emotionally profound testimony to the truth of the incarnation itself, of Jesus being truly one of us to the point of sharing our human need for friendship and our grief at the loss of a friend.

The Gospel writer informs us that those observing Jesus' weeping remarked: "See how he loved him!" This is a telling choice of vocabulary, inasmuch as the Greek word for "love" used here is not the verb form of the expected *agapē*—selfless, self-giving love of which the Johannine corpus is so fond. Rather, Jesus' love for his friend Lazarus is *philia*, the common, everyday Greek word for "friendship," "human affection," or "deep feeling," that ordinary human love we have for our friends. It is to this status as friends that Jesus elevates his own disciples from that of servants a few chapters later in 15:13–15. The early American composer William Billings's "When Jesus Wept" is an especially effective setting of this text to music whether sung by a choir or as a congregational round.[8]

Though Jesus' weeping over the death of his friend Lazarus is the emotional heart of today's Gospel story, its salient homiletical point, particularly as Holy Week approaches, actually occurs at the end of the passage and immediately following. For Jesus' resuscitation of his dead friend, as much as a flash-forward to Jesus' own resurrection as it may be, serves more instrumentally as the final (if figurative) nail in Jesus' coffin.

---

8. William Billings, "When Jesus Wept," in *The New Century Hymnal* (Cleveland: Pilgrim Press, 1995), #192.

The verses that follow report: "But some of them went to the Pharisees and told them what he had done. So the chief priests and the Pharisees called a meeting of the council and said, 'What are we to do? This man is performing many signs. If we let him go on like this, everyone will believe in him, and the Romans will come and destroy both our holy place and our nation.' But one of them, Caiaphas, who was high priest that year, said to them, 'You know nothing at all! You do not understand that it is better for you to have one man die for the people than to have the whole nation destroyed.' . . . So from that day on they planned to put him to death" (11:46–50, 53).

Here again, to the NRSV's translation of Caiaphas's words of advice, "it is better," I prefer the older RSV's more politically ominous "it is expedient." The text reveals that it is political expediency, perhaps even a misplaced patriotic, ethnoreligious solidarity, that prompts Caiaphas to recommend Jesus' death, lest the Roman overlords violently intervene in the life of his—and his God's—people. So the plot leading to Jesus' execution is set in motion as an expedient—meaning, convenient and useful—way of forestalling any threat to the security of the status quo. Church and state connive in the death of yet another innocent, neither the first nor the last scapegoat, neither the most cruel nor the most humane of expedient deaths in that age or any other. The charge against Jesus in bringing him to Pilate according to Luke's Gospel sums it up nicely: "We found this man perverting our nation and forbidding us to give tribute to Caesar, and saying that he himself is Christ a king" (Luke 23:2 RSV).

Caiaphas spoke more than he knew in advising that "it is expedient" for one man to die for the people. The high priest was speaking an ironic truth reverberant with gospel resonances beyond his knowing. In fact, John goes so far as to say that the conniving Caiaphas was unconsciously prophesying (v. 51), both foretelling and forth-telling God's intentions that Jesus should die for the nation. That is just what Jesus' death will turn out to be in what will become the church's theology of atonement (not restricted here to certain "substitutionary" theories):[9] The self-sacrifice of one by whom not only the nation or the Jewish people or even all believers, but the whole cosmos, the whole created order, will be saved. Caiaphas may not have known what he was doing in setting in motion Jesus' expeditious death, but God is sufficiently creative to transfigure even the evil of this innocent's death into the

---

9. See Colin E. Gunton, *The Actuality of Atonement: A Study of Metaphor, Rationality and the Christian Tradition* (London: T.&T. Clark, 1988). On Jesus as scapegoat/sacrifice, see René Girard, *Things Hidden since the Foundation of the World* (Palo Alto, CA: Stanford University Press, 1987).

gospel itself.[10] The beginning of the plot against Jesus that its perpetrators think will find its conclusion on Good Friday begins with Jesus weeping at the death of a friend. Easter will prove to be the real, absolutely unexpected conclusion, in which we will discover what a friend we have not only in Jesus—but in the God who raised him from the dead!

JOHN ROLLEFSON

10. See Gen. 50:20.

Fifth Sunday of Lent

1 Kings 17:8–16

[8]Then the word of the LORD came to him, saying, [9]"Go now to Zarephath, which belongs to Sidon, and live there; for I have commanded a widow there to feed you." [10]So he set out and went to Zarephath. When he came to the gate of the town, a widow was there gathering sticks; he called to her and said, "Bring me a little water in a vessel, so that I may drink." [11]As she was going to bring it, he called to her and said, "Bring me a morsel of bread in your hand." [12]But she said, "As the LORD your God lives, I have nothing baked, only a handful of meal in a jar, and a little oil in a jug; I am now gathering a couple of sticks, so that I may go home and prepare it for myself and my son, that we may eat it, and die." [13]Elijah said to her, "Do not be afraid; go and do as you have said; but first make me a little cake of it and bring it to me, and afterwards make something for yourself and your son. [14]For thus says the LORD the God of Israel: The jar of meal will not be emptied and the jug of oil will not fail until the day that the LORD sends rain on the earth." [15]She went and did as Elijah said, so that she as well as he and her household ate for many days. [16]The jar of meal was not emptied, neither did the jug of oil fail, according to the word of the LORD that he spoke by Elijah.

John 12:1–11

[1]Six days before the Passover Jesus came to Bethany, the home of Lazarus, whom he had raised from the dead. [2]There they gave a dinner for him. Martha served, and Lazarus was one of those at the table with him. [3]Mary took a pound of costly perfume made of pure nard, anointed Jesus' feet, and wiped them with her hair. The house was filled with the fragrance of the perfume. [4]But Judas Iscariot, one of his disciples (the one who was about to betray him), said, [5]"Why was this perfume not sold for three hundred denarii and the money given to the poor?" [6](He said this not because he cared about the poor, but because he was a thief; he kept the common purse and used to steal what was put into it.) [7]Jesus said, "Leave her alone. She bought it so that she might keep it for the day of my burial. [8]You always have the poor with you, but you do not always have me."

⁹When the great crowd of the Jews learned that he was there, they came not only because of Jesus but also to see Lazarus, whom he had raised from the dead. ¹⁰So the chief priests planned to put Lazarus to death as well, ¹¹since it was on account of him that many of the Jews were deserting and were believing in Jesus.

ORDER OF WORSHIP

OPENING WORDS / CALL TO WORSHIP

In times of security and times of uncertainty,   *1 Kgs. 17:8–16*
O Lord, you hear our prayers.
Confident in your faithfulness,
We will ever praise your name.
Through the abundance of your steadfast love
you have gathered us into your house.
In the holiness of your presence,
we bow down to worship and adore you.

HYMN, SPIRITUAL, OR PSALM

CALL TO CONFESSION

[Spoken from the font]
Even in our faithlessness,
God loves us still
and waits in mercy to forgive.
Trusting in the promises given at our baptism,
let us confess our sin before God and one another.

PRAYER OF CONFESSION

Holy God,   *1 Kgs. 17:12–13,*
you promise us a life full of blessing,   *John 12:5–8*
but we do not always believe.
You incite us to hope,
but we fall back into fear.
You urge us to give freely,
but we cling to what we have.
You call us to watch at all times for you,
but we grow lazy and self-absorbed.
Forgive us.

Increase our hope, enlarge our hearts,
and keep us alert to the wonders you work
in the world every day.
For the sake of Jesus we pray. Amen.

DECLARATION OF FORGIVENESS

[Spoken from the font]
Hear the good news!
[Water is poured into the font, visibly and audibly.]
By faith we have been saved,
our guilty hearts washed clean.
Refreshed, revived, and renewed,
empowered by the Holy Spirit,
live as ones who are forgiven and freed,
giving thanks to God.

PRAYER OF THE DAY

God of grace, *John 12:3*
you pour out your mercy with abundance
and your grace with boundless generosity.
Make us ever more faithful,
and ever more grateful,
as we strive to give to others
in the same measure you give to us.
In Jesus' name we pray. **Amen.**

HYMN, SPIRITUAL, OR PSALM

PRAYER FOR ILLUMINATION

Speak to us, O Lord, *1 Kgs. 17:8–16*
your saving Word;
fill us with your Holy Spirit
and feed us with the bread of life. **Amen.**

SCRIPTURE READINGS

SERMON

HYMN, SPIRITUAL, OR PSALM

PRAYERS OF INTERCESSION

We cry to you for help, O Lord,
for you alone have the power to restore our lives.

[Optional response to each intercession:]
Hear us, O Lord,
be gracious to us.

Give bread to those who are hungry
and drink to those who thirst.   *1 Kgs. 17:8–16*

Give life to those who are dying
and grace to those who are sick with sin.

Give justice to those who are oppressed
and peace to those who live in fear.

Give comfort to those who mourn
and hope to those who despair.

As you breathe life into dust
and make dry bones dance with joy,
give new life to this weary world;
through Jesus Christ our Savior. **Amen.**

LORD'S PRAYER

INVITATION TO THE OFFERING

God calls us to share what we have—   *1 Kgs. 17:8–16*
a little bread, a little water—
and God uses those simple gifts
to bring abundant blessing to the world.

PRAYER OF THANKSGIVING/DEDICATION

Thanks and praise to you, O God;
by your grace you bring the dead to life.
Let us use the breath you have given us
to speak your truth and sing your glory;
through Jesus Christ our Lord. **Amen.**

HYMN, SPIRITUAL, OR PSALM

CHARGE
> Your life is a gift of grace;   *John 12:1–11*
> use it to give glory to God!

BLESSING
> Now arise and go with joy!
> God looks with favor upon you.

SONG SUGGESTIONS

"A Prophet-Woman Broke a Jar" (*GTG* 201)
"Come Down, O Love Divine" (*CH* 582, *EH* 516, *ELW* 804, *GC* 471, *GTG* 282, *TNCH* 289, *UMH* 475)
"Fairest Lord Jesus" (*CH* 97, *EH* 383 and 384, *GTG* 630, *UMH* 189)
"Great Is Thy Faithfulness" (*CH* 86, *ELW* 733, *GTG* 39, *TNCH* 423, *UMH* 140)
"How Very Good and Pleasant" (*GTG* 398)
"Savior an Offering Costly and Sweet" (*TNCH* 536)
"Seek Ye First" (*CH* 354, *EH* 711, *GC* 600, *GTG* 175, *UMH* 405)
"Tell Me the Stories of Jesus" (*CH* 190, *UMH* 277)

CHILDREN'S SERMON

Based on John 12:1–8

Jesus was in Bethany on his way to Jerusalem with his disciples to celebrate Passover. They stopped at the home of Lazarus, Martha, and Mary, his good friends. They were giving a dinner for Jesus. Martha had cooked all day and was putting the food on the table. Lazarus was sitting with Jesus and the disciples.

Then Mary did something very unusual. She brought out a jar of nard—expensive oil with a wonderful smell. Nard was one of the oils used to prepare dead bodies for burial. But Mary poured it on Jesus' feet. Then she wiped his feet with her hair. The scent of the nard filled the room. It drew attention to Mary and what she was doing.

Judas, the disciple who took care of the money for Jesus and the disciples, said, "Why was this nard not sold for lots of money that could be given to the poor?"

Mary shrank back a bit. Had she done something wrong? Was Jesus unhappy with her?

"Leave her alone," Jesus said. "She bought this nard so she would have it to bury me. The poor will be with you long after I am gone."

The delicious meal Martha had prepared continued. Mary knew that she had done a good thing for Jesus. But I wonder how Judas felt.

SERMON HELPS

1 Kings 17:8–16

THEOLOGICAL PERSPECTIVE

In a world riven by conflict and urgent need, we thirst for miracles. The story of Elijah and the widow of Zarephath dramatizes the miracle of divine compassion that unfolds when we dare to invite the prophetic word into our midst.

First Kings 17 offers us no fewer than three miracles in twenty-four verses, in a series of vignettes that increase in narrative intensity. The scene is set in 17:6–7, where we see the first miracle: ravens bring bread and meat to Elijah in the morning and in the evening. Many cultures tell of infants, saints, and warriors who are nurtured in the wilderness by feral creatures that normally would represent a threat to humans. The wilderness is a place of testing, as Abraham knew. It is a place of struggle and unexpected gift, as Moses knew. For those who venture into the wilderness, it is a place to meet God. God calls from a flaming bush (Exod. 3); God thunders from atop Sinai (Exod. 19). God's glory illumines the wilderness, leaving Moses's face radiant with the terror and wonder of it (Exod. 34:29–35).

When Elijah emerges from the wilderness, we are alarmed, for he is a wild man (see 2 Kgs. 1:8). In the storytelling of many cultures, the figure of the wild man is set over against cultured society and the conventions of civilization. Think of Enkidu from the Epic of Gilgamesh, Samson and John the Baptist in the Bible, and Tarzan in contemporary Western culture. One theological implication here is that the prophetic word cannot be tamed. The wild Elijah approaches a widow at Zarephath. Her vulnerability underscores the risk that the word of God presents to those who confront it. The potential danger that the widow faces when she meets an unkempt stranger from the wilderness is clear, but she is dangerous to him as well. In stories of wild men drawn into civilization, often women serve as lure and civilizing force. Our text is careful to note that she is Sidonian—of the same ethnicity as Jezebel, who will become Elijah's most potent nemesis. Risk abounds as Elijah steps through the liminal space of the gate at Zarephath. Will he harm her? Will she tame him? We hold our breath, alert and tense.

The emphasis on hospitality increases the dramatic tension in the narrative. Elijah demands water and food from this desperate woman, whose family is at the point of starvation. Now comes the second miracle: her jar of meal and jug of oil are miraculously replenished, day after day. Those who dare to host the wild divine word in their midst are saved from disaster. We are relieved. The story continues; this was only a feint toward closure, and our anxiety mounts once again. The wild-man prophet lingers in the heart of this community. Does another crisis loom?

Indeed it does. The son of the widow dies, and she names the darkest dread that a community can harbor about its prophets: has the presence of Elijah brought the terrible wrath of God upon her? Rather than defend himself, Elijah challenges God on her behalf. Elijah is interceding: imagine not meek hands folded in quiet prayer, but the fierce raging of a wild man. His God has killed the only child of the woman who has been kind to him. This wrenching loss cannot go unaddressed—not here, not in this fragile community that has been brave enough to host the divine word in its midst. God listens to the voice of Elijah.

The widow's cry, "Now I know [*'atah zeh yada'ti*] that you are a man of God, and that the word of the LORD in your mouth is truth" (v. 24), echoes the confession of another outsider, Jethro of Midian, when he saw that God redeemed Israel from slavery: "Now I know [*'atah yada'ti*] that the LORD is greater than all gods, because he delivered the people from the Egyptians" (Exod. 18:11). Her cry echoes the angel's confession after Abraham bound Isaac: "Now I know [*'atah yada'ti*] that you fear God, since you have not withheld your son, your only son, from me" (Gen. 22:12). Because of the wild intercession of Elijah, the exodus unfolds anew and God halts the sacrifice of the beloved. Once again we are delivered. Once again we praise a God whose love defeats death.

Elijah shows God's compassion to those who dare to host the prophetic word. Most striking in this story is not the resurrection of the boy but the intimacy of prophetic presence. The Israelite wild man dwells with the Sidonian widow in abject poverty, not just briefly but for years. His choice to be present with her shows us how we may embody the prophetic word in our own lives: in intimate solidarity with those at risk.

The intertestamental book of Sirach lionizes Elijah as "a prophet like fire" (Sir. 48:1). Elijah's prophetic witness burns like fire through the constraints of our spiritual imagination. God's word is truth, and it is mighty. Boundaries between insider and outsider are as nothing, the desperation of famine is as nothing, before the prophetic word of God's abundant mercy. There is nothing stronger than the wild compassion of God. In welcoming the prophet, we learn that God's power is among us not for judgment but for life.

In the story of the transfiguration (Luke 9:28–36; Matt. 17:1–8), we see Jesus conferring with Moses the lawgiver and Elijah the wild-man prophet. Moses and Elijah together ratify a gospel that is all radical obedience and ferocious compassion. When we dare to host the prophetic word, we are transformed. For we encounter a God who delivers the powerless, a God whose word yields inexhaustible abundance, a God whose compassion is stronger than death. Elijah's prophetic word points to the One who is the way, the truth, and the life. Host that word, know the truth, and live.

CAROLYN J. SHARP

PASTORAL PERSPECTIVE

"The widow, the orphan, and the stranger." These words or categories appear many times in the Scriptures grouped as one social class of voiceless people. Why? What was the thread that united those categories of people? Is it possible that a system of laws designed to protect these people, a system forged under the guidance of the God who is decidedly in favor of the voiceless, nevertheless keeps these very people locked in a perpetual second-class position?

Indeed widows, orphans, and strangers were the poorest of the poor of Elijah's days. Being a widow also meant her child was considered an orphan, the father figure bearing more societal weight than a mother. Widows, orphans, and strangers had this in common: they did not count on the protection offered by a citizen adult male in their family. Thus they were poor and powerless; life was miserable. Much in the OT lets us know of God's care for them, but what kept them powerless?

In North America today there are many laws protecting vulnerable ones. Not strong enough or empowering enough, these laws are attempts in the direction of care for the weak. Are some of these laws also keeping justice at bay? Are we as a nation and as individuals more interested in doing charity than enabling justice for all? Such a thing happened in Elijah's days.

In our story we find a widow and her child—strangers to Elijah, Elijah also a stranger to them. Elijah is physically thirsty and hungry, but, as a fugitive from the anger of King Ahab, he is also emotionally distressed. The widow, a loving mother, is thirsty and hungry, but not only for food and water. She earnestly desires a voice that can be heard and fullness of life for her and her son. We know Elijah's name. We do not know the names of the woman or the child—something common in biblical narratives, yet another sign of injustice. Women and children were, more often than not, referred to as the wife or child of male adults, in those days the only ones with any power in social and religious life. The laws of the land kept things that way. Some of us know how that feels.

No wonder Isaiah clamored:

> Ah, you who . . . write oppressive statutes,
> to turn aside the needy from justice,
>   and to rob the poor of my people of their right,
> that widows may be your spoil,
>   and that you make the orphans your prey!
>
> *(Isa. 10:1–2)*

Too many around us are that widow or that child, literally or figuratively. Too many around us feel lost, hopeless, hungry, and thirsty for something beyond the tangibles of daily living, for more than meager leftovers, scraps of food, love, and justice. Many feel that there is simply no one willing to empower them with healing and grace. The image of a widow also stands for all manner of poor people in the Bible; the psalms are full of such imagery. We see widows in Gospel narratives like today's story of Jesus' encounter with a grieving widow. Widows are also metaphors for spiritual or emotional poverty. Are we not all poor before God? We are all indeed needy, widow, orphan, and stranger in spirit.

We first know ourselves to be the poor, and God is on the side of the poor.

The stranger woman and her child feed Elijah and receive him, glad of the miracle of unending food for life, and oil for healing and light. Then the child dies. The widow's grief is beyond the normal grief of a mother: she knows that without a male adult in her life she will be kept at a level of dependency even more profound than her current situation. Her son was hope for her later years, and now hope is gone. Elijah pleads with God, covers the boy's body with his own—symbolizing God's care for the whole person—and hope and life return to the widow and child.

We are that widow today, but God's countercultural favor and actions on behalf of the poor, love beyond measure, are also in our midst today. See signs of mercy in our Sunday assemblies: in the font, good news of life in unending water; in the anointing, good news of healing and light in unending oil; in the pulpit, good news of justice and salvation in unending Word, Jesus Christ; in the Table, good news of life, grace, and joy in unending bread and wine. All these things are set out for all.

We are the voiceless widows. We are the silenced orphans. We are the homeless strangers. Some translations of the Scriptures refer to strangers as "aliens," today a pejorative, wounding word applied to many wanderers among us; but we are the poor, wayfaring strangers. We die, but God covers us with life, then sends us forth, surprised, to be Elijah. We must not remain silent while political and religious laws keep the poor in our midst locked in poverty and oppression. To strangers who escape a land of known despair and seek a new land of unknown hope, we with God become their shelter. In God's name, we like the widow bring water, oil, bread, and wine for the lost, oppressed, poor, and forgotten. Surprised by joy, we receive life from their hand, for God promises that when we receive the stranger and the poor, we may be receiving angels without knowing it (Heb. 13:1–2).

We first know ourselves to be the real poor.

God is on the side of the poor.

GLÁUCIA VASCONCELOS WILKEY

EXEGETICAL PERSPECTIVE

Today's reading is part of the narrative cycle in 1 Kings 17–19 that tells of the confrontation between King Ahab of the northern kingdom of Israel and Elijah the prophet. Under the influence of his wife Jezebel, Ahab introduced into Israel the worship of the Canaanite god Baal. One of Baal's attributes was giving rain to nurture the crops.

Chapter 17 begins with Elijah's announcement of a drought to Ahab (v. 1). The fact that Baal was responsible for rain makes this announcement a direct challenge to Baal's power and a judgment against Ahab's support of Baal. Having confronted Ahab with this word of YHWH, Elijah is forced to flee.

The rest of chapter 17 contains three stories of Elijah's experiences as he hides from Ahab during the drought. In verses 2–7, YHWH sends Elijah to the Wadi Cherith, east of the Jordan. There the ravens feed him, and he drinks from the wadi until it dries up. In verses 8–16, Elijah is fed by a widow of Zarephath. In verses 17–24, he revives the widow's desperately ill son.

All three stories are prophet legends, designed to praise the prophet's good qualities and to establish the prophet's legitimacy. In all three stories God provides a miracle to sustain life in a situation where death threatens. In the process, Elijah's vocation and power as God's prophet are confirmed.

The structure of verses 8–16 is an interplay of words spoken by one character followed by the response of another character. The stage is set with YHWH's command to Elijah to go to Zarephath, where YHWH has commanded a widow to feed him (vv. 8–9). Elijah obeys, going to Zarephath, where he finds a widow gathering sticks (v. 10a). He requests that she bring him water to drink (v. 10b), and she obeys, setting out to bring the water (v. 11a). Elijah calls to her again, asking for bread (v. 11b). This time the widow protests the request, explaining to Elijah that she has only enough meal and oil to prepare a last meal for herself and her son (v. 12). Elijah reassures her, asks her to feed him first, and proclaims the word of YHWH that the meal and the oil will not fail until YHWH sends rain again (vv. 13–14). The widow obeys, and they all eat for many days (v. 15). The narrative ends with confirmation of YHWH's word concerning the unfailing supply of meal and oil (v. 16).

Elijah is sent by God right into enemy territory: Sidon is the home of Jezebel and the land of Baal. Moreover, God's provision for Elijah's survival during the drought-induced famine is an unlikely choice. She is a widow, left to her own meager resources, with no support from family and with a child to care for. The famine makes her situation even more desperate. She has only "a handful of meal," "a little oil," and "a couple of sticks" with which to prepare a last meal for herself and her son (v. 12). The widow's initial protest to Elijah's request for bread makes clear that she is unaware of YHWH's command for her to feed Elijah. However, she ultimately accepts Elijah's assurance and acts in trust of YHWH's word.

This story speaks of the obedience and trust of Elijah and the widow. It also proclaims the extent of YHWH's power and grace. Even in the home territory of Baal and Jezebel, YHWH is in charge. Even to a poor and desperate widow, who is not one of YHWH's own people Israel, YHWH offers life.

In verses 17–24, the predicament is the illness of the widow's son. This illness "was so severe that there was no breath left in him" (v. 17). The text does not necessarily indicate that the child is dead, but certainly the illness is serious enough that he is on the verge of death.

In addition to the son, a passive participant throughout the story, the characters are Elijah, the widow, and YHWH. The narrative unfolds in three scenes: verses 18–19, the widow and Elijah; verses 20–22, Elijah and YHWH; and verses 23–24, Elijah and the widow.

In the first scene the widow blames Elijah for her son's illness (v. 18). She believes that this illness is divine punishment for some sin of hers and that the presence of Elijah, man of God, in her house has brought her (and her sinfulness) to God's attention. Elijah's response is to take the child from her, carry him upstairs to his own bed (v. 19).

In the second scene Elijah offers a prayer of lament to YHWH (v. 20). His complaint is that YHWH has caused this calamity—"killing" the widow's son despite the fact that she has saved Elijah's life at YHWH's command (vv. 8–16). Elijah then stretches himself out upon the child three times and concludes his prayer with a petition for YHWH to revive him (v. 21). YHWH hears Elijah's prayer, and the boy is revived (v. 22).

In the third scene Elijah takes the revived child back to his mother (v. 23). The widow's response is a confession of faith (v. 24). This confession is not directly about YHWH, but about Elijah's identity as YHWH's prophet (v. 24). In the context of the entire chapter, this affirmation applies not only to the child's revival and to the unfailing food supply (vv. 14–16), but also to Elijah's initial announcement of the drought to Ahab (v. 1).

MARSHA M. WILFONG

HOMILETICAL PERSPECTIVE

The relationship between the kings of Israel and the prophets of God is a storied one. The kings seemed to value—indeed, need—their prophets. They seemed to sense that God liked to be in touch with them. They just did not appreciate the fact that sometimes the prophets' message was, "O Great King, O mighty ruler before whom mere mortals tremble, God has a word for me to speak to you. It is a hard word, for God is not exactly pleased with you. There is a price to be paid for your dance with unrighteousness. There is a score to be settled for your embrace of injustice. God is merciful, yet God is just. Beware, for God is no respecter of persons." Yes, the prophets often found themselves in awkward positions, perpetually asked to bite the hand that fed them. This, of course, led to a life of bold pronouncements interspersed with lingering questions. Sound familiar?

Elijah the Tishbite was the prophet of God when Ahab was king of Israel. The Bible tells us that "Ahab did more to provoke the anger of the LORD, the God of Israel, than had all the kings of Israel who were before him" (1 Kgs. 16:33). We can be sure that Elijah fully expected to spend a lot of time delivering Ahab his failing grades from God and a lot of time running for cover and fearing for his life. In other words, he could anticipate a life of bold pronouncements followed by lingering questions.

As this text begins, Elijah has only recently informed Ahab that his actions have brought a drought upon Israel. This drought will not be lifted except upon God's command. After he delivers this message, God tells Elijah to hide in the Wadi Cherith. The wadi seems to be a pleasant enough place. There is water to drink, and "ravens brought him bread and meat in the morning, and bread and meat in the evening" (1 Kgs. 17:6a). The problem is that because of Ahab's wickedness God has brought a drought on Israel. That drought falls on the just and the unjust. It falls on the Wadi Cherith. It falls on Elijah, who was hiding there. Elijah needs another option. He needs a plan B.

God's plans, particularly God's plan Bs, are always very interesting. They leave us scratching our heads, wondering if we heard God right and wondering if God knows what God is doing. Since there is no water in the wadi, and it does not look as if this is going to change in the foreseeable future, God says to Elijah, "Go now to Zarephath, which belongs to Sidon, and live there; for I have commanded a widow there to feed you" (1 Kgs. 17:9). We don't know if Elijah knew much about Zarephath or Sidon. We know that he would not have been optimistic about a widow feeding him. In the best of times, most widows lived a very tenuous existence. In a time of drought, their need would have been even more pronounced. We cannot blame Elijah if he mutters to himself, "I would rather trust the ravens than depend on the widow. Does God know what God is doing?"

It probably does not help Elijah's confidence much when, upon arriving in Zarephath, he sees the widow gathering sticks, an act not exactly synonymous with wealth and financial security. Maybe because he is tired, thirsty, and hungry, or maybe to assess how bad her situation is, Elijah asks the widow for a drink of water and little bite of bread. How his chest must tighten when he hears her reply, "As the LORD your God lives, I have nothing baked, only a handful of meal in a jar, and a little oil in a jug; I am now gathering a couple of sticks, so that I may go home and prepare it for myself and my son, that we may eat it, and die" (1 Kgs. 17:12). "Oh no," Elijah must be murmuring, "It's worse than I thought, it's as bad as it can be. God, don't you have a plan C?"

Of course, these are not the words that come out of Elijah's mouth. Instead of voicing his questions, Elijah makes a bold pronouncement, that the widow should go ahead and make him a meal and that God will see to it that her jar of meal will not be emptied and her jug of oil will not run out. Where does Elijah find the confidence to speak so boldly and back up his words with deeds?

I know this. I know that Rufus Watson loved this story. Rufus, who lived to be ninety-nine years old, was born in Texas, the son of former slaves. He served his country in the military. He pitched in the Negro professional leagues. He made some money investing in real estate. He witnessed lynchings and spent a lifetime wondering how people commit such atrocities and still go to church and call themselves Christians.

Rufus found comfort in the story of Elijah and the widow. He said if his life was not proof enough, this story showed that God meets people at the bottom of the barrel. "That's where God meets us, Jim, at the bottom of the barrel. God meets us when we've gone so low that all we can do is look up." If Rufus trusted God to meet him at life's low points, if Elijah trusted God to meet him at life's low points, if God met Elijah and the widow at the point where the grain, oil, and rain were running out, I guess we are well advised to do the same. We can hold on to our questions. They are not inconsequential or invalid. Elijah probably held on to his. He just spoke his faith and backed up his words with actions.

Of course let's not forget about Ahab—fuming about Elijah's impudence, wishing someone would do something to make it rain. We could always put our trust in him.

H. JAMES HOPKINS

John 12:1-11

THEOLOGICAL PERSPECTIVE

Following perhaps the most dramatic sign in the Fourth Gospel, the raising of Lazarus, John 12 opens with a countdown to Passover. John 12:1–11 is rich with significant theological themes to explore: (1) the startling image of discipleship; (2) the theological import of "the poor will always be with you" claim made by Jesus; and (3) the theological affirmation that Jesus the giver of life is bound to his death. Let us look at each theme in turn.

Mary as Faithful Disciple. Before heading to Jerusalem, Jesus pauses to feast at the home of his friends Mary, Martha, and Lazarus, "whom he had raised from the dead" (v. 1). The key scene involves Mary's unconventional act toward Jesus, the anointing of his feet. A version of this story appears in each of the Synoptic Gospels, but the differences between those versions and John's are theologically telling. First, John's version is the only place where the woman is named. Second, in Matthew (26:6–13) and Mark (14:3–9), the woman anoints Jesus' head with the oil, while in Luke (7:36–50) the "sinful woman" anoints Jesus' feet first with tears and then with ointment. Here in John, Mary—whose close relationship to Jesus is made apparent in the chapter 11 story of the dying and rising of Lazarus—does not anoint Jesus' feet with oil out of sadness or a need to repent. Rather, the power of Mary's action comes in that it is "an act of faith by a named disciple."[1] Mary's role in this passage has often been underemphasized, but with the rise of feminist theological and biblical scholarship, we see her role in a richer light. Feminist scholars dare to call her a disciple. Mary's faithful act for Jesus functions both as symbolic gesture of thanksgiving for Jesus, who has given new life to her brother, as well as symbolic preparation of Jesus' body for his own burial, as is suggested by Jesus' words in 12:7: "She bought [the perfume] so that she might keep it for the day of my burial."

This image of Mary as faithful disciple does not stand unchallenged within the text, however. Judas Iscariot, the one who will betray Jesus, is also present at this meal, and he objects to Mary's extravagant act, saying, "Why was this perfume not sold . . . and the money given to the poor?" (v. 5). A legitimate question, perhaps, but the narrator quickly clues in the reader that Judas's qualification as faithful disciple or honest questioner is in serious doubt. The narrator explains in verse 6, "He said this not because he cared about the poor, but because he was a thief." Jesus responds to Judas's question, siding unequivocally with Mary. Rebuking Judas, Jesus says, "Leave her alone. . . . You always have the poor with you, but you do not always have me" (vv. 7–8). While Judas carries the official status of disciple, clearly he fails to live up to the role. This unfaithful disciple's challenge to Mary's loyal act serves only to highlight the contrast between the two. A female follower is the one whom Jesus praises as exemplary disciple, offering us an unconventional model of discipleship today.

The Poor with Us. Before moving to the remainder of the passage, let us pause and consider more fully Judas's question to Jesus. While we can appreciate that Judas's question stems from unreliable motives, asking, why perfume instead of giving to the poor? remains a theologically significant question. Indeed, according to liberation theologians, Christians have all too often embraced Jesus' claim that "the poor will always be with you" as tacit support of the status quo. Is this what Jesus is suggesting? Very likely not. For Jesus' rebuke of Judas is, first of all, in support of Mary's preparation of Jesus for burial. Time before his death is short, and Mary's gesture helps prepare for and signify what lies ahead. Judas, it becomes clear, cannot accept what it means to live according to the economy of God, where followers like Mary "give as God gives." Rather, Judas is "surrounded by those from whom he takes, victims of his self-centered greed."[2] Jesus' words to

1. Dorothy Lee, *Flesh and Glory: Symbol, Gender, and Theology in the Gospel of John* (New York: Crossroad, 2002), 198.

Judas—"You always have the poor with you"—illumine the economy to which Judas himself adheres, the this-worldly economy of scarcity, thievery, and death, rather than the economy of God, which offers the promise of life abundant. Jesus does not here approve of poverty. Rather, Jesus points to a different way of being in the world—an extravagant, self-giving love that emerges out of death. We will soon see that this way of being threatens more than simply Judas Iscariot.

Jesus the Giver of Life. Many would argue that the raising of Lazarus stands at the center of John's Gospel. This event, which does not appear in any of the Synoptics, clearly identifies Jesus as the life-giver to all who believe in him (cf. 1:12; 3:16; 5:24). What are the theological implications of this sign? In verses 9–11, we see that the sign serves to turn us toward the imminence of Jesus' death. In these verses we hear of the growing sentiment among the chief priests to kill both Lazarus and Jesus. Thus, the raising of Lazarus is a "revelation of the identity and mission of Jesus" in and through a concrete action of Jesus.[3] The irony at play here is that the religious authorities commit to killing Jesus because he gives life to others. Yet the paradox remains: his death, the gospel tells us again and again, is what will bring new life to all.

DEANNA THOMPSON

PASTORAL PERSPECTIVE

The story begins in an idyllic way. Lazarus and his sisters Mary and Martha host an intimate party among friends. Jesus is the honored guest, and the event promises to be one of great joy. The Gospel writer does not say explicitly why this is no ordinary dinner party. Though Jesus has likely dined in this home, with these dear friends, on many occasions, this party is special. The difference is not because of the time of year, just before Passover, or because of Jesus' presence. The presence of Lazarus, recently raised from the dead, makes this dinner a special celebration. The recently empty place at the table has again been filled by Mary and Martha's brother. Healthy and alive, Lazarus hosts a party to honor the miracle worker Jesus and to give thanks to him for the gift of new life.

What a beautiful scene: fellowship, good food, time to linger at the table, and opportunities to express gratitude with words and with actions. Here we see an idyllic portrait of church fellowship. We yearn for the church to

---

2. Anthony J. Kelly and Francis J. Moloney, *Experiencing God in the Gospel of John* (New York: Paulist Press, 2003), 252.

3. Sandra M. Schneiders, *Written That You May Believe: Encountering Jesus in the Fourth Gospel* (New York: Crossroad Publishing, 1999), 160.

be a warm and inviting place. We long for a church where we gather around the table to be fed, not only by the bread and the cup, but by the presence of family and friends and, most of all, by the presence of Jesus. This is a place where Jesus is honored and those who gather are filled with gratitude and love for the gift of new life in Jesus. This is heaven on earth.

There is just one problem. The Gospel writer continues the story in a way that disrupts this happy scene. Conflict arises. Offering the very best she has, Mary anoints Jesus' feet with costly perfume made of pure nard. The perfume and her devotion captivate everyone in the room. Judas Iscariot takes offense at this—not because a woman touches a man in public, but because he thinks this is a tremendous waste of money. In his view, Mary should have used the money spent on perfume for something more important, like caring for the poor. The Gospel writer whispers to us what we cannot be sure the dinner party guests know: Judas is actually more interested in dipping his hand into the treasury for his own purposes than in caring for the poor.

There we have it: trouble in paradise. Both Mary and Judas are followers of Jesus. Among Jesus' chosen band are Simon, a Zealot, and Matthew, a tax collector. These two men represented groups that fought bitterly.[4] The first community of believers did not always live in harmony, and Christians do not always live peacefully today. Conflict exists in congregations. Jesus Christ calls diverse people into the church. With diversity come differences of opinions, split votes, competing priorities, and different ways of expressing devotion to Jesus.

Some have seen in this passage the ongoing tension in some Christian communities between acts of piety and acts of social justice. It often comes to the surface when the church budget is being discussed. Jesus cared for the poor and the marginalized. Should we then give all we have to ministries of justice and compassion? Are there legitimate times to pour our resources into renovating the sanctuary, purchasing a new organ, or expanding our Christian education facilities? How do churches work through the values that lie behind such struggles?

Clearly, Mary's pious act of devotion is lauded by Jesus. The church of Jesus Christ today must give time, attention, and dollars to the programs that help people connect to Jesus in personal ways so that, like Mary, they may worship and adore him. Mary's love and devotion, enacted in the anointing of Jesus' feet, developed over time and through a personal relationship with Jesus. Worship and education are often primary places where

---

4. Hans Weder, "Disciple, discipleship," in *The Anchor Dictionary of the Bible*, ed. David Noel Freedman et al. (New York: Doubleday, 1992), 2:208.

this relationship is developed.

Encountering Jesus in the proclamation of the Word and in the celebration of the sacraments nurtures faith. Our connection to Christ grows stronger as we listen attentively to Jesus in prayer and in Bible study. The life of discipleship entails bringing our joys and our sorrows to the feet of our Lord. Mary's anxiety, anger, and sorrow over the death of Lazarus are important parts of her growing relationship with Jesus. All that she has learned from Jesus and all that she has experienced in her life bring Mary to her knees in that amazing act of love and devotion. She anoints Jesus' feet and wipes them with her tresses. There is nothing wasteful about that.

What about the poor? Should this not be considered, even if the concern is raised by one whose integrity is questionable? Jesus intervenes on Mary's behalf as Judas challenges Mary's act of love. He does not, however, dismiss the value of helping the poor. Judas is not wrong for advocating for the needs of the most vulnerable members of our communities. He is wrong for creating a competition between acts of justice and compassion, born from a love of Jesus Christ, with other forms of devotion and discipleship. It must also be noted that Judas is in the wrong because of the deceit of his heart, though Jesus does not confront him about this.

Before us, then, is a first-century dinner party seen as a microcosm of the modern church. The threat of death and the joy of life sit side by side. The richness of worship and the poverty of the world rub shoulders. The quiet and contemplative disciples sit at table with social activists. Sometimes the table feels a bit crowded, and the mood slips from gratitude to pious judgmentalism. So long as Jesus is the honored guest and the focus of the party, the church will live out its life as those called to follow him.

NANCY A. MIKOSKI

EXEGETICAL PERSPECTIVE

In John's portrayal of Jesus' journey to the cross, the account of Mary anointing Jesus' feet plays a pivotal role. The temporal reference that introduces this story (six days before Passover) reminds the reader that the hour of Jesus' death is getting closer, especially in light of the references to Jesus' death that surround this text (the high priests' plot to kill Jesus in 11:47–53 and the death threat against Lazarus in 12:10). Moreover, the reference in verse 1 to Lazarus, who was raised by Jesus from the dead, sets the tone for the rest of the narrative, assuring the reader of the paradoxical truth that there is life in the midst of death.

John's version of the woman anointing Jesus contains elements of both the accounts in Mark 14:3–9 and Luke 7:36–50. However, for many people Mary of Bethany, who in John 12 anoints Jesus' feet with costly perfume and wipes his feet with her hair, has become the sinner woman of Luke 7—even though nothing is said about her character in John's version. This interpretive amalgamation has contributed to a large-scale confusion that exists to this day between Mary of Bethany, Mary of Magdala (Mary Magdalene), and the sinner of Galilee. In the Catholic liturgical tradition this amalgamation results in a singular saint's day honoring a fusion of all three of these women.[5] This confusion diminishes the contribution of the manifold women in Jesus' ministry and falls prey to the tendency to equate all women with sinners.

A central question of this text is, what does it mean to follow Jesus? The story of Mary anointing Jesus' feet offers different models for responding to Jesus; it contrasts belief with unbelief. Specifically, the women in this passage are held up as model believers; they expand the typical understanding of discipleship.

At the start of the narrative, we find Martha serving (*diēkonei*)—a term that is often used in the biblical text to refer to ministry (cf. Acts 6:1–6, where "deacon" is considered an ordained position). Moreover, her sister Mary functions as the prime example of true discipleship. Her loving faith is expressed by the gift she brings—expensive perfume or ointment made from real (lit. "faithful," *pistikos*) nard, that is, a substance that was typically used for incense, cosmetics, perfume, medicines, and burial preparation. John underscores the extravagant nature of her sacrifice when he focuses on the cost of the ointment (three hundred denarii, with one denarius equaling a day's wage) and the quantity (a pound constituting an abundance of perfume). John presents Mary as a woman who is prepared to give everything to Jesus. The strong scent of the perfume serves as a powerful symbol of this woman's devotion and love that spreads throughout the house and the world, serving as a public witness to Jesus.

Mary's action of anointing Jesus' feet is typically understood in light of the context of Jesus' imminent death as a prophetic act foreshadowing Jesus' death and burial, thereby signifying a tender act of preparing a loved one for burial. Jesus' interpretation of Mary's deed lends support to this understanding. He says that Mary should be left alone in order that she might keep the ointment for Jesus' burial (v. 7), the meaning of "to keep" being far

---

5. Raymond Brown, *The Gospel according to John (I–XII)*, AB 29 (Garden City, NY: Doubleday, 1966), 452. For a good overview of the Mary Magdalene legends that grew out of this early conflation, see Jane Schaberg, "Thinking Back through Mary Magdalene," in *A Feminist Companion to John*, vol. 2 (Sheffield: Sheffield Academic Press, 2003), 167–89.

from clear.[6] It is important to note that in contrast to Mark's Gospel, where the anointing by the unnamed woman would be the only preparation for burial that Jesus would receive, John's Gospel records Joseph of Arimathea's provision of an elaborate burial (19:38–42). It seems that in John's version, Mary's action anticipates or prefigures the final anointing.

Mary's act of anointing Jesus' feet is further significant when John uses exactly the same word to describe Mary's action of wiping Jesus' feet with her hair (v. 3) that he uses to describe Jesus' action of wiping the feet of his disciples with a towel (13:5). This correspondence between Mary's and Jesus' actions gives broader significance to her deed. Mary serves as an example of a true disciple, particularly because she knows how to respond to Jesus without being told. Even before Jesus gives the love commandment to his disciples (13:34–35), Mary fulfills the obligation of showing self-sacrificial love to others. In our world, where greed and consumerism reign supreme, Mary's unselfish love sets the tone for the mutuality and devotion that should mark believers' interaction with one another.

Mary as faithful disciple is juxtaposed with the greedy and self-centered male disciple, Judas. Judas harshly critiques Mary's actions, based upon his apparent concern for the poor. However, the narrator's assessment sheds negative light upon Judas and hence discredits him (the reminder that Judas would betray Jesus [v. 4] as well as the accusation that Judas was a thief who often stole from the common purse [v. 6]). Over against Jesus' condemnation of Judas stands his commendation of Mary's actions. This creates a contrast between a life of self-centeredness and greed and a model of self-sacrificing love, one of the central tenets of John's message that is today more relevant than ever.

Mary's act of anointing Jesus' feet further contrasts with the high priests' resolve to kill Jesus and his influence. The high priests serve as the ultimate expression of unbelief, actively seeking to erase any reminders of Jesus' deeds. Their actions stand over against the very public action of Mary pouring the fragrant ointment on Jesus' feet—the strong scent drawing attention to Jesus, thereby serving as a public witness to Jesus' identity and purpose.

L. JULIANA M. CLAASSENS

HOMILETICAL PERSPECTIVE

In today's reading, Jesus comes for dinner at the home of Mary and Martha, together with their brother Lazarus, whom Jesus had raised from the dead. Important turning points in the ministry of Jesus tend to take place at

---

6. Gail R. O'Day, "Introduction, Commentary and Reflections on the Gospel of John," *The New Interpreter's Bible: Luke–John*, vol. 9 (Nashville: Abingdon Press, 1995), 702.

dinner tables.

Mary anoints *the feet* of Jesus with precious ointment of great cost. Something very costly is about to unfold and the anointing of feet is a clue. Kings and priests were anointed on the head, and guests were lavished with perfume on the upper body. In preparing a body for burial, the anointing began with the extremities, the hands and feet. The precious ointment heightens our attention to the great cost that Jesus will soon bear in his body. The anointing of Jesus' feet anticipates his burial and the visit of the women to the tomb on resurrection morning to complete the care of his body.

Judas, the treasurer of Jesus' mission, objects to the extravagance of Mary's care for Jesus. Like many who betray, Judas appears to be concerned for others, but in truth he is concerned only for himself. Loyalty to another, even to Jesus, is often limited by our own self-interests and selfish motives. Few things are more painful, more costly in human terms, than the betrayal of loyalty.

"Leave her alone" (v. 7). Jesus knows what is coming, and so does Mary. Why else would she go to such extremes? The poor will need our care and concern long after Jesus is no longer with us. We can get back to that in due time. Right now, all of our attention must be on Jesus.

Jesus draws crowds. This simple family dinner in Bethany is drawing a crowd. Some want to see Jesus. More want to see Lazarus to make sure the rumors they have heard about his being raised from death to life are really true. Even in times of great promise, skepticism runs deep. Some find believing easy; others find believing very difficult. Most of us live somewhere in the middle: we want to see Jesus, but we also want to see Lazarus (i.e., what Jesus can do).

The folks in power are threatened. The chief priests have limited vision. In the confines of their world, dead people stay that way. Jesus' raising of Lazarus from the dead was not helpful. It raised too many questions. People were flocking to Jesus. More people were claiming him as their Messiah with each passing day. Lazarus must be put to death, again. The chief priests were worried. What if they caused Jesus to be killed, buried, and his body secured in a rock-solid tomb? This was no time to take chances. It was not just Lazarus that they wanted dead.

This Gospel gives us clues about what is coming in the days ahead for Jesus, heightens our awareness, and calls us to pay close attention to the details as Holy Week draws closer.

Every time I read the story of Mary anointing the feet of Jesus with costly, perfumed ointment, and Judas's reaction to her doing so, I cannot help but recall the church's ministry to the seafarers on the docks of London in the middle of the nineteenth century. It was a desperate time in many ways. The industrial revolution and the mass production of manufactured goods were placing an enormous burden on the English shipping industry. The English colonists around the world were anxious to receive boatloads of comfort and familiarity from home.

Being a dockworker was a dangerous vocation. Loading and unloading the ships was tricky business, and a careless moment of inattention or the simple misstep of a coworker could cause severe injury and often death. The seafarers who worked on the ships would be gone for months at a time, and one never knew when one might be taking their final sailing. The areas around the docks were filled with widows and orphans. Poverty and disease was rampant. In many ways it was "progress" at its worst.

In the midst of all this, however, there were beautiful churches adorned with great art and breathtaking stained glass. No expense was spared to provide fine organs and support great choirs. The liturgical vestments were often quite lavish, much grander than in the churches in the wealthy areas. It was all a very costly ointment.

There were soup kitchens too, and church-run schools for the orphans. There were societies for the support of the widows. There were social justice ministries around every corner. The church reached out to "the poor that we will always have with us."

In the dismal surroundings of the London docks, if the people were going to have any beauty in their lives, it was going to have to be at the church. If the people were going to see any great art, it was going to have to be in church. If the people were going to hear any beautiful music, it was going to have to be the organ and choir. If the people were going to be treated to great oratory, it would have to be the great preaching of the church. If the people were going to be anointed with God's beauty, then the church was going to have to provide copious amounts of costly perfumed ointment in the midst of their desperate, needy, seemingly hopeless neighborhood.

Imagine what could have been done if the churches on the London docks had spent all of their resources on something other than costly perfumed ointment. Then imagine what the dockworkers and the seafarers and their families would have missed. Imagine how dreadful our religion might have turned out to be if we did not have Mary of Bethany, and so many like her through the centuries, reminding us by their sacrificial gifts of the extravagance of God.

J. NEIL ALEXANDER

Sixth Sunday of Lent (Palm Sunday)

1 Samuel 16:1–13

¹The LORD said to Samuel, "How long will you grieve over Saul? I have rejected him from being king over Israel. Fill your horn with oil and set out; I will send you to Jesse the Bethlehemite, for I have provided for myself a king among his sons." ²Samuel said, "How can I go? If Saul hears of it, he will kill me." And the LORD said, "Take a heifer with you, and say, 'I have come to sacrifice to the LORD.' ³Invite Jesse to the sacrifice, and I will show you what you shall do; and you shall anoint for me the one whom I name to you." ⁴Samuel did what the LORD commanded, and came to Bethlehem. The elders of the city came to meet him trembling, and said, "Do you come peaceably?" ⁵He said, "Peaceably; I have come to sacrifice to the LORD; sanctify yourselves and come with me to the sacrifice." And he sanctified Jesse and his sons and invited them to the sacrifice.

⁶When they came, he looked on Eliab and thought, "Surely the LORD's anointed is now before the LORD." ⁷But the LORD said to Samuel, "Do not look on his appearance or on the height of his stature, because I have rejected him; for the LORD does not see as mortals see; they look on the outward appearance, but the LORD looks on the heart." ⁸Then Jesse called Abinadab, and made him pass before Samuel. He said, "Neither has the LORD chosen this one." ⁹Then Jesse made Shammah pass by. And he said, "Neither has the LORD chosen this one." ¹⁰Jesse made seven of his sons pass before Samuel, and Samuel said to Jesse, "The LORD has not chosen any of these." ¹¹Samuel said to Jesse, "Are all your sons here?" And he said, "There remains yet the youngest, but he is keeping the sheep." And Samuel said to Jesse, "Send and bring him; for we will not sit down until he comes here." ¹²He sent and brought him in. Now he was ruddy, and had beautiful eyes, and was handsome. The LORD said, "Rise and anoint him; for this is the one." ¹³Then Samuel took the horn of oil, and anointed him in the presence of his brothers; and the spirit of the LORD came mightily upon David from that day forward. Samuel then set out and went to Ramah.

John 13:1–17, 34–35

[1]Now before the festival of the Passover, Jesus knew that his hour had come to depart from this world and go to the Father. Having loved his own who were in the world, he loved them to the end. [2]The devil had already put it into the heart of Judas son of Simon Iscariot to betray him. And during supper [3]Jesus, knowing that the Father had given all things into his hands, and that he had come from God and was going to God, [4]got up from the table, took off his outer robe, and tied a towel around himself. [5]Then he poured water into a basin and began to wash the disciples' feet and to wipe them with the towel that was tied around him. [6]He came to Simon Peter, who said to him, "Lord, are you going to wash my feet?" [7]Jesus answered, "You do not know now what I am doing, but later you will understand." [8]Peter said to him, "You will never wash my feet." Jesus answered, "Unless I wash you, you have no share with me." [9]Simon Peter said to him, "Lord, not my feet only but also my hands and my head!" [10]Jesus said to him, "One who has bathed does not need to wash, except for the feet, but is entirely clean. And you are clean, though not all of you." [11]For he knew who was to betray him; for this reason he said, "Not all of you are clean."

[12]After he had washed their feet, had put on his robe, and had returned to the table, he said to them, "Do you know what I have done to you? [13]You call me Teacher and Lord—and you are right, for that is what I am. [14]So if I, your Lord and Teacher, have washed your feet, you also ought to wash one another's feet. [15]For I have set you an example, that you also should do as I have done to you. [16]Very truly, I tell you, servants are not greater than their master, nor are messengers greater than the one who sent them. [17]If you know these things, you are blessed if you do them." . . .

[34]I give you a new commandment, that you love one another. Just as I have loved you, you also should love one another. [35]By this everyone will know that you are my disciples, if you have love for one another."

ORDER OF WORSHIP

OPENING WORDS / CALL TO WORSHIP
> Awake to the day of triumph for our Savior!
> Give thanks for this day that leads to the cross!
> Come with your branches, hosannas, and songs!
> Fill the air with welcome to the Lord!
> Blessed is the one who comes in the name of the Lord.

HYMN, SPIRITUAL, OR PSALM

CALL TO CONFESSION

The Lord sees our hearts   *1 Sam. 16:7*
and knows our innermost thoughts.
We can deny our wrongs to ourselves
but we cannot hide them from God.
As we confess our sins, let us do so knowing
we say nothing that is not already known to God,
who is not fooled by our strength, but loves us
   in our weakness.

PRAYER OF CONFESSION

Lord Jesus Christ,   *John 13:1–17, 31b–35*
how well you know our hearts,
and still you love us—
you have loved us to the end.

We have denied you,
and we have denied our calling
to serve one another.

We have betrayed you,
and we have betrayed your commandment
to love one another.

Pour out your Spirit of grace upon us.
Teach us to love and serve you faithfully
and to love and serve one another
by the example you have set for us;
in your holy name we pray. Amen.

DECLARATION OF FORGIVENESS

Now the Lord Jesus Christ has been glorified,   *John 13:31*
and God has been glorified in him.
Now the promise is fulfilled,
and love's redeeming work is done:[1]
In Jesus Christ we are forgiven.
Thanks be to God!

1. Charles Wesley, "Christ the Lord Is Risen Today!" *Glory to God* (Louisville, KY: Westminster John Knox Press, 2013), 245.

PRAYER OF THE DAY

Lord Jesus Christ,
as you upturn all expectations
make us ready to follow you,
whatever that path might bring,
loving and serving one another
in your name. **Amen.**

HYMN, SPIRITUAL, OR PSALM

PRAYER FOR ILLUMINATION

Let your Word, O God, break open our hearts this day
through the power of the Holy Spirit,
that we may enter into the coming Holy Week
ready to meet Jesus as he is, not what we expect him to be. **Amen.**

SCRIPTURE READINGS

SERMON

HYMN, SPIRITUAL, OR PSALM

PRAYERS OF INTERCESSION

Our Savior comes to us humbly,
riding a donkey and proclaiming a message of peace.
Let us pray for the church,
for Earth and all its creatures,
and for all people in need, saying,
God of mercy, hear our prayer.
[A time of silence may follow each petition.]

That Christians hear and share the word of God as true disciples,
God of mercy, **hear our prayer.**

That all ends of the earth receive the words of the king of peace.
God of mercy, **hear our prayer.**

That all leaders, of church and of state, prefer humble service
to empty power.
God of mercy, **hear our prayer.**

That all people live with gratitude
for the gifts of nourishment, friendship, family,
trust, patience, and hope
with the courage and wisdom to change whatever fails
    to be life-giving.
God of mercy, **hear our prayer.**

That those who see the cross starkly revealed in their lives
draw strength from the name that is above every other name.
God of mercy, **hear our prayer.**

That we might live with gratitude for our ancestors
whose faith and witness have nourished our own,
that all who mourn today will be comforted,
and that we, who hope to greet Jesus when he comes again,
will be ready and filled with joy.
God of mercy, **hear our prayer.**

God our creator, you show your sons and daughters
the way to freedom through the gentle obedience of your Son,
    Jesus Christ,
in whose name we pray.
Amen.

LORD'S PRAYER

INVITATION TO THE OFFERING
Let our hosannas to the one who brings liberation
take form in our tithes and offering.

PRAYER OF THANKSGIVING/DEDICATION
God of all good gifts,
we thank you for showing us how to care
    for each other.   *John 13:1–17*
May these gifts lead to great feasting
for those who have no banquets set before them.
May these gifts build shelters and places of prayer
for those who are homeless.
May these gifts proclaim your desire
that all your creation live in peace.

Give us grateful hearts, O God,
in the name of the one who came to draw all people
   to himself,
Jesus Christ, our Savior.
Amen.

HYMN, SPIRITUAL, OR PSALM

CHARGE

Let the same mind be in you   *1 Sam. 16:7*
that is in Christ Jesus, our Lord.
Look not at outer appearances, be they humble
   or grand,
but at the heart, to see and serve the child of God
that lies in each one of us.
Listen to the word of the Lord,
and believe.

BLESSING

Go in peace, assured of God's presence with you,
with the mind of Christ Jesus as your path and guide,
and the constant companionship of the Holy Spirit.

SONG SUGGESTIONS

"All Glory, Laud, and Honor" (*CH* 192, *EH* 154 and 155, *ELW* 344, *GC* 421,
   GTG 196, *TNCH* 216 and 217, *UMH* 280)
"An Upper Room Did Our Lord Prepare" (*CH* 385, *GTG* 202)
"Come Now You Blessed, Eat at My Table" (*GTG* 186)
"Filled with Excitement" (*GTG* 199, *TNCH* 214, *UMH* 278)
"Hosanna, Loud Hosanna" (*GTG* 197, *TNCH* 213, *UMH* 278)
"O Blest Are They Who in Their Love" (*GTG* 208)
"You Walk Along Our Shoreline" (*GTG* 170, *TNCH* 504)

CHILDREN'S SERMON

Based on 1 Sam. 16:1–13, John 13:1–17, and John 12:12–19

Imagine with me a day when everything seems like the opposite of the way it usually is. Maybe you wake up early and make breakfast for your parents, then walk *them* to the bus stop, where they ride the bus to school and sit at *your* desk all day! Imagine, maybe, that your principal and the school janitor switch places, so the principal mops the floors and cleans up when kids get sick, and the janitor gets to sit in a nice office and make the morning announcements over the loudspeaker! Or maybe the kid who usually gets picked last in gym class because he is not so great at basketball gets to be the team captain!

Well, I think God would really like a day like that, because there are stories all over the Bible about God doing things just like that!

There is a story about a prophet named Samuel who goes to visit a family with eight sons, because God told him that one of those sons is going to be the next king of Israel. Samuel looks at the sons and thinks it must be the oldest, tallest, strongest son. He sure looks like a king! But God tells Samuel, "Nope, it is not him!" Samuel keeps guessing which son it might be, and he keeps guessing wrong. It turns out that God had chosen the youngest, littlest son in the family to be the next king!

There is another story in the Bible about Jesus and his friends having dinner together. Even though Jesus is the Son of God, and much wiser and holier than all the other people at the dinner table, Jesus grabs a towel and a bowl of water and starts washing his friends' feet because they were all dusty from walking around. That is something a servant would usually do!

Today is Palm Sunday, when we remember how Jesus rode into Jerusalem on a donkey. That is a story about God doing the opposite of what you would expect, too. Usually, kings and army generals and other really important people would ride into town on fancy horses and the town would have a big parade where all the most important people came out to celebrate them. But Jesus rode in on a lowly little donkey. The most important people in town did not like Jesus and definitely would not throw him a parade, but the people who liked Jesus got excited and waved palm branches to celebrate him. They made their own parade!

God is just full of surprises.

SERMON HELPS

1 Samuel 16:1–13

THEOLOGICAL PERSPECTIVE

If theology consists of giving God names that adequately describe God's ways, then the first biblical character to practice this art was Hagar, the slave woman who, on the basis of her experience, calls God "El-roi," "the God who sees" (Gen. 16:13). Neither distance nor time imposed limits on God's seeing, Hagar observed. Her own contemptuous looks had rendered her a fugitive, but the Lord had mercifully found her in the wilderness and looked far into the future of the seed growing within her.

Centuries later, the Lord would see the distress and remember the prayers of yet another maidservant, a barren wife named Hannah. As a consequence, she too would bear a son (1 Sam. 1:11, 20). This child, Samuel, would become a judge and prophet, but he would also call himself a seer, one who sees (1 Sam. 9:19). Although he saw what some could not, even Samuel did not see as God sees, and some elements within his story serve as a sobering lesson concerning human limitations, particularly as they apply to the work of theology.

At God's direction, Samuel had anointed Saul as Israel's first king. The story's narrator never states God's rationale for this choice, but readers do learn that Saul is the tallest, most handsome man in all Israel (1 Sam. 9:2). When Samuel eventually presents Saul to the people as the new ruler whom they have requested, the prophet seems to assume that looks and stature suffice to make one a leader. "Do you see the one whom the LORD has chosen? There is no one like him among all the people," Samuel tells the assembly (1 Sam. 10:24).

When the time comes for Samuel to anoint Saul's successor, God and Samuel see things very differently. For one thing, Samuel cannot fully understand God's rejection of Saul. The tense, heart-wrenching quality of the account that reports this debacle (1 Sam. 15) suggests that the narrator may have attributed to Samuel his own perplexity over this tragedy. In any case, Samuel grieves the rejection of Saul, upon whom the prophet would never again lay his eyes.

For another thing, God tells Samuel, "I have seen me a king" among the sons of Jesse (1 Sam. 16:1, my wording), but Samuel trusts his own eyes and also the visual appeal of beauty and stature as identifying qualities for a new king (v. 6). In rebuke, God contrasts divine and human seeing. "The LORD does not regard appearances, but sees into the heart" (v. 7), God explains to the visually impaired prophet. Indeed, God has seen and chosen one whom Samuel cannot see at all, the shepherding son who remains at some distance in the field.

These observations do not exhaust this reading's optical issues. Another level of theological probing begins when someone fetches the absent but chosen lad so Samuel can anoint him, and the narrator then carefully describes David's appearance. He is ruddy and good-looking, with beautiful eyes (v. 12)—or was it an eye for beauty?

David's eyes too would see, or not see, in ways that led to trouble. From his rooftop, he would look upon Bathsheba. Though he lacked nothing and already had numerous wives, his eyes convinced him that he must have another man's wife (2 Sam. 11). Still later, David would see the same wanton look in the eyes of his son Amnon, but he would not recognize it. As a consequence, he would send his daughter Tamar, the delectable object of Amnon's hungry eyes, into a terrible trap (2 Sam. 13). All through this story, the sons of David die for the sins of their father, including those that stemmed from the blindness of his beautiful eyes.

If we cannot trust the eyes of prophets or the vision of one like David, "a man after God's own heart," as the Scriptures call him (1 Sam. 13:14), then we must learn to practice a certain wariness of all theologians and anybody else who claims to know God's mind or discern God's will. Theology, after all, is made on earth, not in heaven. Accordingly, it suffers from all the flaws and limits that characterize the perceptive capacities of a species whose most stunningly nimble skill is self-deception.

We live in an age in which theologians and prophets, including many of the self-appointed variety, rarely hesitate to make pronouncements about the will of God and the theological messages they discern in current events. Seers on either end of the political spectrum find warrants aplenty for calling down God's judgment on those whose sins they decry, or interpreting the most recent disaster as heaven's blow against evildoers of the sort that they have helped God identify. Others among the prophetic band claim as well to know whom God would have us elect or appoint as leaders.

Theologians, prophets, and Pharisees of all stripes would do well to ponder the story of Samuel and David, in which, ironically, an ancient, anonymous theologian who practiced his art through narrative reminded readers, including peers and colleagues of every age, that God does not see as mortals see. God sees what human observers can never discern, including the hidden depths of their own hearts (1 Sam. 16:7). By making that point, this storyteller also confesses his own blindness and the limitations of his and every other writer's analysis and depiction of human or divine affairs, whether published, perished, scriptural, apocryphal, or otherwise. In so doing, this exemplary narrator also engages in the safest, sanest response to the inevitability and depth of his own blindness. His confession is a form of repentance.

FREDERICK NIEDNER

PASTORAL PERSPECTIVE

What was God thinking? What was Samuel thinking? What do any of us think as we attempt to lead a congregation toward God's will and way? In preceding chapters we learn that Samuel's first attempt at "king making" did not end well.

We read in 1 Samuel 9:1–10:1 that God will send Samuel a man to anoint as Israel's first king. That very day a Benjaminite named Kish lost his herd of donkeys. Kish had a son named Saul who was very handsome (a GQ type) and very, very tall. He stood head and shoulders above his peers. Saul was a bit of a Jewish giant! Kish instructed Saul to find the donkeys with the help of a boy. Along the way, Saul ran out of food and money and turned toward home before Kish began to worry about him. The boy produced some coin and persuaded Saul to continue to the village at the top of the hill, where a seer with a pretty good reputation for being right lived. Some young girls near a well directed them to Samuel, and the rest, as they say, is history.

Saul had early victories and did win the approval of his people; but he let the prerogatives of power go to his head. Kingly control emboldened Saul to assume authorities not ascribed to him in his anointing: his call and covenant with God and the people. At Gilgal (13:7–10) he arrogated the priestly role offering sacrifices, an offence to God and irritation to Samuel. God then spoke to Samuel, lamenting the choice, "I regret that I made Saul king, for he has turned back from following me, and has not carried out my commands" (15:11). Samuel chastised Saul, saying, "Has the LORD as great delight in burnt offerings and sacrifices, as in obedience to the voice of the LORD? Surely, to obey is better than sacrifice, and to heed than the fat of rams. For rebellion is no less a sin than divination, and stubbornness is like iniquity and idolatry. Because you have rejected the word of the LORD, he has also rejected you from being king" (15:22–23).

Boundary issues are almost a given for life in the church. Usurping power and territory with or without malice is commonplace. Such trespasses may cause a member to look for a new church or a church to look for a new minister. It truly is better to ask permission than forgiveness—especially over time.

Still grieving over Saul, Samuel received marching orders. God had identified yet another Benjaminite, whom God saw (now?) from the inside

rather than the outside. Despite his grief over the results of his first anointing, his fear of being killed by Saul, the apparent coup being planned, the
subterfuge—using sacrifice as cover for meeting with Jesse to anoint a new
king—Samuel chose obedience and filled his horn with new oil. With a
heifer in hand for cover, Samuel traveled to Bethlehem.

The circle of sacrifice began well. Jesse and his sons were sanctified by
Samuel, and a parade of the potentials began. Samuel, however, still saw with
his eyes. Eliab, the first presented, was tall and easy on the eye. Samuel began
to think his work was done! God rejected Eliab, and the other six, because
God was looking for a leader with heart.

Heart was not the center of emotions for the ancients, although it was
included. Heart was the center of one's being: emotion, intelligence, discernment, wisdom, commitment, and character were all elements of heart—perhaps what we call soul. The right combination was absent in these seven
sons. Samuel asked for more. Surely, he had been obedient to God's command. God had said one was already chosen, so there must have been at
least one more. Samuel would not close the circle until even the least likely
was presented.

The ruddy youngest was fetched from the flock he was shepherding. The
boy with beautiful eyes passed by them all and, even knowing that God was
looking internally, Samuel (or the narrator) could not help but comment on
the lad's appearance. The beauty of one's heart, the loveliness of one's soul
surpasses its physical container and is often seen through its portal to the
world: one's eyes. David's name was finally used and he was anointed.

While the story line of our text is the anointing of David, the subtext of
this passage, as well as its larger narrative, is about God and Samuel and
obedience in leadership. Samuel heard God speak and his first response
was protest and inquiry. Samuel wanted to understand the parameters and
responsibilities, the realities and consequences, and gain assurance that God
understood them too. At times, God responded with more detail or altered
plans, giving the impression that it was a cocreative process. At other times,
God responded, "We will cross that bridge when we come to it. Go!" Samuel
now acted in knowledge and faith, walking where God directed and doing
as God instructed. God's call was not to blind obedience, but cocreated purpose, toward which Samuel walked at a steady and healthy pace.

Life in the church may also be a cocreative process, a kind of dance of
leadership in which either party may lead from time to time with more
detail or an enlarged vision. Perhaps that is why David liked to dance so
much; he was dancing out the details with God.

In the life of the church, too often conflicts erupt, opportunities are missed, people are hurt and/or disheartened, and the community takes several steps backward because the boundaries of our covenant and purpose are ignored and broken. Leadership needs to be vigilant about training, informing, and recovenanting with volunteers to make clear the vision and mission of individual and faith community tasks. It really is better to get permission than forgiveness. We know our need for daily forgiveness; that much more do we need permission.

What were God and Samuel thinking? Apparently, they first thought it took a giant to slay giants. The larger story reveals that it really took a faithful, dancing heart. Remember, it was David who slew Goliath. Faithful, dancing hearts are what the church needs too.

DONALD P. OLSEN

EXEGETICAL PERSPECTIVE

This account of the anointing of David by Samuel stands at a critical turning point in the books of Samuel. The preceding chapters have described the failed kingship of Saul and God's rejection of him (15:10–35), though Saul will not die until chapter 31. Now David is privately—even secretly—anointed, and the chapters that follow recount his complex relationship with Saul and his rise to become king over Israel (1 Sam. 16:14–2 Sam. 5:10).

The act of anointing with oil is a ritual that establishes a covenantal relationship between the partners. The one who anoints pledges support to the one who is anointed. Later the men of Judah (2 Sam. 2:4) and the elders of Israel (2 Sam. 5:3) will themselves anoint David, thus obligating themselves to him. God's anointing of David through the prophet Samuel serves as a sign of God's election of and commitment to David. By placing this account at the beginning of the story of David's rise, all that happens is seen through the lens of David's election by God.

The short narrative is a masterful combination of psychological drama, political realism, folkloristic color, and careful intertextual allusion, all designed to point to the freedom of the divine choice in the selection of a king. The story divides into four sections: (1) the initial conversation between God and Samuel (vv. 1–4a); (2) Samuel's arrival at Bethlehem (vv. 4b–5); (3) the review of Jesse's seven sons (vv. 6–10); and (4) the anointing of David (vv. 11–13).

Much of the story's *psychological interest* focuses on Samuel. The prophet had been something of a father figure to Saul and yet had been required to tell him that God had rejected him from being king. Poignantly, the preceding chapter closed with the note that Samuel never saw Saul again before his death but that he grieved for Saul (15:35). Nevertheless Samuel the grieving mentor is required to put aside his own feelings to carry out his duties as God's prophet. God sternly reminds him of this in 16:1. As the story proceeds, God will educate Samuel about the qualities needed in a king who can succeed.

The *political realism* of the narrative is evident in the sense of danger that overshadows events. To anoint a new king while the old one lives would be seen by Saul as treason; consequently Samuel fears for his own life (v. 2). Similarly, when Samuel arrives at Bethlehem, the elders who greet him tremble in alarm (v. 4). As a prophet, Samuel is a figure of uncanny power, and now he is an enemy of the king. No wonder his presence creates anxiety. God, however, has provided Samuel with a cover story: he has come to conduct a sacrifice (vv. 2–3, 5)—though one wonders if it is particularly plausible. The anointing itself (v. 13) is apparently conducted with only David's immediate family present. Saul remains ignorant of what has taken place, though he later draws his own conclusions about God's intention and David's future (23:17; 24:21).

The *folkloristic element* in the story concerns the motif of the overlooked or neglected child who becomes a king or queen. It is, in short, the Cinderella story. The motif is used cleverly in the narrative. Already in verse 1 the reader and Samuel know that God has selected a king from one of the sons of Jesse, but which one is not indicated. When Samuel reviews Jesse's sons, Samuel starts with his own intuitions. He is impressed with Eliab's appearance and height.

The reader who knows the folkloristic convention already knows that none of the favored sons will be the chosen one. The story uses the motif to make a theological point. People tend to judge by outward appearances; but God judges by the "heart," that is, the inner character of a person (v. 7). All of Jesse's sons (or so the reader is led to believe) are brought before Samuel. God, however, has indicated to Samuel that none of these is the one. How can that be? Samuel perseveres and asks if there is some other son. That David has not been included is an indication of his status within the family. His father identifies him as "the youngest," a term that could also be translated "the smallest" or even "the least" (v. 11). His job in the family—shepherd—has, however, a strong metaphorical resonance. Shepherd is a common metaphor that ancient Near Eastern kings used to describe their relationship to their peoples. The fact that David is a shepherd is symbolic of his future role in relation to the Israelite people.

The story of the selection of David both echoes and contrasts with that of the selection of Saul. Samuel is initially drawn to Eliab's handsomeness and tall stature, which are similar to Saul's kingly appearance (9:2; 10:23).

The "yes/no" word that God gives to Samuel is similar to the lot by which Saul was chosen (10:17–27a). Just as Saul was missing at the crucial moment of his selection (10:21–22), so David is also not on the scene. Of course, it is Samuel who anoints each of them (10:1). Also, just as Saul was seized by the spirit of the Lord (10:6, 10; 11:6), so is David (16:13), though in the case of David, the empowering spirit of the Lord remains with him as a lasting charisma (v. 14).

David's introduction is both climactic and ironic. Although the reader familiar with the history of Israel has known from the beginning—even before Samuel did—that it is David who will be God's choice, David's name is mentioned only in the final verse (v. 1). Though Samuel has been warned not to look on the outward appearance as an indication of kingliness, David is introduced by the narrator in terms of his good looks (v. 12)! Here is someone in whom both the inward and the outward qualities come together. The human and the divine desires for an ideal king seem to intersect, but David will prove to be anything but an ideal king and will receive both divine and human disapproval (2 Sam. 11–12).

CAROL A. NEWSOM

HOMILETICAL PERSPECTIVE

In many worship services, children are provided their own children's sermon. After this they are then excused from suffering through the sermon preached to the grownups. How ironic that the church systematically excludes its youngest sons and daughters from the hearing and interpretation of this text. They already have more in common with the absent David than they know. Whether tending sheep or having snacks in the fellowship hall, the smallest have gone missing.

All children know how it feels to be excluded. Many have experienced the peculiar agony of being picked last for a sports team. The youngest, smallest, least coordinated are forced to watch as one by one the taller, stronger, more athletic specimens are chosen by the captains. A teenage girl knows the pain of being the one who is not asked to a dance. A boy whose birthday falls in the summer watches as each of his friends gets a driver's permit. Drawing on these rich and all-too-common experiences, a preacher can use this text as a guide for speaking directly to the socially *non*-elect, whatever their age.

Instead of segregating the congregation by sermon type—children's or adults'—Palm Sunday and this text provide an ideal opportunity for the intentional inclusion of all members in participation in the sermon, from the youngest to the oldest. One could forgo the usual grown-up sermon in favor of elevating the children's sermon to the proclamation for the day. This liturgical adjustment itself would be an implicit proclamation of the text. With only a little creativity, this Scripture—and the Gospel text as well—could be enacted through drama, just as Jesus' triumphal entry traditionally is on this day. A hopeful Jesse could call strapping sons one by one before a crusty old Samuel, who inspects them for height, strength, and any number of additional, more humorous traits, some planned and some improvisational. Can this one sing opera? Does this one have good teeth? Can this one disco dance? One by one, each is rejected, perhaps by the children of the congregation playing the part of God, shouting down each one in succession. Finally a young David appears before the jury, and the whole congregation is encouraged to yell and shout approval.

The reason this Scripture passage is inherently funny is because the older, stronger, better sons are passed over. The proud, the vain, the predictable winners are humiliated, while the one child everyone has discounted, or even forgotten, is selected by God. "Do you have *any* other sons, Jesse?" "Well, um, there is one more, I think. I kind of forget about him most days." Hooray for David! Hooray for the little guy! Hooray for the ostracized, the outcast, the dismissed, the forgotten, the missing. At this critical point, a playful sermon turns deadly serious.

The homiletician must remain keenly aware that even in a humorous presentation, this text, like God, sees and speaks to the heart. Anyone who has been the victim of a social pecking order carries scars that run deep. Human groups are not as patient as God. Any social organization is by its nature exclusive, but exclusion is particularly painful in the church. Many church people choose to self-exclude before a clique does it for them. So those who do not see well stop attending worship. Those who depend on walkers or wheelchairs sit near the back, arriving late and leaving early, so as not to be an obstacle to the crowd. Those whose skin color or sexuality is different go elsewhere, wherever that may be. After a while, the church forgets these people, not on purpose, not in malice. We just forget.

A congregation's sins of omission may require awakening, prophetic speech. On occasion, the preacher may need to step into the role of Samuel, boldly pointing out the congregation's implicit sin and saying, "No!" to those who unwittingly perpetuate the cycle. On the other hand, the injuries of those who have known exclusion are slow healing and easily reopened. The preacher who steps into the ever-present, serious side of this text need not tread too heavily upon the hearts of those who know rejection. Simple acknowledgment of their pain may well be enough. Rather, this is a time to commend those who have felt the hurt of a church's discrimination for the tremendous courage it takes just to show up on a Sunday morning. This is a chance to applaud the strength of those who wait, and wait, for someone's approval. While it may feel like small consolation to know that God, at least, sees their hearts, it is consolation nonetheless.

While we might and should laugh at our own vanity, we must also pay close attention to its consequences and, as Christ taught, cry with those who cry. This is not a complicated concept. Even children understand that friends sometimes stop playing with them, although the reason for the change is more difficult to grasp. We laugh at that which scares us. We rejoice when that which we thought was lost is found, whether that lost thing is a person, a relationship, or our own dignity. In proclaiming the gospel of this text, the preacher joins his or her voice in Scripture's central and highest themes of salvation and restoration. That even a child can understand these concepts is cause to rejoice.

JAMES MCTYRE

John 13:1-17, 34-35

THEOLOGICAL PERSPECTIVE

This entire Gospel can be summed up in the hospitable act of friendship where an extraordinary master takes the place of servant to his own servants (vv. 2b–5). The towel-clad Jesus has extraordinary knowledge, authority, divine origin, and destiny. Yet in this "hour" of anticipated execution and glorification, the disciples will witness what was already declared to some of them by the baptizer John: "Here is the Lamb of God who takes away the sin of the world!" (1:29b, 36b). Will they understand these things?

Do we understand? Where do we locate ourselves in the story of the dirty foot washing? Are we servants of Jesus and God? Or does the demonized figure of Judas live in us as well? The poet Eva Gore-Booth wrote of human-kind, "What all men share must all men execrate."[2] Are we as citizens of "this world" the ones who corporately have handed over to imprisonment, torture, and execution the enemies of the state and the religious fanatics who threaten our fanaticism for secular regimes with global reach?

Like Simon Peter, *what if* the act of our teacher and Lord washing our feet, cleansing us from head to toe, is too intimate, too close to erotic love? There are boundary issues when it comes to feet. (In historical perspective, "the washing of a master's feet could not be required of a Jewish slave,"

2. Eva Gore-Booth, *Shepherd of Eternity and Other Poems* (London: Longmans, Green & Co., 1925), 97, as quoted by Mark Edwards, *John*, Blackwell Bible Commentaries (Malden, MA: Blackwell, 2004), 130.

although on occasion loving disciples might serve their teacher in this way.)[3] Even when the foot washer pronounces us "entirely clean" before "his hour" has run its course, realizing "the end" (eschatology) *before* the execution and resurrection, we turn around and deny we even knew this intimate servant and messenger of God (18:15–18, 25–27). We did not know the one who knew our feet!

When the dirty foot washing in the mixed company of the unclean and clean is over, what do we do with this act of service? Is it merely a moral example of good pastoral, pedagogical, familial, and social behavior? Can such a radical love be proscribed as a formula for action in a world where service debases rather than liberates—where love between those who differ in power often opens the less powerful lover to coercion and abuse?

Sandra Schneiders finds a prophetic and symbolic act in the foot washing and its interpretation by Jesus (13:12–17) that is summed up in "a new commandment" (13:34–35; 15:12–14). This act of service in the context of Jesus' "hour" was read by the author of John and other NT writers in light of the Suffering Servant Songs in Isaiah (42:1–4; 49:1–6; 50:4–11; 52:13–53:12). However, what is service?

For Schneiders, the ideal is "self-gift . . . an expression of love" that may be taken to the extreme of laying "down one's life for one's friends" (15:13).[4] In ordinary daily life, though, we experience at least three models of service. (1) There is *service as obligation* in a pattern of domination or patriarchy. The server is bound in a relationship of social power to serve a privileged other: children / parents; slaves / masters; woman / man; subject / ruler; the poor / the wealthy. Even when these relations are well intended, the acts of service continually reinforce the imbalance of privilege. Imagine Jesus' facing Pilate in John 19:10–11. (2) In Schneiders's *existential model*, the server acts freely on behalf of the served because of a perceived need that the server has "the power to meet": mother / child, teacher / student, professional / client or patient, clergy / laity, rich / poor, strong / weak. Here again the relations are structured by a fundamental inequality. Children meet our "need to be needed," students feed our egos, clients or patients build up our careers, and laity fill our need to be perceived as "good shepherds." As long as we can keep others in relationships of neediness to us, our self-esteem is validated, while they long for escape or rebellion. (3) The model of *friendship* subverts the obligation of the first model and the privilege of meeting the

---

3. Raymond E. Brown, *Gospel according to John, XIII–XXI*, Anchor Bible 29A (Garden City, NY: Doubleday, 1970), 564.
4. Sandra M. Schneiders, *Written That You May Believe: Encountering Jesus in the Fourth Gospel* (New York: Crossroad, 1999), 170–72. Later Schneiders quotes are from the same source.

needs of others less privileged, as in the second model. For "friendship is the one human relationship based on equality." Seeking the good of the friend becomes mutually beneficial. Although friendship may begin between two or more who do not share the same power and prestige, over time the community of friends can subvert the economy of inequality and neediness. The politics of friendship at its best can build bridges over chasms of ideological, religious, racial, and social conflicts. Unfortunately, such friendships are rare and difficult to maintain, as the other models of service structure so many of our daily relationships with others.

Schneiders rereads John's theology of "the hour," the unity of cross and resurrection in light of Jesus' service to the disciples and command to love as friends love. The distinctive motifs of atonement in this Gospel are not the cross as "sacrifice or retribution" but the cross as Jesus' gift of himself to his friends. In this self-gift, symbolized the night before the execution by the foot washing and new commandment, God's love for the world becomes flesh and blood.

Some Christians, looking back over our history of persecution of "the Jews" (13:33), colonization of other religions, and the tendency of our forms of service and family to perpetuate inequality, call our attention to the many and horrific abuses of the cross. Schneiders's close reading of the foot washing that precedes the passion narrative places us on a better path to understand the cross and atonement as the ultimate degree of friendship and beloved community. To live in the light of this cross and this Friend is to seek relations of mutual respect that refuse to use and abuse those less powerful and privileged than ourselves, so that all might become the friends of God.

ROBERT A. CATHEY

PASTORAL PERSPECTIVE

Pastorally speaking, this traditional Holy Thursday text invites the disciples of Jesus in every age to gather for a meal, have their feet washed, love one another, bid farewell to a dear friend, suffer through his death, and grieve their own loss. Is there anyone among us who has not shared a meal, said good-bye, or suffered a loss? For the preacher who is also a pastor, there may be no better time to gather the people of God around these everyday human experiences, celebrating the common union that is ours in Christ.

This text, which comes to its climax with Peter's horror at Jesus' servanthood, begins with a meal. Jesus is at the table with his disciples, all of them reclining, propped up on their elbows, dipping pita bread into bowls of savory hummus and smacking their lips, licking their fingers. The sounds of conversation fill the room, punctuated from time to time by loud laughter or the clink of one clay cup against another. Oil lamps flicker, their light reflected in the shining eyes of the disciples, and while all of this is going on Jesus gets up from the table, strips off his outer robe, wraps a towel around his waist, pours water into a basin, and begins to wash the disciples' feet.

It would not be unusual if he were one of the household servants; the disciples have probably had their feet washed before. However this is their teacher, their Lord! As he moves from one to another, they fall silent, until all you can hear is the splash of water being poured into the basin over dusty, callused feet. Peter objects, but Jesus persists. In the end Jesus puts his robe back on to join them at the table. "Do you know what I have done to you?" he asks (v. 12). Apparently not. No one says a word. "I have set you an example," Jesus says. "If I, your Lord and Teacher, have washed your feet, you also ought to wash one another's feet" (v. 14).

On one level this action is symbolic, representing the pendulum swing of the prologue (1:1–18) in which Jesus removes the outer robe of his glory, wraps around himself a towel of human flesh, suffers and dies for the sake of the world, reclothes himself with glory, and resumes his rightful place in the bosom of the Creator. This may be what Peter and the other disciples will understand "later" (13:7). On another level, though, this action is personal and pastoral. The disciples need to have their feet washed. No one else has volunteered to do it. Perhaps, as in the Synoptics, they have been arguing about which one of them is the greatest, and for any one of them to volunteer would be to lose the argument. So Jesus gets up to do it—shocking them all by his disregard for social and cultural convention. As Peter implies by his objection, foot washing is slave labor. However when Jesus has finished he says: "If I, your Lord and Teacher, have washed your feet, you also ought to wash one another's feet" (v. 14).

It is a good reminder for a church that still argues over who is the greatest. We are not here to lord over one another; we are here to wash one another's feet! Sometimes on Holy Thursday we try to do this literally, in the context of worship, and it almost always comes off badly. It is awkward, embarrassing, and in some cases (since the invention of panty hose), practically impossible. Maybe the real problem is that we do not do it often enough to be good at it—not actual foot washing, necessarily, but those countless small acts of humble service Christians can offer to one another on a daily basis.

I still remember talking to a well-respected pastor at a ministers' conference when he looked down and noticed that my shoe was untied. Before I could do anything about it, he had dropped to one knee to tie it for me. I was embarrassed—like Peter—but when he stood up again, he resumed the conversation as if nothing had happened. Maybe that was why he was so well respected. Maybe that is why Jesus says to his disciples: "Do not be afraid to stoop down and offer the most humble service imaginable to one another. It is no more than I have done for you."

I see this kind of thing in my own church from time to time. One of our members has cerebral palsy, is confined to a wheelchair, and is not able to feed himself. He also has a thousand-watt smile and a wonderful sense of humor, which is good, because when we have potluck luncheons once a month, someone has to volunteer to feed him, and often those people have better intentions than results. I watch out of the corner of my eye as they ease a spoonful of food into his mouth and then dab at his face with a napkin, tentatively. They have never done this before, but they are trying, and he is grinning, and for those who have eyes to see it, some foot washing is going on.

"If I have washed your feet, you also ought to wash one another's feet," Jesus says. Then he goes one better. "If I have laid down my life for you, you also ought to lay down your lives for each other." That is not exactly the way he puts it, of course. He says, "I give you a new commandment, that you love one another," but in the next phrase he says, "Just as I have loved you, you also should love one another" (13:34). Then in chapter 15 he says, "No one has greater love than this, to lay down one's life for one's friends" (v. 13). The connections seem clear: love is laying down our lives for one another; foot washing is one of those small, everyday acts of humble service; and both of these reveal us to be the disciples of Jesus.

JIM GREEN SOMERVILLE

EXEGETICAL PERSPECTIVE

Johannine commentators commonly recognize chapter 13 as the opening of "Act II" in this Gospel's drama. The action in John 1–12 has revolved around miraculous "signs" of Jesus' identity as God's Son (2:11; 3:2; 4:54; 6:2), eliciting division among his antagonists (5:9b–18; 7:40–52; 9:13–34; 10:19–21; 11:45–53) and extended discourses by Jesus, whose truth sails over his listeners' heads but registers among the Gospel's faithful readers (3:3–21; 5:19–47; 6:35–59; 10:22–39). From chapter 13 onward, the narrative concentrates on the preparation of Jesus' followers for his resolute march to Golgotha, where on the cross his glory will be revealed fully, albeit ironically (17:1–5). The lectionary wisely assigns John 13 for meditation on Holy Thursday. Not only does this passage recount the Fourth Evangelist's version of Jesus' Last Supper with the Twelve; in many ways it crystallizes the dominant theme of John's passion narrative.

Unlike the Synoptic Gospels (Matt. 26:17–19; Mark 14:12–16; Luke 22:7–15), John identifies Jesus' last meal as *prior to* the Passover (13:1a), not as its celebration. John's focus lies elsewhere, namely, on Jesus' washing of his disciples' feet—not described in the Synoptics—and an interpretation of that event's significance. The events that follow the foot washing itself show that the point is not merely that Jesus "loved his own who were in the world . . . to the end" (v. 1b), but that he did so in the face of Judas's betrayal (vv. 18–30) and Peter's eventual denial and abandonment of his Lord (vv. 36–38). The significance of Jesus' action is heightened by the tension between the Son's fidelity to the Father and his followers' infidelity to their Lord.

Among a slave's most menial responsibilities in antiquity was washing the master's feet (see 1 Sam. 25:41; John 1:27). Simon Peter's incredulous protest (13:6, 8a) acknowledges the humiliating impropriety of what Jesus is doing for his disciples. For John, such outlandish flouting of social expectation is significant both christologically and ecclesiologically. The latter is more obvious: Jesus, Lord and teacher, is modeling the radically subservient love that his followers should express toward one another (vv. 12–15). That point is driven home in verses 34–35: Jesus' disciples are so recognized when they love one another precisely as, and to the ultimate degree that, he has demonstrated his love for them (15:12–13).

The basis for the church's conduct does not lie, however, in its natural aptitude. The church can be the church only if it is washed by its Lord and participating in his love (13:8b, 34; 15:9–10). Such self-sacrificial love (*agapē*) looks both backward and forward. It recalls the same love God has expressed in the sending of his only Son for the world's redemption (3:16–17), for the Son speaks only as the Father has taught him (8:28–29; 14:10) and does only the will of the One who has sent him (5:30; 6:38–40). The cross on which Jesus will give his life for the world (see 1:29) is anticipated at 13:4, when Jesus lays aside [*tithēsin*] his garments and takes [*labōn*] a towel: "For this reason the Father loves me, because I lay down [*tithēmi*] my life, that I may take [*labō*] it again" (10:17). The christological and ecclesiological dimensions converge at 13:16: "Truly, truly I say to you: a slave is not greater than his lord, nor an envoy [*apostolos*] greater than the one who has sent him"—even as the Father is greater than the Son (14:28b) and apart from Jesus his disciples can do nothing (15:5).

All this remains true despite the disciples' inability to comprehend it. The answer to Jesus' question, "Do you know what I have done for you?" (13:12) has already been revealed in Peter's fumbling request that his Lord not merely wash his feet but give him a bath (v. 9). In this Gospel, the disciples do not and cannot understand the import of Jesus' actions until after

Easter (2:22; 7:39; 12:16; 14:26). Even then, their faith still falters (20:19–29; 21:20–23). Unlike gnostic writings, in John the disciples' divine election and sustenance do not depend on how much they understand. Their faith is perfected, not in knowledge, but in how much they love their fellow lambs (21:15–19; cf. 1 Cor. 13:12–13).

Some interpreters see in the Fourth Gospel a constriction of love to love "for one's friends" (15:13)—within the church's confines—in contrast with the Synoptic Jesus, who teaches love for one's enemies as well (Matt. 5:44; Luke 6:27, 35). Up to a point that reading is justified, since in John "the world" is a hostile environment that cannot receive the Father's revelation through Jesus (1:10; 15:18–20; 16:33; 17:14, 25). On the other hand, the world, however benighted, is the realm that Jesus has come to save (3:16–17; 4:42; 6:33, 51; 12:47). John does not so much contradict the Synoptics as focus on the love that disciples, in alignment with their Lord, are commanded to offer one another.

The eschatological context in which the Fourth Evangelist locates the foot washing resists all attempts to sentimentalize that episode. The "hour" of the Son's glorification of the Father on the cross has finally tolled (13:31–32; cf. 7:30; 8:20; 12:23–27; 17:1). The devil has commandeered one of Jesus' disciples to betray him (13:2, 11; see also 6:70–71). When Judas leaves the table, "it was night" (13:30), whose darkness is now exposed by "the light of the world" (8:12; 9:5; 12:46; see also 1:5; 3:18–21; 11:9–10). Because Jesus is preparing to return to God, his disciples will soon be unable to see him (13:33; 16:16–28). As the cosmos turns on its hinges, the incarnate Word, who was with God in the beginning (1:1–2, 14), stoops to love to the bittersweet end those whom the Father has entrusted to him (17:24). It is a shattering moment of blessing. "If you know these things, blessed are you if you do them" (13:17).

C. CLIFTON BLACK

HOMILETICAL PERSPECTIVE

The Passover feast is approaching, and Jesus has gathered for a final meal with his disciples. As John sets the scene, before Jesus departs from the world and returns to God, he wants to leave his disciples with something to show the full extent of his love.

If we did not already know the rest of this story, we might anticipate a climactic ending more like that found in the life of the Old Testament prophet Elijah. About to depart the world in a literal blaze of glory, Elijah asks Elisha what gift he would like to receive before his master is taken from him. "Let me inherit a double share of your spirit," the disciple replies (2 Kgs.

2:9). Elijah obliges. Before departing for heaven in a chariot of fire, he leaves behind the mantle he has just used to part the waters of the Jordan. Elisha picks up the mantle. Holding it over the river, calling upon Elijah's God, he discovers that he too can make waters part at his command.

Can we not imagine a similar hope from Jesus' followers? "If you want to show us how much you love us, then let us inherit a double portion of your power. Give us some memento infused with magical properties, some token of our future greatness in the world." What a shock for the disciples—what a shock for us, if we rehear the story with fresh ears—when Jesus does not pass on a mantle of authority, but a towel.

A towel. Jesus rises from the meal, lifts off his outer garments, and wraps a towel around his waist. Then he proceeds on all fours around the table, washing his disciples' dirt-encrusted feet. According to the *Mechilta,* one of the oldest works of midrashic commentary, not even a Hebrew slave was expected to perform such menial service. While numerous scriptural passages refer to foot washing as an ancient form of hospitality, they show water being brought so that guests may wash *their own* feet. The only exceptions, notably enough, are acts by *women:* Abigail who washes the feet of David's servants (1 Sam. 25:41); the unnamed woman who washes Jesus' feet in the home of Simon the Pharisee (Luke 7:38); later, the widows in 1 Timothy 5:10. How low Jesus is stooping, both metaphorically and literally!

A towel: something used to dry dishes, wash children, wipe tables, clean wounds, cool fevers, warm aching joints, swaddle babies, mop up sweat, blot away tears. The mantle of Jesus' authority is a tool of women's work—of practical, daily, unglamorous service. A sermon about John's account of the Last Supper could fruitfully explore this imagery in three directions.

Lessons in Humility: Learning to Receive. When Jesus first approaches Peter, the disciple protests: "You will never wash my feet" (John 13:8). Peter is embarrassed, reluctant to have a highly respected person perform a menial job for him. While his resistance initially sounds like modesty ("surely I am not worthy . . ."), it ultimately masks a form of pride. Like Peter, many of us resist vulnerability, preferring to remain in control, to choose what gifts we will gratefully accept. Yet a fundamental fact of our humanness is our dependency: as infants, we all submitted to being wiped clean by someone else; in illness or old age, many of us will confront such dependency again (recall, for example, the moving portrait of a man slowly dying of Lou Gehrig's disease in Mitch Albom's *Tuesdays with Morrie*).[5] Jesus points out that

5. Mitch Albom, *Tuesdays with Morrie* (New York: Doubleday, 1997). See, e.g., 49 and 115–16.

those who cannot with grace receive the gift of physical cleaning are scarcely in a position to receive the even more humbling cleansing of sin that occurs in his even more humiliating death on a cross. It is worth pondering what other gifts we are too proud to let ourselves be given.

Lessons in Hospitality: Learning to Serve. Significantly, this is not the first but the second lesson of John's Gospel story. Before Jesus commands the disciples to follow his example in washing one another's feet (vv. 14–15), he first insists that they experience what it is like to be on the receiving end of service. Unless we are aware of our own vulnerability, our care for others is in danger of coming across as condescension. Furthermore, unless we are thoroughly instructed by the images of the towel and the basin of dirty water, we are in danger of neglecting the small, exhausting, inelegant demands of service while seeking out instead the spectacular and showy. It is worth recalling that the ministerial stole has its symbolic origins in the towel and in the yoke over the neck of a beast of burden. How are we all being called to the towel and the yoke of extending God's hospitality to the world?

Lessons in Hope: Learning to Reconcile. Jesus does not simply wash the feet of the faithful disciples; in full knowledge of the impending betrayal, he washes Judas's feet as well. Those who embrace the dual humility of being served and of reaching out to serve others are those with the suppleness to act as agents of reconciliation. For such reconciliation, the symbolism of foot washing has not lost its potency. At the 2004 Forum on World Evangelization, a dramatic foot-washing ceremony featured members of formerly divided communities: Hutu and Tutsi, Israeli and Palestinian. In 2006, a former official of the South African government washed the feet of anti-apartheid activists as an act of public apology and a gesture of hope for the restoration of right relationships.[6] As if in anticipation, Alan Paton offered a powerful fictional account of foot washing in the context of apartheid South Africa in his novel *Ah, But Your Land Is Beautiful.*[7] Before coming to Christ's Table for a foretaste of the heavenly banquet, we should give careful thought to those in our world who need reconciling—including ourselves.

MARY LOUISE BRINGLE

6. Eve Fairbanks, ""I Have Sinned against the Lord and against You! Will You Forgive Me?" *New Republic* (June 18, 2014), http://www.newrepublic.com/article/118135/adriaan-vlok-ex-apartheid-leader-washes-feet-and-seeks-redemption.
7. Alan Paton, *Ah, But Your Land Is Beautiful* (New York: Scribner's, 1981), 232–39.

Easter Sunday

¹⁷For I am about to create new heavens
    and a new earth; the former things shall not be remembered
        or come to mind.
    ¹⁸But be glad and rejoice forever
in what I am creating; for I am about to create Jerusalem as a joy,
    and its people as a delight.
¹⁹I will rejoice in Jerusalem,
    and delight in my people;
no more shall the sound of weeping be heard in it,
    or the cry of distress.
²⁰No more shall there be in it
    an infant that lives but a few days,
    or an old person who does not live out a lifetime;
for one who dies at a hundred years will be considered a youth,
    and one who falls short of a hundred will be considered accursed.
²¹They shall build houses and inhabit them;
    they shall plant vineyards and eat their fruit.
²²They shall not build and another inhabit;
    they shall not plant and another eat;
for like the days of a tree shall the days of my people be,
    and my chosen shall long enjoy the work of their hands.
²³They shall not labor in vain,
    or bear children for calamity;
for they shall be offspring blessed by the LORD—
    and their descendants as well.
²⁴Before they call I will answer,
    while they are yet speaking I will hear.
²⁵The wolf and the lamb shall feed together,
    the lion shall eat straw like the ox;
    but the serpent—its food shall be dust!
They shall not hurt or destroy
    on all my holy mountain,

                                                    says the LORD.

¹Early on the first day of the week, while it was still dark, Mary Magdalene came to the tomb and saw that the stone had been removed from the tomb. ²So she ran and went to Simon Peter and the other disciple, the one whom Jesus loved, and said to them, "They have taken the Lord out of the tomb, and we do not know where they have laid him." ³Then Peter and the other disciple set out and went toward the tomb. ⁴The two were running together, but the other disciple outran Peter and reached the tomb first. ⁵He bent down to look in and saw the linen wrappings lying there, but he did not go in. ⁶Then Simon Peter came, following him, and went into the tomb. He saw the linen wrappings lying there, ⁷and the cloth that had been on Jesus' head, not lying with the linen wrappings but rolled up in a place by itself. ⁸Then the other disciple, who reached the tomb first, also went in, and he saw and believed; ⁹for as yet they did not understand the scripture, that he must rise from the dead. ¹⁰Then the disciples returned to their homes.

¹¹But Mary stood weeping outside the tomb. As she wept, she bent over to look into the tomb; ¹²and she saw two angels in white, sitting where the body of Jesus had been lying, one at the head and the other at the feet. ¹³They said to her, "Woman, why are you weeping?" She said to them, "They have taken away my Lord, and I do not know where they have laid him." ¹⁴When she had said this, she turned around and saw Jesus standing there, but she did not know that it was Jesus. ¹⁵Jesus said to her, "Woman, why are you weeping? Whom are you looking for?" Supposing him to be the gardener, she said to him, "Sir, if you have carried him away, tell me where you have laid him, and I will take him away." ¹⁶Jesus said to her, "Mary!" She turned and said to him in Hebrew, "Rabbouni!" (which means Teacher). ¹⁷Jesus said to her, "Do not hold on to me, because I have not yet ascended to the Father. But go to my brothers and say to them, 'I am ascending to my Father and your Father, to my God and your God.'" ¹⁸Mary Magdalene went and announced to the disciples, "I have seen the Lord"; and she told them that he had said these things to her.

ORDER OF WORSHIP

GREETING

[From the doors of the church]
Early on the first day of the week,   *John 20:1*
the disciples of Jesus went to the tomb

where he had been buried
only to find that the stone had been rolled away
and the tomb was empty.
Friends, we gather here as Christ's disciples,
on the first day of the week,
to celebrate the good news of the gospel:
Jesus Christ has risen from the dead!

OPENING WORDS / CALL TO WORSHIP

Beloved church,
behold the victory of our God:
Jesus, our Lord, has conquered the grave.
Christ is risen! Alleluia!
Sin and death shall reign no more.
Christ is risen! Alleluia!
Let this place resound with joy.
Christ is risen! Alleluia!
Thanks be to God.

CALL TO CONFESSION

God has opened to us the gates of righteousness
that we may enter through them.
Confident in God's love, let us confess our sin.

PRAYER OF CONFESSION

Lord Jesus, through the power of the Holy Spirit
we have been raised from the waters of baptism
to share in your glorious resurrection.
Yet we have not lived as Easter people.
We are unsure of your promise,
confused about your will,
and afraid in the face of danger.
Like Mary, we weep at the tomb, but do not
recognize your presence.   *John 20:11*
Call us by name, risen Lord, that we may know
you with confidence.   *John 20:16*
Whenever we are tempted to fear death,
give us courage to confess your Easter victory.
Whenever we are distracted by petty conflicts,
keep our minds on your reconciling love.

Whenever we are overwhelmed by the power of evil,
reveal again to us your triumph over the destructive powers
of oppression.
Forgive us our sin
and let our lives be a testimony to your salvation
through the love of God and by the power of the Holy Spirit.
Amen.

DECLARATION OF FORGIVENESS

Listen, church:
God who raised Jesus from the dead has not
given us over to death.
In the name of Jesus Christ, we are forgiven.

PRAYER OF THE DAY

Alleluia! We praise you, O God,
for the power of your saving love
revealed in the resurrection of our Lord.
We await with gladness your new heaven and new earth.
As you have raised Jesus from the dead
give to us the gift of everlasting life,
that we may worship you forever;
through Christ, our risen Savior. **Amen.**

HYMN, SPIRITUAL, OR PSALM

PRAYER FOR ILLUMINATION (OPTIONAL)

SCRIPTURE READINGS

SERMON

HYMN, SPIRITUAL, OR PSALM

PRAYER FOR ILLUMINATION

Living God, by your Holy Spirit,
open our eyes to see the new light of this day;
open our lips to tell of the empty tomb;
open our hearts to believe the good news;
through Jesus Christ our Lord. **Amen.**

PRAYERS OF INTERCESSION

[Possible response to each intercession:]
Living God, hear our prayer: *Isa. 65:18–25*
Make of this world your new creation!

Before we call, you answer, O Lord.
Before we speak, you know our words.

Let there be joy in Jerusalem,
and peace among all nations.

Let sounds of weeping and cries of distress
turn to shouts of joy and laughter.

Let infants grow and thrive;
let the old dance like children.

Let every person find a home
and enjoy the fruit of their labor.

Let the wolf and the lamb live in peace;
let no one hurt or destroy another.

Show us, O God, the holy mountain you have prepared,
the new heaven and new earth you have promised,
so that we may be glad and rejoice in your presence forever;
through Jesus Christ, our risen Lord. **Amen.**

LORD'S PRAYER

INVITATION TO THE OFFERING

God has given us life in the resurrection of our
    Lord Jesus Christ.
In gratitude, let us offer our hearts and the fruit
    of our labor to God's service.

PRAYER OF THANKSGIVING/DEDICATION

Almighty God,
by your grace, accept the fruit of our labor
and the offering of our lives

in union with our risen Lord
who lives and reigns with you forever.
Amen.

HYMN, SPIRITUAL, OR PSALM

CHARGE

Receive the good news: Christ is risen from the dead.
Tell the good news: the power of death shall no more oppress us.
Live the good news: we are free to love as he has loved us.

BLESSING

May God who raised Jesus from the dead bless you
and by the power of the Holy Spirit raise you with
    him in glory.

SONG SUGGESTIONS

"Christ Is Risen, Shout Hosanna" (*CH* 222, *ELW* 383, *GC* 449, *GTG* 248,
    UMH 307)
"Christ the Lord Is Risen Today" (*CH* 205, *ELW* 355 and 363, *GC* 439, *GTG*
    242, *TNCH* 228, *UMH* 302)
"Good Christians All, Rejoice" (*EH* 205, *ELW* 385, *GTG* 239)
"In the Darkness of the Morning" (*GTG* 229)
"Jesus Christ Is Risen Today" (*EH* 207, *GC* 457, *GTG* 231, *TNCH* 233)
"O Sons and Daughters, Let Us Sing" (*EH* 203 and 206, *ELW* 376 and 377,
    GC 446, *GTG* 235, *TNCH* 236, *UMH* 317)
 "Up from the Grave He Arose" (*CH* 224, *UMH* 322)
 "Woman Weeping in the Garden" (*CH* 223, *GTG* 241)

CHILDREN'S SERMON

Based on John 20:1–18
Just before the sun was in the sky, Mary of Magdala got up and went to the
tomb where Jesus had been buried. The tomb was like a little cave, with
the opening covered by a big rock. When Mary got to the tomb, she saw that
the rock had been moved from in front of the cave, so it was open!

    Mary ran and told some of the other disciples—Peter and John—what she had seen. "They have taken Jesus' body, and I do not know where they took it!"

So John and Peter and Mary took off running as fast as they could back to the tomb but stopped short at the opening of the tomb, where the big rock had been. They leaned over and craned their necks, nervously looking inside. Could it really be? Was Jesus' body gone? Where did it go? Was Jesus alive again?

John peered inside the tomb but would not go in. Peter summoned his courage and went inside. He saw all the cloth that had been wrapped around Jesus' body lying there, but no Jesus! Then both men ran back home. They did not know what was going on!

But Mary stayed right there, outside the tomb, and started crying because she was so confused. She wiped tears away from her eyes as she looked inside the tomb again. When she did, she saw two angels wearing shining white clothes. They asked her, "Why are you crying?" and she told them, "Someone took Jesus away, and I do not know where they took him!"

She turned away from the tomb and saw a man standing there. She thought it must be the gardener. Was this the man who took Jesus' body away? "Sir, if you took Jesus' body away, please tell me where you took it. I will find a new place to bury him."

The man just said to her, "Mary."

How did this gardener know her name? Wait a second! She looked closer at the man's face and realized it was Jesus!

"Teacher!" she cried. She tried to hug him, but he said, "Go and tell the other disciples that I am alive."

SERMON HELPS

Isaiah 65:17–25

THEOLOGICAL PERSPECTIVE

Isaiah launches the reader into God's new creation. New life in this text is defined in terms of "new heavens and a new earth." God's new creation is cosmic, and a new order is at hand. While many believers circumscribe the resurrection to life after death, the prophet reminds us that resurrection is God's power to create a new reality for all creation. This new creation reconfigures relationships. Here the prophet points to a new cosmic matrix: the new cosmos reveals how the transformation of relationships and the transformation of space and time are mutually dependent. Relationships change because space and time change; space and time change because relationships change. Context and relationships embody God's creative power. This matrix is not a linear, sequential, and cumulative progression of goodness, in which relationships transform context or context transforms relationships. God's creative power transforms both, unleashing the goodness of God's power on God's new cosmos.

God's new cosmos has at least three dimensions: (1) the joy of God in creating new heavens and a new earth; (2) the transformed character of life in God's new cosmos; and (3) the reordering of cosmic relationships in the new creation. Perhaps the preacher can focus on one of these characteristics or allow them to interact with each other, emphasizing the cosmic matrix—the transformation of context and relationships—made possible by God's creative power for new life, rather than limiting this power to the individual hope for life after death.

The Joy of God in Creating New Heavens and a New Earth. God delights in creating a new space, a new context, a new Jerusalem. The old space, the old Jerusalem, is not to be remembered. The new Jerusalem is full of joy. God's joyful nature overwhelms God's created new space. God is joy. God's new space, the new Jerusalem, is joy. *"Mi Dios es alegre"* (My God is joyful) says the refrain of a popular rhythmic hymn sung in many congregations in the Latin Caribbean. People sing the refrain over and over, assuring the community that the nature and character of God is joy. Congregational space becomes party space, because the reign of God is a party. God delights in the joy of a new space that celebrates God's creative power.

The Character of Life in God's New Cosmos. The new Jerusalem is not an abstract ideal, and Isaiah gives us strong grounding for God's joy. First, God's new creation generates *good* life. With new space comes new relationships. Sobs of distress are heard no more, and weeping is unreal in the new Jerusalem. We may imagine a space where the conditions of evil and suffering are eliminated; in this new place, our relationships can engender only goodness and joy.

Time is also transformed. Any student of astrophysics recognizes that a change in space produces a change in time. *Chronos,* our linear time frame, collapses. Time becomes unending, eternal, but not in the sense of something *otherworldly* juxtaposed against the *this-worldly.* God's new creation is a total transformation of the spatial and chronological setup of our daily lives. Life is long, abundant, and joyful. God transforms the context.

The Cosmic Relationships in the New Creation. Who could live long if deprived of shelter and food? Who could live joyfully if exploited? Who could enjoy work, only to come home to poverty and misery? Who could rejoice in a newborn, if the future held only suffering and death? Such questions show the interplay between context, content, space/time configuration, and relationships.

In Guatemala, many Amerindian mothers do not name their children until the age of three years. The marginalization and exploitation of Amerindian communities create an uncertainty of life for the young. Mothers resist naming their children, creating a shield of love against love itself. Their strategy is to keep a human and emotional distance from the pain of the child's imminent death. On the one hand, this distant relationship between mother and child prevents further pain. There is already enough pain when most Amerindian mothers "bear children for calamity." On the other hand, it resists the temptation to surrender life to a cynical cycle of tragedy. Amazingly and as a testimony of faith, these women expect the blessing of the Lord upon them and their descendants.

Just imagine these Amerindian women reading Isaiah: "No more shall there be in it an infant that lives but a few days. . . .They shall not labor in vain or bear children for calamity" (vv. 20a, 23a). Isaiah nourishes the hope of longevity with the goodness that comes from justice: time and relationships are embodied in the image of a child growing old, not in the frequently justified theology of life after death, when injustice is the cause of death.

This new cosmic creation reconfigures the way we relate to God and God relates to us. God responds to our needs even before we name them, because God knows. From a Christian perspective, the resurrected one is also the one who has lived among us, suffered among us, and died among us. Jesus' resurrection is not only a witness to the promise of life after death. It is also a testament to the promise of resurrection grounded in a life given to others against all manifestations of evil.

This new cosmic order reshapes the natural order. Predator and prey eat together. The two are reconciled. Once more, spatial dynamics are reconfigured to radiate an image of new cosmic relationships. Context and content embody no hurt or destruction. In the new cosmic matrix, relationships embody the joy of God's creative power.

How might our communities participate in God's joy of the new cosmos this Easter season? Will it be necessary to change our configuration of space and time, our architecture, the setup of our seats, our worship time? Will it be necessary to develop new relationships? How might we embody God's creative joy in our midst, as we live into the reality of new heavens and a new earth?

CARLOS F. CARDOZA-ORLANDI

PASTORAL PERSPECTIVE

"They shall not labor in vain or bear children for calamity," God declares through the prophet, in the Jerusalem that will be created as a joy. There people will rejoice when women no longer bear children to be kidnapped into militias, or to take up swords, or to be shattered by invasion, war, conquest, or deportation. Male children will not have their arms chopped off if they do not sign up as boy soldiers, nor will female children be gang raped or sold into slavery. These calamities greet many children in this world on Easter morning.

"Bear children for calamity" flickers on and off like a searchlight today, begging for an interpretation that cries for justice—not only for peace, not only for personal resurrection or the rebirth of spring (which is not a biblical notion). Isaiah captures creation's part in the rejoicing of a restored Jerusalem. New heavens and a new earth herald this action of God, which concludes with the friendship of predators and prey, and defanged serpents. There will be no more torture or destruction (of animals or humans) on the holy mountain of the Lord.

Yet suddenly it is Easter Day, with new frocks, suits, and ties; lamb or pork on the table; parades, dancing, and games in the streets; and folk on front porches drinking mimosas and Bloody Marys. Elsewhere in the world, children are born, not for dancing and new dresses, but for bloody, heart-wrenching calamity.

What does Easter—beyond personal resurrection and the promise of eternal life—have to do with justice? This text invites us to declare that resurrection has become the key to understanding justice and restoration as God's way in a tortured world. Resurrection is the act of God, the beginning of a new creation. With the resurrection of Jesus from death, God has answered definitively, before we called. God has spoken with finality, while we were standing at the tomb in doubt and fear or were muttering to each other and to the seemingly ignorant stranger on the road to Emmaus.

We did not expect resurrection. The women were on their way with spices and ointments to minister to the corpse of Jesus. Things were as they had always been: the powerful crushing the innocent; the fearful finding a scapegoat to assuage their anxiety about social upheaval and persecution; the energetic followers running away at the moment of crisis; and the one who loudly claimed to be the most loyal of all the disciples denying that he ever knew the man who was charged with blasphemy and sedition. We did not expect resurrection. Human life was unfolding, as T. S. Eliot wrote, "from birth to copulation to death," with the more than occasional ordinary acts of public and private cruelty interrupting the course of ordinary days.[1]

Yet when the resurrection came, everything was "thrown off balance," as Flannery O'Connor's Misfit said of Jesus. "Jesus is the only One that ever raised the dead . . . and He shouldn't have done it. He thrown everything off balance. If He did what He said then it's nothing for you to do but to throw everything away and follow Him, and if He didn't, then it's nothing for you to do but enjoy the few minutes you got left the best way you can—by killing somebody . . . or doing some other meanness to him."[2]

God threw the cosmos off balance by raising Jesus Christ from death. The world was turned upside down. Things have never been the same since: not the stars in their courses, not the future of this planet, not the relationship of human life to the rest of creation, and not the people of God—who are now defined by relationship to Jesus Christ in Word and water, bread and wine. God not only entered the created order as a human being, God overcame the "meanness" that we did to the Incarnate One.

Just so, the prophet declared that God was doing something new—that in God's new world order there would be no more meanness, no more crying and lamentation, but a new heaven and a new earth, with a new social order that excluded not only war between humans but also war among the creatures. All creation (thrown off balance by human disobedience) is now at peace with itself and thereby reflects the character of Israel's God.

Is this merely pious nonsense for returned exiles or the church? Is this salve that soothes burdened cynicism, helping the poor and those with tender consciences endure the troubles of this world while we await the resurrection? Is such yearning what Marx claimed, and what the "new atheism" declares, to be the opiate of the people? Or is this trustworthy verbal evidence—backed up by hopeful actions all over the world, even in the glutted despair of the overdeveloped world—that human life does not and has never completed itself?[3] The prophet knew that reality, and so declared God's salvation. The church maintains that faith and—here and there, now

---

1. T. S. Eliot, "Fragment of an Agon," in *The Complete Poems and Plays 1909–1950* (New York: Harcourt, Brace & World, 1952), 80.
2. Flannery O'Connor, "A Good Man Is Hard to Find," in *The Complete Stories* (New York: Farrar, Straus, & Giroux, 1971), 132. I first saw this used in a similar fashion by Buddy Ennis in a sermon printed in *Journal for Preachers*.
3. Paul D. Hanson, *Isaiah, 40–66*, Interpretation series (Louisville, KY: John Knox Press, 1995), 241–46.

and then—makes real the claims of resurrection by our obedience. In spite of the arrogance and danger to life of all fundamentalisms everywhere, there arise Martin Luther King Jr., Desmond Tutu, Mother Teresa, and Mahatma Gandhi (and hundreds of thousands of unknown faithful people) who give evidence that the Spirit of God is completing what God intends for all creation.

It is a challenging business to preach on an apocalyptic Old Testament text when the church celebrates resurrection. However, the reward is rich and sure. We proclaim a God who is the same today, yesterday, and forever, until the wolf and the lamb shall feed together.

O. BENJAMIN SPARKS

EXEGETICAL PERSPECTIVE

The setting of Isaiah 65:17–25 is difficult to determine. As a part of what scholars have termed Third Isaiah (Isa. 56–66), it can be roughly placed in the early postexilic period following the return of the exiles from Babylon. The general tone of these chapters suggests the first century of Persian rule (538–424 BCE).[4] The exiles who returned to the province of Yehud (Judah) had high expectations of a renewed Jewish existence, expectations that were fed by the prophecies of Second Isaiah (Isa. 40–55). The realities of postexilic life failed to live up to these expectations, however, leading to a rethinking of the Isaianic tradition. Drawing on earlier passages in the book of Isaiah, Isaiah 65:17–25 is full of hope, offering a vision of the new world that God is creating.

The text appointed for this Sunday opens with language that draws heavily on the Priestly creation story in Genesis 1. The same verb for creation is used in both passages (Heb. bara'). This word is found frequently in the Isaianic tradition, particularly within Second Isaiah, where it refers not only to the creation of the world but also to YHWH's creation of Israel (Isa. 40:26–28; 41:20; 42:5; 43:1, 7, 15; 45:7–8, 12, 18; 48:7; 54:16). Here God is said to be creating new heavens and a new earth. The new creation will be so spectacular that the Israelites will no longer remember "the former" (Heb. ri'shonoth), an obvious allusion to the original creation "in the beginning" (Heb. re'shith, Gen.1:1).

In verse 18 the Israelites are called to rejoice over the new creation, for it is not just the world that is being renewed. Both Jerusalem and the Israelites are being recreated as well. The verbs for rejoicing alternate with the verb for creation, creating a chiastic structure in this verse:

4. Joseph Blenkinsopp, Isaiah 56–66, Anchor Bible 19B (New York: Doubleday, 2003), 42–43.

But be glad (*sisu*)	A
and rejoice (*gilu*) forever	B
in what I am creating (*bore'*);	C
for I am about to create (*bore'*)	C'
Jerusalem as a joy (*gilah*)	B'
and its people as a delight (*masos*).	A'

Due to the different English words used to translate the noun and verb forms of the words for being glad / delight (*sis*) and rejoicing / joy (*gil*), the chiasmic structure does not come through in the NRSV. In verse 19a, it is God's turn to rejoice over Jerusalem. God's pleasure is expressed using the same words as in the previous verse (Heb. *sis* and *gil*), which unites God and the people in their happiness over the new creation.

In verses 19b–24, the specifics of life in God's new creation are laid out. No more will weeping or the cry of distress be heard in Jerusalem. Although crying would have been found in Jerusalem in any period, no doubt the first readers would have thought back to the weeping and distress found in Jerusalem after its destruction at the hands of the Babylonians in 587 BCE. In verse 20, the people are promised long life. As with much of the creation language employed in this passage, the promise of long life calls to mind the conditions of the primeval history (Gen. 1–11), when lifespans often covered several centuries. God's new creation will reflect the ideal life that was found after the first creation.

With verses 21–22 the passage turns to the idea of security within the home. No longer will people build houses and plant vineyards, only to have them taken away by someone else. The loss of home and the fruits of one's labor are frequently mentioned as calamities in the Old Testament (Lev. 26:16; Deut. 28:30), but given the location of this passage in the postexilic period, it is likely that the original hearers would have thought back to the destruction of Jerusalem in 587 BCE, when their ancestors' houses and vineyards, for which they had worked so hard, had been taken away for generations. Third Isaiah promises a new creation in which this loss can never be repeated.

Neither shall they bear children only to see them die. Instead, verse 23 promises that the birth of children will be a blessing. The Israelites are to be a seed blessed by YHWH. Although the connections with creation language are not strong in this verse, it is possible—though far from certain—that the reference to the offspring ("seed," Heb. *zera'*) echoes the language of the curse after the fall in Genesis 3:15. Isaiah 65:23 may be alluding to a creation in which the curse of the fall is reversed. In verse 24, God promises that the Israelites' prayers will be heard and answered even before they finish speaking.

The final verse in this passage picks up on the imagery employed in Isaiah 11:6–9. In both of these passages, the authors foresee a future in which the conditions of the first creation have been reestablished. In Genesis 1:30, God gives plants to the animals as their food. Although it is not explicitly stated, the implication is that they do not eat meat. Isaiah 65:25 sees a return to that ideal. No longer will animals eat one another. Instead, even the fiercest of them—the wolf and the lion—will dine on vegetation. The restoration of the heavens and the earth is a blessing not only for humans but for the animal world as well. No one, whether animal or human, will hurt or be hurt on God's holy mountain, that is, Mount Zion in Jerusalem. The location of this ideal existence in Jerusalem picks up on earlier traditions in Isaiah that point to a future in which Jerusalem will be the center of the world (Isa. 2:2–3), an image reflected in the new Jerusalem of Revelation 21:1–2.

KEVIN A. WILSON

HOMILETICAL PERSPECTIVE

Leading a service of worship in witness to the resurrection is the minister's task both on Easter Day and at funerals. Every funeral service seeks to bring pastoral care and comfort to the grieving, but the circumstances of the person who has died may make that task vary in difficulty. If the funeral is for a person who has lived to "a ripe old age," whose family can look back across a life of accomplishment and blessing, then death may seem to be less the unwelcome intruder. In the case of a young person who dies suddenly or violently, the grieving are more likely to say, "She had her whole life ahead of her." Pastoral care must be attentive to these differences, while the proclamation of the resurrection remains urgent.

Isaiah 65:20 takes some account of the life span issue. It agonizes over "an infant that lives but a few days" and proclaims, "No more." Even the long and well-lived life—at whose ending North American culture may often judge that excessive grief is unseemly, if not unwarranted—this too is protested: "One who falls short of a hundred [years] will be considered accursed."

The Old Testament reading for Easter Day is not likely to be the primary preaching text, but it portrays the new heaven and new earth in images familiar to the present earth: inhabiting one's own house and eating the fruit of one's own vineyard. The text thereby addresses a theological question on the mind of the Easter Day worshiper, whether that worshiper is present every Sunday or on Easter only. It is the old question that refuses to go away: Why is there suffering, injustice, and death in a world fashioned by a good Creator? That question per se may not be best answered in the Easter sermon. Preachers may save theodicy for another time, but the Isaiah text is aware of the problem. In it, suffering, injustice, and death make the human heart long for God's new creation.

Both preacher and hearer may detect some discontinuity between the tangible and this-worldly vision in Isaiah 65 and the less easily grasped truths found in the Easter Gospel and Epistle. The proclamation of and belief in the resurrection of Christ teeter between the familiar and the utterly novel. In Isaiah 65, at least, the concepts are readily understandable: babies no longer die (v. 20); children no longer suffer (v. 23b); work is always rewarded and rewarding (v. 22b–23a); weeping and cries of distress are no more (v. 19b). The passage even proclaims a new thing throughout the animal kingdom, in an echo more associated with Advent: "The wolf and the lamb shall feed together."

Some will be so bold as to ask, if Christ is raised from the dead, then why are these promises in Isaiah not found among the benefits of the resurrection here and now? Alas, the burden and the glory of preaching consist in proclaiming things that are not yet fully realized, but the hope for them holds a powerful grip upon the faithful imagination. By following where the risen Christ leads, some of the faithful have realized portions of Isaiah's vision in some measure, in some places. More children do live longer and freer of disease, and more people have useful, creative work, because of advances achieved in places where the Gospel of Christ has been proclaimed and received. As expressed in the Confession of 1967, "Already God's reign is present as a ferment in the world, stirring hope in men and preparing the world to receive its ultimate judgment and redemption. With an urgency born of this hope the church applies itself to present tasks and strives for a better world."[5]

However in the not-yet-ness of the Easter proclamation, heaven has not yet arrived on earth. We receive the vision of Isaiah 65 by faith and in hope that remains beyond our reach here below. As the Confession of 1967 continues, "It [the church] does not identify limited progress with the kingdom of God on earth, nor does it despair in the face of disappointment and defeat. In steadfast hope, the church looks beyond all partial achievement to the final triumph of God."

As part of the scriptural witness to Easter, Isaiah 65 "fleshes out" the believer's response to faith in the resurrection. The preacher may move the focus of the sermon beyond the scientific plausibility of Christ's resurrection and beyond even the need, as some see it, of putting away our critical

---

5. "The Confession of 1967," in *The Book of Confessions* (Louisville, KY: Office of the General Assembly of the Presbyterian Church (U.S.A.), 2002), 262.

thinking for this grand hour of Easter worship. Isaiah 65 engages the issue of what difference the Easter message will make to those who have heard it on the day *after* Easter. Will those who are convinced of the resurrection of Christ understand that it has effects beyond the gift of life in a world to come for the individual? Resurrection faith sends its adherents toward work and witness here and now, in the service of Isaiah's vision of the redeemed life of creation.

The Easter sermon that keeps some focus on Isaiah 65 can be just the occasion to connect a congregation's faith and works. Imagine that belief in the resurrection of Christ energizes a church to share the risen life of Christ and support a shelter for victims of domestic violence or begin an after-school tutoring program for children in the nearby public school. So "shall be offspring blessed by the Lord—and their descendants as well" (v. 23). Dare we also hope that the Easter-only worshiper actually comes back to worship the next Sunday as well? Then we may well "be glad and rejoice forever in what I am creating" (v. 18).

J. MICHAEL KRECH

John 20:1–18

THEOLOGICAL PERSPECTIVE

The Easter texts were written and told in order first to bring judgment on a hopeless world and then to save a faithless one. Such texts are prophetic, and those who preach them are called to be prophets. Prophets? We should use that title cautiously. Novelist Saul Bellow, who back in the 1960s heard many civic activists referred to as "prophets," wearied of such use of the term. Many of them were sincere and well-intentioned speakers, but as he heard them, most activists of any sort were people who talked not about God but about themselves, their causes, or the evil of their foes. I heard Bellow say in a lecture, "Being a prophet is nice work if you can get it. But to be a prophet, sooner or later you have to talk about God."

Preachers can easily get in the habit of forgetting that "*sooner.*" It is tempting for them to talk first about themselves and their opinions or about world affairs or movies. They may then forget about God entirely, or speak in such unsure and muffled tones that no one hears or gets the point or experiences God's power from them. So the corrective reminder has to be emphatic: it *is* more efficient and effective to talk about God *sooner*. Notice that the theological theme that prompts the "God-talk" of this text from John 20 focuses on the crucial theme of what God does to turn an ancient story into a prophetic word that will help make the conversion of humans possible.

So we talk about conversion. To make a textbook case out of this, we recall that the Hebrew word for "convert" is *shub*, meaning to "turn back," to "return," or that the Greek is *metanoia*, which also implies a 180-degree turning. Both indicate the involvement of the heart and not just the head—though conversion includes a change of mind or intellectual dimension. This conversion can occur when people hear testimony as the word is preached, become aware of the presence of God in the sacraments, or are moved by the generous activity of people who have already turned or been turned. Christians believe that their baptism represents and effects such a turning, a newness in Christ.

In the tradition of the Reformation, which was in some continuity with older Catholic interpretations, while conversion occurred in churchly contexts of preaching and the sacraments, special stress was placed on the personal dimension, in which divine grace worked in the human heart. Sometimes conversion occurred in an instant, as in this text. Here we find the model of Mary Magdalene's conversion, and then that of a disciple and Peter. They turned or were turned from being uncomprehending to knowing emphatic faith. For other people through the ages, conversion resulted from a long process that might involve resistance before there is acceptance. Believers come to know and to testify that conversion, the opening of the eyes and hearts plus the openness to faith and hope and love, is not something one can accomplish through her own purpose or strength. Converts like to speak, instead, of the Holy Spirit being active.

Now we can look more closely at the story that suggests this theological theme. If we remember that conversion refers to turning around, to being turned, we will be informed and moved by two case studies here. The first is that of Mary Magdalene. She had to be converted from the sincere and well-intended business she had generously undertaken, to take charge in a hope-less memorial act for the dead Jesus. Then, we are told, she looked and "saw." Did she really yet see? Notice that there was no reference to God, no God-talk in her statement to Peter and the other disciple. No, she said that an anonymous *"They* have taken the Lord out of the tomb" (v. 2), and *"they"* must have laid him somewhere. So, unturned, unconverted, she quite naturally wept outside the tomb, engulfed in her puzzlement and her grieving. When asked about what was going on, we heard her say again that "they" must have done something, not that God *had* done something and was doing it now. Her response was passive and ordinary. Then when she turned around, she saw Jesus; but still, with unconverted eyes and heart, she did not recognize him. She believed in the presence of a gardener but had not yet believed in or felt the presence of God in the risen Christ. She heard an ordinary word, simply, her name, but it was spoken with a theological intention,

to quicken her faith and hope: "Mary!" Then, *"She turned"* her face to him
(v. 16) and then really "turned," which is exactly what conversion means and
is about. She now had to tell others.

In the process, she had gotten ahead of them, so she turned before those
two disciple insiders got there. They began to "see," in a beginning of conversion, but this is still not the end of our story. The process next took several
turns. The first of two disciples peeked into the tomb, "but he did not go
in" (v. 5) to where the action had been and the evidence lay. (You cannot be
converted if you are not open to stirrings and signs.) Then, we hear, when
Peter *did* go in, he saw something and did some deducing. Whatever it was
that Peter did moved the first disciple to open himself and now to explore.
This disciple "went in, and he saw and believed" (v. 8).

The process still was only half completed. The disciple and Peter did not
know what to make of the experience, "for as yet they did not understand the
scripture, that [Jesus] must rise from the dead" (v. 9). They simply and sadly
went home. They did not yet do what Mary Magdalene could do and did, for
she "went and announced to the disciples, 'I have seen the Lord!'" (v. 18). She
told them that he had said certain things to her, thus providing a case study
in the phenomenology of conversion and its positive consequences.

MARTIN E. MARTY

PASTORAL PERSPECTIVE

The narrative here seems almost two separate stories, that of the woman
Mary and that of the two men, Peter and the other disciple, the one whom
Jesus loved.

I call the disciples "men," but the word that comes more quickly to mind
is "boys." There seems such a childish competition between them. When
they get word of the missing body, they run to the tomb, but their racing is
not presented just as a run to arrive: it is reported as a race, with care taken
to tell that the "other disciple," the one with whom the author identifies, outran Peter and got there first. He won the race, even though Peter, typically
brash, was the one who forged first into the tomb. So yes, the common claim
that Peter was the first of the male disciples at the actual site of the resurrection may have some truth, but only by a technicality. The other one, John,
was really first, and the faster runner. Besides, he was the one whom Jesus
loved. Perhaps I overstate the comic quality of John's account here, but it is
hard to ignore at least the suggestion of such childish, such boyish, competition between these two iconic figures.

The story of Mary Magdalene, on the other hand, has nothing of such
comedy. Arguably, there *is* something of comedy in the classic sense in the

confusion about Jesus and the gardener, but that is very different from the boys-will-be-boys rivalry that brings a smile of recognition at the footrace. What we have in the Magdalene story, rather, is deep and intimate emotion. Unlike the empty-tomb stories of the other evangelists, John's account gives us just one woman, one who comes to the tomb alone. She comes out of her own desire to be where the body of Jesus is. She is bereft that he has been taken away, not just by death but by the disappearance of his body. She grieves, she yearns, she weeps. Her words are poignant, and we can feel the hurt and longing in them: "They have taken away my Lord, and I do not know where they have laid him" (v. 13).

Try as I might, I cannot help but hear a resonance of the Magdalene's voice in *Jesus Christ Superstar*, that of the amazed and devoted lover of the man who has moved her so deeply. Volumes have been written on all that is problematic with that tradition of imagining Mary Magdalene, both as it has diminished her likely importance as an apostle in her own right and as it has played out as a paradigmatic male fantasy about women. This story, like other images of feminine devotion to a messianic male figure, is fraught with danger, with both a history of and a potential for misappropriation. Let the teller of the tale take care! Cognizant of such risk, however, I am moved once more by this woman who loves with such longing for a lost beloved. Lurid legends or prurient speculation about the Magdalene set aside, this *does* seem the depiction of an intimate and deeply embodied affection.

Is it not both curious and wonderful that these two stories—one of the boys and one of the woman, the comic and the passionate—sit here, one within the other? While we might opt to preach primarily from the one or the other, why not let both play upon us, reminding us that the encounter with the resurrection can be experienced differently by different people at different times, its music in different keys and danced in different ways?

The empty tomb found by the disciples is a place pregnant with potential meaning not yet understood. What it means is still unknown, but what it will mean transforms both past and future for the eager disciples who run to it. They see nothing within but empty wrappings, the leavings of one who left, and only later will they understand what presence that absence bodes.

Mary, on the other hand, has not raced with curiosity or hope but has come to pay grief's necessary homage to one she loved. When she looks in, she sees not only the emptiness but the angels who make the slab no longer a mere place of absence but a vision of the mercy seat and the ark of God's presence (Exod. 25:17–22). Yet, after responding to the angels and telling her grief, Mary turns *away* from the tomb; even with angels, with religious symbolism, with supernatural promise and implications, it cannot hold her interest. It does not compensate for the reality of Jesus, does not dissolve her grief. He is not there, and she turns away. It is when she turns around that she encounters the one whom she seeks, in reality and not just potential. At first she does not recognize him—we may think of all the different reasons we also do not recognize our Christ—but he calls her by name. Then she sees and exclaims her greeting in return, *"Rabbouni, my teacher."*

There is tenderness of affection here and the joy of a real presence, but there is finally that *Noli me tangere* and a new incompleteness: she may not hold on to him, perhaps not even touch him. He is going away, and as she seems to reach for him, he retreats from her. She will be his apostle to the disciples, but he does not stay to be held. That withdrawal is also part of the story.

There is much that may engage our reflection here, much familiar from our parish experience—comedy and devastation, symbol and realities, encounters and absences, the dance of nearness and distance in relationships—all of it laid out, not as the tired story of human life through the generations, but as it shines in the transfiguring light of the resurrection morning. May we preachers see it, and show it, so freshly new.

JOHN K. STENDAHL

EXEGETICAL PERSPECTIVE

John's Easter morning sequence is surely one of the most memorable. In the Synoptics, Mary Magdalene is accompanied by other women to the tomb (see Matt. 28:1; Mark 16:1; Luke 23:55–24:1, 10). Here, she is alone. Mary comes while it is still "dark." This may be John's way of underlining, once again, the dark/light symbolism first announced in 1:5. The time of Mary's arrival may also be seen to mirror both the darkness of her despair and the depth of confusion her discovery engenders.

That Mary found the tomb's stone "removed" invites comparison with the circumstances surrounding Jesus' raising of Lazarus (11:38–41), where the stone needed to be taken away. Mary's alarm, her summons to Peter and the "other" disciple ("the one whom Jesus loved," the Beloved Disciple), suggest that she fears the work of grave robbers.

Those who detect a rivalry between Peter and the Beloved Disciple in what follows overlook the sheer narrative energy this passage manages to convey—*and* the ambiguity with which it concludes. Peter leaves for the tomb first, followed by the "other disciple." Then, for a time, they are running together. What amounts to a footrace ensues, with the other disciple outrunning Peter, arriving at the tomb first. He looks in, balks, but does not enter. Peter does. He observes the particulars of the evidentiary remains, apparently concurring with Mary's initial assessment (grave robbery). The Beloved Disciple weighs the material effects differently.

The disposition of the burial cloths is peculiar. Again, a contrast with Jesus' raising of Lazarus (11:41–44) is surely meant to be drawn. Not only did Lazarus's stone have to be removed; Lazarus emerged from the tomb "bound hand and foot" in grave clothes, his face wrapped with a cloth. Onlookers were charged with the task of disentangling him. For the Beloved Disciple, this tidiness augurs for an interpretation other than a case of mere robbery. It seems not to be a matter of resuscitation.

The Beloved Disciple "believes"—but what? The discovery, as it presents itself, does not yet add up to a fully articulated belief in Jesus' resurrection. The evangelist underscores this by noting that "as yet they did not understand the scripture, that he must rise from the dead" (20:9). Indeed, the men return to their homes. Their investigation of the tomb has *not* served, as many claim, to corroborate or to provide a legally valid (Deut. 19:15) confirmation by two male witnesses of an insufficient, singular, inferior, female report.

Mary remains at the tomb, outside, distraught. When she peers in, grave clothes do not arrest her attention. The tomb is no longer empty! There are "two angels in white, sitting where the body of Jesus had been lying, one at the head and the other at the feet" (v. 12; cf. Mark 16:5; Matt. 28:2–3; Luke 24:4). The angels, whom Mary does not acknowledge as such, are reverencing an empty space. Perhaps this cenotaphic tableau is an *ironic* evocation of the ark of the covenant: God's presence is absent in this place of death. When they ask her why she is crying, she persists in her assumption that a heist has occurred.

Mary backs out of the tomb, turns around, and encounters a human figure. She thinks it is the "gardener" (Gk. *kēpouros*—a *hapax legomenon* in the NT and LXX). Is this meant to evoke the rather different garden encounter between God, Adam, and Eve in Genesis 3:8? Sticking to her guns that the body of Jesus has been relocated, she begs him for information of its whereabouts. We anticipate a Homer-like recognition scene (e.g., Odysseus's nurse catches sight of the hero's telltale scar and welcomes his return). Rather, Jesus calls her by name: "Mary!" Suddenly, it is clear to her: she is face to face with the (literally "my") "Teacher." The reader is expected to remember that when Jesus was teaching in Jerusalem before his death, he said, "I am the good shepherd," who "calls his own sheep *by name* and leads them out" (10:11, 3). They follow him because they "know his voice" (10:4). Jesus needed to call Mary by name for her to recognize him.

However, recognizing Jesus is not the same as apprehending his resurrected nature. Apparently, Mary attempts some sort of physical confirmation. How so? We are not told exactly; the text is silent (even if many commentators—and novelists—are not). This we do know: she is *rebuffed*. "Do not keep on trying to hold me," Jesus says, in effect. Mary learns from her Teacher that she is being caught up into a larger drama that includes Jesus' death, resurrection, *and* ascension. This is *not* merely a story about a reunion, case solved. It is about ultimate destinies: Jesus' and Mary's—and the disciples' destinies too. Jesus tells her: "I am ascending to *my* Father and *your* Father, to *my* God and *your* God" (20:17). The story has not concluded; it is still unfolding. She must relate *that* to the disciples.

In John's Gospel, the evangelist wants his audience to recognize that Jesus is, utterly, a "God-related being."[6] Jesus has a uniquely intimate relationship with God, whom he calls "Father." The evangelist is also at pains to make clear that God is a "Jesus-related Being," that is, God works redemptively in and through all that Jesus does and undergoes. Hence, Jesus is the Father's "Son," but the Gospel goes further. It says that those who have the eyes of faith to perceive this can themselves become "children of God"—both "God-related" *and* "Jesus-related" persons. "To all who receive him, who believe in his name, he [gives] power to become children of God, . . . born, not of blood or of the will of the flesh or of the will of man, but of God" (1:12–13).

That is why Mary cannot hold on to Jesus. Her story and his, his experience and hers, cannot be anchored in the past. Nor is it singular. Instead, he calls her by name to announce to the disciples—and, by extension to all who would believe—a new creation, an unimaginable future. The good news that she reports to the disciples is only the beginning of an ongoing revelation of what resurrection and its implications might mean.

GREGORY A. ROBBINS

HOMILETICAL PERSPECTIVE

Although John's account of the resurrection is by no means the earliest in the canon (that honor belongs to the creedal statement quoted by Paul in 1 Cor. 15:3–5), it has held great influence throughout the ages. This is true not only because of its place in the Revised Common Lectionary (in which it is featured every year as the Gospel reading for Easter worship) but also because of the author's fine attention to dramatic and narrative detail,

---

6. To use David H. Kelsey's felicitous turn of phrase in *Imagining Redemption* (Louisville, KY: Westminster John Knox Press, 2005).

drawing readers into its scenes and offering them the same choices once given to Mary, Peter, and the Beloved Disciple. Countless hymns have been composed and pictures painted about this scene at the tomb. So it remains the Easter classic. Each preacher will have to determine whether she or he can preach it every year or turn to another Gospel's account of Jesus' followers at the empty tomb.

In the first two verses, the narrator reintroduces the three characters whose responses dominate John's version of the story. Mary Magdalene finds the tomb with its stone rolled away. When she runs to tell the others that the body has disappeared, Peter and the Beloved Disciple take off to see for themselves before Mary returns to make her own discoveries. It is in the responses of these three model disciples that we find homiletical riches for our Easter preaching.

The Beloved Believes. The minute the Beloved Disciple hears Mary's news, he jumps up to see what has happened, arriving at the tomb before Peter. His actions seem perfectly understandable, since in the Fourth Gospel he always represents the most appropriate way to respond to Jesus and his message. After all, he stayed with Jesus all the way to the bitter end; why would he not want to see what has happened now? Because the Beloved Disciple serves as the faithful witness, the source of the irreplaceable knowledge for belief in this Gospel, he must see for himself the linen cloths and the bodyless tomb. He instantly believes without full comprehension or explanation of what it all means.

We know people like this today; every church needs them to survive. These are the people who have no evidence to believe that the boy who messes up the sound equipment in the sanctuary will be anything but trouble, yet insist that he is headed toward a brilliant career in sound engineering. These are the people who see service possibilities in broken-down playgrounds and faded fellowship halls. These are the people who require no proof that eternal life trumps death and smile inwardly every time they hear the word "resurrection." Although they may often annoy us with their boundless optimism and refusal to face facts as we see them, we secretly cheer for them and draw strength for our own faith journeys from their unwavering trust that God will work good, even out of a crucifixion.

Peter Runs. Peter's reaction to Mary's news about an open tomb is less easy to understand in this Gospel. We are not sure why he joins this outlandish footrace to Jesus' tomb; after all, he has just spent the last few days running away from Jesus. Why is he running toward him now? Although the Fourth

Evangelist does not speculate, we may make some guesses. Perhaps it is simple jealousy, a desire to prove that he is as good as the faithful Beloved Disciple. Or perhaps guilt motivates Peter to run out the door so that he can say he is sorry—for denying Jesus after boasting about his loyalty, for not being present at the cross, for running away when the chips were down. Or maybe Peter felt a hopeful curiosity. With all the other disciples, he was present at the raising of Lazarus. Could it be possible that the same thing has happened to Jesus?

Many of us live with Peter in this complex of emotions. We harbor petty jealousies in our souls for those who seem so blessed by the love of God, so full of confidence and joy. We are resentful of the success of others. Or we promise ourselves that we will not fall away from whatever God has given us to do, but the minute we are threatened in some way, we leave. With Peter we are hurrying to confess our shortcomings. Or maybe we remember something remarkable and life-giving from our past, running to see if it might happen again, if new life is possible even for those of us caught in a web of conflicting feelings and actions.

Mary Speaks. Then there is the Magdalene who shows up at the tomb after her male companions have returned home, weeping for what is gone. She obviously expects nothing to happen; she has come to mourn the loss of life, of a body to touch, and to bid good-bye. In her grief she can hardly think clearly. She sees two angels and does not recognize their otherworldly origins. She sees Jesus and mistakes him for the gardener. Then he speaks her name, and she suddenly knows exactly who this mysterious stranger is. She responds to the call of her name; "Teacher," she replies. Then Jesus commissions her to go and tell what she has seen, just as he commissioned the woman at the well way back at the beginning of his ministry.

Scholars often remind us that the resurrection narratives are really commission stories, sending believers out into the world to tell everyone that death is not the last word. Otherwise, no one would ever know what happened, and Easter would be just a reunion story with tears and hugs all around. However, Mary obeys the risen Jesus, fighting her impulse to cling to a familiar body, and leaves the garden to tell what she knows to be true. An expected ending is now a beginning—of telling the truth about life to those who want to deal only in death, of offering living water and the bread of life to those who want only to buy and sell commodities that perish. Mary speaks, and in her speaking we find our own voice.

NANCY CLAIRE PITTMAN

❧ MIDWEEK SERVICES ❦

Introduction

The following devotional services are designed for use during a brief midweek gathering such as a lunch-hour worship or Wednesday night fellowship. If your congregation does not have an established midweek gathering suited for this series, a new short-term worship gathering could be offered for the season of Lent. The first service is designed for Ash Wednesday and includes additional liturgical elements specific to that observance. The following weeks feature simply an opening psalm, focus Scripture and homily, and prayers for confession, intercession, and dismissal.

The focus Scriptures for these services examine circumstances and instructions related to fasting, food, and self-denial. Exploring these themes will enhance participants' Lenten disciplines with examination of why and how one abstains from certain foods or diversions and the spiritual implications of such a practice. The congregation might consider a common fast, with everyone invited to abstain from alcohol and sweets during Lent, or the fellowship might be accompanied by a simple meal devoid of meat and dessert.

The final service of this midweek series is intended to fall during Holy Week and does not replace traditional Maundy Thursday, Good Friday, or Holy Saturday services. Orders of worship for those services are included later in this volume.

Midweek Service: Week One (Ash Wednesday)

Isaiah 58:1–12

¹Shout out, do not hold back!
   Lift up your voice like a trumpet!
Announce to my people their rebellion,
   to the house of Jacob their sins.
²Yet day after day they seek me
   and delight to know my ways,
as if they were a nation that practiced righteousness
   and did not forsake the ordinance of their God;
they ask of me righteous judgments,
   they delight to draw near to God.
³"Why do we fast, but you do not see?
   Why humble ourselves, but you do not notice?"
Look, you serve your own interest on your fast day,
   and oppress all your workers.
⁴Look, you fast only to quarrel and to fight
   and to strike with a wicked fist.
Such fasting as you do today
   will not make your voice heard on high.
⁵Is such the fast that I choose,
   a day to humble oneself?
Is it to bow down the head like a bulrush,
   and to lie in sackcloth and ashes?
Will you call this a fast,
   a day acceptable to the Lord?

⁶Is not this the fast that I choose:
   to loose the bonds of injustice,
   to undo the thongs of the yoke,
to let the oppressed go free,
   and to break every yoke?
⁷Is it not to share your bread with the hungry,
   and bring the homeless poor into your house;

when you see the naked, to cover them,
and not to hide yourself from your own kin?
[8]Then your light shall break forth like the dawn,
and your healing shall spring up quickly;
your vindicator shall go before you,
the glory of the Lord shall be your rear guard.
[9]Then you shall call, and the Lord will answer;
you shall cry for help, and he will say, Here I am.

If you remove the yoke from among you,
the pointing of the finger, the speaking of evil,
[10]if you offer your food to the hungry
and satisfy the needs of the afflicted,
then your light shall rise in the darkness
and your gloom be like the noonday.
[11]The Lord will guide you continually,
and satisfy your needs in parched places,
and make your bones strong;
and you shall be like a watered garden,
like a spring of water,
whose waters never fail.
[12]Your ancient ruins shall be rebuilt;
you shall raise up the foundations of many generations;
you shall be called the repairer of the breach,
the restorer of streets to live in.

ORDER OF WORSHIP

OPENING WORDS / CALL TO WORSHIP

We come to worship God as the Lenten season begins,
aware of our frailty and our failings.
We come seeking God's mercy,
acknowledging our mortality.
Having received the waters of baptism,
we come to be marked now with ashes.
May we humble ourselves before God   *Isa. 58:5–6*
not with a yoke of burden
but a mantle of freedom in Jesus' name.

HYMN, SPIRITUAL, OR PSALM

CALL TO CONFESSION

God desires truth in the inward being
and receives a broken spirit, the contrite heart.
Seeking abundant mercy,
let us confess our sins before God. *Ps. 51:1, 6, 17*

PRAYER OF CONFESSION (PSALM 51)

Have mercy on me, O God,
according to your steadfast love;
according to your abundant mercy
blot out my transgressions.
Wash me thoroughly from my iniquity,
and cleanse me from my sin.

For I know my transgressions,
and my sin is ever before me.
Against you, you alone, have I sinned,
and done what is evil in your sight,
so that you are justified in your sentence
and blameless when you pass judgment.
Indeed, I was born guilty,
a sinner when my mother conceived me.

You desire truth in the inward being;
therefore teach me wisdom in my secret heart.
Purge me with hyssop, and I shall be clean;
wash me, and I shall be whiter than snow.
Let me hear joy and gladness;
let the bones that you have crushed rejoice.
Hide your face from my sins,
and blot out all my iniquities.

Create in me a clean heart, O God,
and put a new and right spirit within me.
Do not cast me away from your presence,
and do not take your holy spirit from me.
Restore to me the joy of your salvation,
and sustain in me a willing spirit.

Then I will teach transgressors your ways,
and sinners will return to you.
Deliver me from bloodshed, O God,
O God of my salvation,
and my tongue will sing aloud of your deliverance.

O Lord, open my lips,
and my mouth will declare your praise.
For you have no delight in sacrifice;
if I were to give a burnt offering, you would not be pleased.
The sacrifice acceptable to God is a broken spirit;
a broken and contrite heart, O God, you will not despise.

Do good to Zion in your good pleasure;
rebuild the walls of Jerusalem,
then you will delight in right sacrifices,
in burnt offerings and whole burnt offerings;
then bulls will be offered on your altar.

DECLARATION OF FORGIVENESS
According to God's steadfast love,   *Ps. 51:1, 4b*
according to God's abundant mercy,
God does not pass judgment on us
the judgment we deserve.
God creates in us clean hearts   *Ps. 51:10, 13, 14b*
and gives a new and right spirit.
In the grace of Jesus Christ,
we return to God forgiven.
Praise God for our salvation!

PRAYER OF THE DAY
God of our salvation,
we long to be reconciled to you.
Help us to clear away any obstacle
that prevents us from accepting the grace of Christ.
No matter what we face in this life,
increase in us knowledge and patience,
kindness and holiness of spirit,
genuine love and truthful speech,
so that, by the power of God at work in us,

we may live even as we are dying
and rejoice even in our sorrows.
Though it may seem that we have nothing,
if we are reconciled to you,
we possess everything,
through Jesus Christ our Lord. **Amen.**

PRAYER FOR ILLUMINATION (OPTIONAL)

SCRIPTURE READING

HOMILY

Ash Wednesday marks the beginning of the forty days of Lent. It is traditionally a time for Christians to enter a period of self-reflection, prayer, and preparation in anticipation of the celebrations of Easter. The symbolism of forty days has many roots, including the flood and forty years of wilderness wanderings, but inspiration for this time is probably taken from Jesus' forty days in the wilderness where he, like Moses and Elijah before him, sojourned in preparation for his ministry.

Fasting was one of the notable features of Jesus' forty days in the wilderness. A common practice throughout the Bible, fasting was believed to be a humbling act of commitment or repentance that was intensified when combined with prayer. Fasting has become a favored spiritual discipline for a wide variety of people who believe this effort can help eliminate earthly distractions as they seek to draw nearer to God. John Wesley, Mohandas Gandhi, Dorothy Day, Cesar Chavez, and Thomas Merton all regularly fasted; Roman Catholics are required to fast on Ash Wednesday; among Jews, Hindus, Muslims, and Buddhists, many fast. In contemporary Protestant religious practice, during Lent many persons practice some kind of fasting or a more popular (and, alas, regularly abused) idea of "giving up" something for the duration. Reasons for fasting abound—nearness to God, weight loss, detoxification—but they are often misunderstood (many forget that nothing we can do will draw us any nearer to God—God is already with us). Today's reading from Isaiah 58 helps us with this precise point.

Isaiah is preaching to Israel at the end of their exile when they are overwhelmed with a sense of defeat and abandonment by YHWH. We know from Zechariah 7 that Israel's religious habits have become rote and empty. Walter Brueggemann calls it a kind of "pseudo-holiness." Thus, when people complain that God is not hearing their prayers or responding to their fasting, Isaiah confronts them with the hypocrisy of their humility. He is direct: fasting should never be understood as an end in itself or a substitute for righteous living. Indeed, it is arterially related to righteous living. Our private devotions are inextricably linked to our public lives. True devotion to God demands both. If we are not living righteously, then our spiritual disciplines lose their meaning.

Isaiah pointedly condemns any quest for righteousness before God that overlooks the plight of the poor and contrasts such an unfaithful "fast" to God's concern for loosening "the bonds of injustice" and letting "the oppressed go free." The fast God chooses is radically self-forgetful. "Why do we fast, but you do not see?" by contrast, is the question of an anxious idolatry eager to make God "useful," worshiping God for the sake of something else, in this case, one's own salvation. Lusting for such a possibility was the great threat that continually confronted Israel and continues to tempt us today in both liberal and conservative garb. All desire the power to save themselves. All.

The form of fasting that God chooses is strangely free of this affliction. It is distinguished from idolatry in its lack of anxiety. It is free to engage another, to see the other, and to see the other not as something to be used or merely as an object of pity or duty but as a gift.

That is why Karl Barth begins his treatment of human freedom not by talking of rights or duties but by speaking first of being set free for God, a freedom manifest in the way we keep the Sabbath day. How we understand what that day is for is the central clue to our understanding of what human beings are for. Isaiah 58 does not offer moralistic wisdom at this point. Rather, "the fast God chooses" describes a new vision of humanity. In the presence of this One, we are saved from the loneliness of our self-justifying ways, even as we are forbidden to give ultimate loyalty to our own agendas, however pious or political. Instead, we are invited to receive ourselves and others as gifts, discovering in God's engagement with us a life that can only be a life together. The end of such Sabbath freedom leads not "to the individual in isolation, but in relationship to his fellows."

All true joy in life derives from this free decision of God to seek fellowship with that which is not God, just as all human fellowship is rooted in the triune love of Father, Son, and Holy Spirit. That is where Ash Wednesday's journey is taking us, the place where God's fast pours itself out for the sake of the whole world. There God's fast becomes our food, and we are set free to sit at table with others whom we have not chosen and would never choose, to eat and even delight in this fearful mercy.

Strangely, the prophet is very clear about this mercy and this irrepressible joy: "Then your light shall break forth like the dawn, and your healing shall spring up quickly. . . . Then you shall call, and the LORD will answer; you shall cry for help, and he will say, Here I am." In commenting on this passage Calvin writes, simply, "The chief part of our happiness" is that "God listens to us." What the prophet knows, but the self-absorbed pietist and the ideologue forget, is that the God whose fast is to loosen the bonds of injustice delights in the life together that is the gift that belongs to all his children.

The season of Lent begins with ashes, as we recall our mortality and fragility before God, but this does not mean it is a season devoid of joy. Whatever we choose as a Lenten discipline, let it be part of a freedom journey, not wallowing in gloom but practicing justice and joy in fellowship with God and one another. Let us make that journey together, exploring how we can turn the casual cultural concept of "giving up something for Lent" into a meaningful act of devotion.

HYMN, SPIRITUAL, OR PSALM

THE LITANY OF ASHES
We bow our heads before you, O God,
aware of our sinfulness and our shortcomings.
Remembering our baptism,
the watermark of the cross upon us,
we also receive this ashen cross
upon our foreheads—
another sign
that in life and in death,
we belong to you.
In the name of Jesus Christ,
crucified, risen, and coming again,
we pray. **Amen.**

IMPOSITION OF ASHES
Remember that you are dust,
and to dust you shall return.

PRAYERS OF INTERCESSION
God in the highest,
you came to us in a human being
who humbled himself like a slave.   *Phil. 2:7–8*
**The stone that the builders rejected
has become the chief cornerstone.**   *Ps. 118:22*

We pray for the nations that worship power and might;
may they be ruled by humility and peace.
The stone that the builders rejected
has become the chief cornerstone.
We pray for the church and its leaders,
that we may have the mind of Christ.   *Phil. 2:5*
The stone that the builders rejected
has become the chief cornerstone.
We pray for the victims of human tragedies and
    disasters of nature.
The stone that the builders rejected
has become the chief cornerstone.
We pray for those who are in prison—
the repentant and the unrepentant
and those falsely accused.   *Luke 23:32*
The stone that the builders rejected
has become the chief cornerstone.
We pray for those who are ill or infirmed
or are rejected because they are seen to be weak.
The stone that the builders rejected
has become the chief cornerstone.
God of compassion,
through Jesus Christ you have come to us and shared
    our common lot.
Mold us into people who show your mercy
and keep us obedient to him whose name is above
    all other names—   *Phil. 2:9*
Jesus Christ, in whose name we pray. **Amen.**

HYMN, SPIRITUAL, OR PSALM

DISMISSAL
Dedicate yourselves to the fast God chooses,   *Isa. 58:6–9*
loosening the yoke of bondage,
declaring freedom to the oppressed,
offering food to the hungry
and shelter to the homeless.
Then your light shall break forth like dawn,
and the glory of the Lord will shine upon you.
He will hear your cry and be at your side, now and forevermore.

Midweek Service: Week Two

Matthew 6:1–6, 16–21

[1]"Beware of practicing your piety before others in order to be seen by them; for then you have no reward from your Father in heaven.

[2]"So whenever you give alms, do not sound a trumpet before you, as the hypocrites do in the synagogues and in the streets, so that they may be praised by others. Truly I tell you, they have received their reward. [3]But when you give alms, do not let your left hand know what your right hand is doing, [4]so that your alms may be done in secret; and your Father who sees in secret will reward you.

[5]"And whenever you pray, do not be like the hypocrites; for they love to stand and pray in the synagogues and at the street corners, so that they may be seen by others. Truly I tell you, they have received their reward. [6]But whenever you pray, go into your room and shut the door and pray to your Father who is in secret; and your Father who sees in secret will reward you. . . .

[16]"And whenever you fast, do not look dismal, like the hypocrites, for they disfigure their faces so as to show others that they are fasting. Truly I tell you, they have received their reward. [17]But when you fast, put oil on your head and wash your face, [18]so that your fasting may be seen not by others but by your Father who is in secret; and your Father who sees in secret will reward you.

[19]"Do not store up for yourselves treasures on earth, where moth and rust consume and where thieves break in and steal; [20]but store up for yourselves treasures in heaven, where neither moth nor rust consumes and where thieves do not break in and steal. [21]For where your treasure is, there your heart will be also."

ORDER OF WORSHIP

OPENING WORDS / CALL TO WORSHIP

Psalm 36: 1–10

Transgression speaks to the wicked
    deep in their hearts;

there is no fear of God
before their eyes.
For they flatter themselves in their own eyes
that their iniquity cannot be found out and hated.
The words of their mouths are mischief and deceit;
they have ceased to act wisely and do good.
They plot mischief while on their beds;
they are set on a way that is not good;
they do not reject evil.

Your steadfast love, O Lord, extends to the heavens,
your faithfulness to the clouds.
Your righteousness is like the mighty mountains,
your judgments are like the great deep;
you save humans and animals alike, O Lord.

How precious is your steadfast love, O God!
All people may take refuge in the shadow of your wings.
They feast on the abundance of your house,
and you give them drink from the river of your delights.
For with you is the fountain of life;
in your light we see light.

O continue your steadfast love to those who know you,
and your salvation to the upright of heart!
[A time of silence may follow for centering prayer.]

CALL TO CONFESSION

In quiet trust, in simple words,   *Matt. 6:6*
we enter a space for prayer.
As we confess our sins,
both secret and public,
the door to God's heart is open,
and we enter into grace and mercy.

PRAYER OF CONFESSION

O God, you see our secret hearts.   *Matt. 6:1–6,*
You see through our vain attempts at righteousness,   *16–18*
when we do the right thing for the wrong reason.
Forgive us when we seek to please others,
instead of pleasing you.

Do not see us for our faults,
and do not go away from us.
Keep us always in your presence
so that we may be restored to the joy of your salvation.
Sustain in us a willing spirit to treasure what you desire;
then our hearts will be opened in joy and gladness.
In Jesus Christ, our Treasure, we pray. Amen.

DECLARATION OF FORGIVENESS

Friends, our God who sees all our hidden parts
also cleanses every part.
Trust in God's forgiveness
that you may serve with pure hearts
in Christ's name. **Amen.**

PRAYER OF THE DAY

God of our salvation,
we long to be reconciled to you.
Help us to clear away any obstacle
that prevents us from accepting the grace of Christ.
No matter what we face in this life,
increase in us knowledge and patience,
kindness and holiness of spirit,
genuine love and truthful speech,
so that, by the power of God at work in us,
we may live even as we are dying
and rejoice even in our sorrows.
Though it may seem that we have nothing,
if we are reconciled to you,
we possess everything,
through Jesus Christ our Lord. **Amen.**

PRAYER FOR ILLUMINATION (OPTIONAL)

SCRIPTURE READING

HOMILY

Lent is a season of awareness of sin and death and of the possibilities of new
life in Jesus Christ. For many, it is also a time of increased devotion—extra
prayer services (like this one), added prayer disciplines, and fasting from a

certain meal, food, or other indulgence. Within this attention to devotion and discipline, today's text from the Sermon on the Mount offers a stern warning: the dangers of sin are as close as the expression of piety to which we are called. "Beware," says Jesus, "of practicing your piety before others."

Three specific warnings follow, concerning almsgiving, praying, and fasting. In each case, the disciples are not to allow anyone to see what they are doing; their practice is to be done "in secret; and your Father who sees in secret will reward you." At issue is the *focus* of the disciples' piety.

Jesus assumed that his disciples would fast, pray, and give alms; these were the marks of a good Jew and would have been deemed worthy of praise in both Jewish and Gentile society. They are commended also for the followers of Jesus and the church of Matthew's day. The difference for followers of Jesus was not the acts themselves but rather the motives and manner in which they were to be carried out. Instead of being done with fanfare that would attract attention and admiration from other people, these deeds were to be done modestly and in secret. In that way they became a challenge to the "honor" and competition that characterized Roman society and that Matthew accuses the local synagogue of adopting.

Fasting is not so common today as it was in Jesus' day, when people often fasted as a sign of penitence or mourning. Most of us today only fast during Lent, and then it is only a partial fast—chocolate, coffee, wine, maybe Facebook or TV? In our culture of abundance and indulgence, even these small abstentions can feel significant, and they certainly can be significant when they are authentically given over to God. But how much more significant do we make them out to be when we whine about how much we miss chocolate, or tweet about our forty-day departure from social media?

The craving, boredom, or restlessness we feel when fasting is meant to point to and symbolize the hunger only God can fill. We can grow so enchanted with our own fasting, the small void we temporarily create in ourselves, that we forget there is One who means to fill us. God gladly will give us God's own self. Whether we know it or not, our deepest hunger is for God. Augustine knew this, praying, "O Lord, you made us for yourself, and our hearts are restless until they rest in you."

Our fasts are not an end unto themselves, nor is Lent intended to confine our piety to a single season. Jesus was describing a lifestyle of quiet devotion: praying without grandstanding, giving our money without showing off. Praying and tithing are fairly common in our congregation, and generally done without fanfare; but we have other works of devotion we like to do noisily. Serving on committees. Assisting with worship. Teaching Sunday school. Volunteering at the food bank. Our motives for these things are usually mixed. A genuine love of God and God's people can sit side by side with a desire for self-aggrandizement, a passion for justice with a selfish need for control, a commitment to service with a heap of martyrdom and a dash of guilt.

It is for people like us that Jesus spoke these words of warning we read today. Unbelievers and occasional churchgoers may suffer many temptations (as do we all) but not the temptation to overzealous piety. The temptation that comes with being religious people is to substitute religion for God. We mistake our road map for our destination. We turn the means into an end. God gives us the good gifts of almsgiving, prayer, fasting, teaching, service, etc., so that we may draw near to God, and we anxiously transform them into performances. To people like us, who take our religious discipline seriously, Jesus offers an irreverent parody.

"Here come the almsgivers into the courts of God," Jesus effectively says. "They are accompanied by the brass section of the symphony. They give a few dollars to this cause, and the trumpets fanfare; a few dollars more to another cause, and the trombones blare a salute!

"Over there stand people praying. People blocks away may hear their praying, and the words go on and on and on, always stretching for one more crumb of emotion and another shred of humility.

"Here come the people who gave up chocolate for Lent. You know they are fasting by their gaunt faces and eyes crazed from lack of sugar!

"And there are the people who chair five committees, teach Sunday school, and never miss choir practice! You know them by their constant rushing and loud laments that they are 'soooo busy.'"

Jesus parodies our religious behavior in the hope that we may be caught laughing at ourselves. We need to laugh at ourselves. Our selves are the problem. These selves we are—these fragile, tragic, needy selves that can scarcely imagine that we are dust.

What reward are we seeking in our fasting, our generosity, our busyness? Of each of the pious people Jesus describes—the almsgivers sounding their horns, the pray-ers piling up words, the fasters in ashen misery—Jesus says, "Truly I tell you, they have received their reward." They have been recognized for their religiosity. That recognition is their reward.

The "treasures" Jesus warns against storing up on earth include not only literal treasures that can be stolen or destroyed but also the praise and honor accorded by one's culture, which can prove utterly fickle. "Treasures in heaven," on the other hand, do not refer to rewards reserved for after death but the valuable treasures that one finds in company with God and in accord with God's sovereign will. The quest for that kind of reward is what guides our devotion to God during Lent and throughout the year, as we prepare to follow Jesus in a life committed to God's reign.

PRAYERS OF INTERCESSION

In peace let us pray to the Lord, saying, Lord, have mercy.

For the church throughout the world,
that all who bear the name of Christ
may find true repentance for their sins
and walk in the ways of the peace,
let us pray to the Lord.
Lord, have mercy.

For the nations of the world,
wherever there is poverty, war, or oppression of human spirit,
that all people may repent of the evil they do to one another,
let us pray to the Lord. **Lord, have mercy.**

For the planet Earth, God's gift to humankind,
that we repent of selfish or thoughtless exploitation
and tend it with care so that all may share justly in its bounty,
let us pray to the Lord. **Lord, have mercy.**

For the leaders of the nations,
that they may work for the common good of all people
and repent of arrogant nationalism,
let us pray to the Lord. **Lord, have mercy.**

For our enemies,
that we may learn to love them with regard for God's compassion,
forgiving wrongs and seeking reconciliation,
let us pray to the Lord. **Lord, have mercy.**

For those who are sick or in trouble,
for the defenseless, the weak, and the poor,
that they may find help in time of need,
and that the church may heed their cry,
let us pray to the Lord. **Lord, have mercy.**

Loving God, hear the prayers of your people for the sake of our world.
With our prayers, accept the dedication of our lives
that we may minister to the world in the name of Jesus,
through whom we pray. **Amen.**

DISMISSAL

Practice your piety not before others, *Matt. 6:1–2, 5–6,*
but before God. *16–17, 19–21*
Give generously, but quietly;
pray constantly, but confidentially;
fast with gratitude to God;
and store up that which is in your heart;
for it cannot be taken from you.
And may the blessing of God, who hears when you call,
remain with you in these Lenten days
and for all your days,
and forevermore.

Midweek Service: Week Three

Joshua 5:2–12

²At that time the LORD said to Joshua, "Make flint knives and circumcise the Israelites a second time." ³So Joshua made flint knives, and circumcised the Israelites at Gibeath-haaraloth. ⁴This is the reason why Joshua circumcised them: all the males of the people who came out of Egypt, all the warriors, had died during the journey through the wilderness after they had come out of Egypt. ⁵Although all the people who came out had been circumcised, yet all the people born on the journey through the wilderness after they had come out of Egypt had not been circumcised. ⁶For the Israelites traveled forty years in the wilderness, until all the nation, the warriors who came out of Egypt, perished, not having listened to the voice of the LORD. To them the LORD swore that he would not let them see the land that he had sworn to their ancestors to give us, a land flowing with milk and honey. ⁷So it was their children, whom he raised up in their place, that Joshua circumcised; for they were uncircumcised, because they had not been circumcised on the way.

⁸When the circumcising of all the nation was done, they remained in their places in the camp until they were healed. ⁹The LORD said to Joshua, "Today I have rolled away from you the disgrace of Egypt." And so that place is called Gilgal to this day.

¹⁰While the Israelites were camped in Gilgal they kept the passover in the evening on the fourteenth day of the month in the plains of Jericho. ¹¹On the day after the passover, on that very day, they ate the produce of the land, unleavened cakes and parched grain. ¹²The manna ceased on the day they ate the produce of the land, and the Israelites no longer had manna; they ate the crops of the land of Canaan that year.

ORDER OF WORSHIP

OPENING WORDS / CALL TO WORSHIP

Psalm 104, Selected Verses
Bless the Lord, O my soul.
O Lord my God, you are very great.

You are clothed with honor and majesty,
  wrapped in light as with a garment.
You stretch out the heavens like a tent,
  you set the beams of your chambers on the waters,
You make springs gush forth in the valleys;
  they flow between the hills,
giving drink to every wild animal;
  the wild asses quench their thirst.
You cause the grass to grow for the cattle,
  and plants for people to use,
to bring forth food from the earth,
  and wine to gladden the human heart,
oil to make the face shine,
  and bread to strengthen the human heart.
The trees of the Lord are watered abundantly,
  the cedars of Lebanon that he planted.
In them the birds build their nests;
  the stork has its home in the fir trees.
The high mountains are for the wild goats;
  the rocks are a refuge for the badgers.
The young lions roar for their prey,
  seeking their food from God.
Your creatures all look to you
  to give them their food in due season;
when you give to them, they gather it up;
  when you open your hand, they are filled with good things.
May the glory of the Lord endure forever;
  may the Lord rejoice in his works—

I will sing to the Lord as long as I live;
  I will sing praise to my God while I have being.

Bless the Lord, O my soul.
Praise the LORD!
[A time of silence may follow for centering prayer.]

CALL TO CONFESSION
  Trusting the grace promised to us in Jesus Christ,
  let us confess our sins before God and one another.

PRAYER OF CONFESSION

Merciful God,
we confess that we have strayed from your ways.   *Josh. 5:5–7*
We have seized our independence, forgetting
**   your provision.**
You gave us the earth for our home,
but we squander earth's resources and hoard
**   its bounty.**
You gave us neighbors to love, but we pursue
**   selfish ambitions.**
You gave us the commandments that lead to
**   human flourishing,**
but we break your law and forsake your love.
Forgive us our sin and bring us to repentance.
Draw our wandering hearts back to you
that we may find freedom in obedience to your love.
Through Christ our Lord we pray. Amen.

DECLARATION OF FORGIVENESS

Sisters and brothers,
Your disgrace has been rolled away,   *Josh. 5:9*
like the stone from Christ's tomb.
God offers forgiveness of our sins and
    the grace of repentance.
Accept God's grace, repent of your sin,
    and be restored to abundant life.

PRAYER OF THE DAY

Creator God,
you have formed us as your own,
so whether we are weeping or laughing,
hungry or well-fed, dreaming or shouting for joy,
we are always coming home to you.
For all this and more, we thank you in Jesus' name. **Amen.**

PRAYER FOR ILLUMINATION (OPTIONAL)

SCRIPTURE READING

HOMILY

Lent is a wilderness journey. It lasts forty days (not including Sundays) because of Jesus' forty days of fasting and temptation in the wilderness, and to a lesser extent in reference to the Israelites' forty years of wandering in the wilderness of Sinai, on their way out of slavery in Egypt. Today's passage in Joshua details how the Israelites' wilderness wandering comes to an end. They have been wandering for forty years, having escaped the oppression of the Egyptians. Moses led the people capably and was memorialized as "unequaled for all the signs and wonders the Lord sent him to perform," but as they prepared to cross over into the promised land, they had a new leader named Joshua.

Our passage begins just after the people have passed through the Jordan River on dry ground (an effective bookend to Israel's time in the wilderness, as it mirrors Moses's miraculous parting of the Red Sea forty years before). God's promise to the Israelites was that they would enter and possess a land of milk and honey, and their entering the land shows that God's promise to them is real and effective. Despite the fact that the Israelites have not always been good, God has always been good to them. In the wilderness they were fed manna, a direct provision from God. They wandered for years in utter dependence upon God. Now the land of promise lies before them, a land of opportunities.

Yet Joshua is aware of the dangers of new opportunities. With their independence from Egypt may come independence from God. The people need to be reminded that, in spite of all they wish to leave behind, God must not be thrown by the wayside. The Lord declares to Joshua, "Today I have rolled away from you the disgrace of Egypt." It is language that can propel our hearts forward across centuries to another time and place, where God will again roll something away, a stone from the entrance of a tomb. Neither the disgrace of Egypt nor the darkness of sin and death can finally stand as obstacles to the power of God's love to redeem and give life. God is able to bring forth life out of death and disgrace.

This time and place are marked by ritual and remembrance. All the males, all the warriors, who had come out of Egypt had died. None of the people born on the journey had been circumcised. Now standing at the edge of the promised land, this new generation is circumcised, accepting the physical sign of their covenant relationship with God. Then they observe the Passover. "On the day after the passover, on that very day" they eat (v. 11), and the food opens their eyes to wonder about their journey and their dependence on God, who is the giver of land, food, and life.

On that day the menu changes: no more manna. I wonder if they secretly breathe a sigh of relief. Thank goodness. Wow, I was sick and tired of that stuff. Or maybe they miss it and start to remember it fondly. After all, manna was the gift of life. Manna reminds them how God provided for them in the wilderness, but manna is a part of the past in a new land flowing with milk and honey. Manna requires neither settlement nor work; it merely needs to be gathered. The promised land, however, is to be developed. The manna ceases and they eat the crops of the land of Canaan. It is a new time, a new stage in life, calling for a different flavor, a new local cuisine.

The message of the food remains familiar. The food is more than fuel for their bodies. The bread points them to the bread giver, who is also the promise giver, who is also the life giver: the Lord. That message remains the same whether one is eating manna that falls from the sky or bread produced by farmers and bakers, shipped to a store, and sold out of aisle 9—but it is a lot easier to remember the role God played in providing that food without all the middlemen.

Most of us with the luxury of reading this book are financially more secure than the rest of the world. Yet wealth is both blessing and temptation. It is wonderful to live in a land flowing with milk and honey, but it is also easy to rely more on the land than on the Giver of the land. Our riches can lure us to celebrate ourselves rather than the Holy One who provides for us, calling us to seek our treasures first in heaven rather than on earth. Our truest calling is to watch and pray and work for the reign of God. There we can enjoy milk and honey; there we can even drink living water.

But first, we must covenant afresh with the God who leads us into new and challenging futures. Before we can begin our new endeavors, ministries, and missions, we must circumcise our hearts, cutting away the old foreskins of past sins and past failures. We must also be careful to dethrone our modern idols. Our reliance upon such idols leaves us open to sudden and terrible reversals. The land still has milk and honey, yet we know that we cannot live on milk and honey—or bread—alone, but only by every word that proceeds out of the mouth of God.

Our Lenten fasts should remind us of these truths. By eating simple foods and abstaining from foods we love, the difference between needs and wants becomes more apparent, and we become ever more aware of God's provision in our lives. This way of being requires prayer, meditation, confession of sins, and repentance. Once we have prepared ourselves to follow God into the wonderful provisions of our promised land, we are better prepared to enjoy both the land and the feast, when the time comes, in the presence of the One who makes and gives it all.

PRAYERS OF INTERCESSION

God our Provider,
out of your fullness you cause life to spring up in barren landscapes;
you have power to control troubled waters, making a path of safety;
you hear our cries and receive our tears;
you restore us to joy and laughter.
You have done great things for us, O God,
and are continually making all things new.
We thank you, O God:
you are making all things new.

We thank you for the gift of your Son, Jesus Christ,
whose life and ministry has guided us through this Lenten season
and guides us in every season of life.
In his suffering and death, he knows full well
the troubles and pains we face in this earthly life.
In his resurrection is the hope of our own.
Surrounded by your overflowing love, we are not alone.
We thank you, O God:
you are making all things new.

We pray for people who wait in difficult places.
For those who are suffering and those at life's end;
for people struggling with employment and financial worries;
for those estranged from loved ones;
for those trapped in the grip of addiction;
for people enduring emotional or spiritual turmoil.
Because you are able to make a way in every wilderness,
we thank you, O God:
you are making all things new.

We pray for the needs of the world.
May peace invade places of war and justice crowd out
    oppression and cruelty.
Protect soldiers and citizens alike from harm's way and
    make all conflict cease.
Bless leaders of communities, states, and nations,
that they may speak the truth and work with others
    for the common good.

Pour out healing on the earth itself, depleted and injured
by our careless consumption and intentional greed.
Comfort those devastated by natural disasters;
strengthen those supplying shelter, food, and aid.
Amid the chaos of this world, your Spirit intercedes with
    sighs too deep for words.
We thank you, O God:
you are making all things new.

We pray for the church, the body of Christ in the world,
that we may proclaim your Word boldly.
Lead us, by the power of your Spirit, to witness to your truth,
for we remember and proclaim that death does not have
    the last word—
in our lives, in the church, or in the world.
We thank you, O God:
you are making all things new.

We pray in the name of Jesus Christ, crucified and risen. Amen.

DISMISSAL

Friends, God loves and cares for each of us.
Therefore, trust in the Lord
and give thanks in all things,
so that we may remain steadfast in faith with Christ,
who supports and strengthens us in all things.

And may the abundance of God bless you,
the strength of Christ keep you,
and the Spirit of glory, which is the Spirit of God,
shine upon you forever.

Midweek Service: Week Four

Luke 4:1–13

[1]Jesus, full of the Holy Spirit, returned from the Jordan and was led by the Spirit in the wilderness, [2]where for forty days he was tempted by the devil. He ate nothing at all during those days, and when they were over, he was famished. [3]The devil said to him, "If you are the Son of God, command this stone to become a loaf of bread." [4]Jesus answered him, "It is written, 'One does not live by bread alone.'"

[5]Then the devil led him up and showed him in an instant all the kingdoms of the world. [6]And the devil said to him, "To you I will give their glory and all this authority; for it has been given over to me, and I give it to anyone I please. [7]If you, then, will worship me, it will all be yours." [8]Jesus answered him, "It is written,

> 'Worship the Lord your God,
>   and serve only him.'"

[9]Then the devil took him to Jerusalem, and placed him on the pinnacle of the temple, saying to him, "If you are the Son of God, throw yourself down from here, [10]for it is written,

> 'He will command his angels concerning you,
>   to protect you,'

[11]and

> 'On their hands they will bear you up,
>   so that you will not dash your foot against a stone.'"

[12]Jesus answered him, "It is said, 'Do not put the Lord your God to the test.'" [13]When the devil had finished every test, he departed from him until an opportune time.

ORDER OF WORSHIP

Psalm 91

You who live in the shelter of the Most High,
    who abide in the shadow of the Almighty,
will say to the Lord, **"My refuge and my fortress;**
    my God, in whom I trust."
For he will deliver you from the snare of the fowler
    and from the deadly pestilence;
he will cover you with his pinions,
    and under his wings you will find refuge;
    his faithfulness is a shield and buckler.
You will not fear the terror of the night,
    or the arrow that flies by day,
or the pestilence that stalks in darkness,
    or the destruction that wastes at noonday.
A thousand may fall at your side,
    ten thousand at your right hand,
    but it will not come near you.
You will only look with your eyes
    and see the punishment of the wicked.
Because you have made the Lord your refuge,
    the Most High your dwelling place,
no evil shall befall you,
    no scourge come near your tent.
For he will command his angels concerning you
    to guard you in all your ways.
On their hands they will bear you up,
    so that you will not dash your foot against a stone.
You will tread on the lion and the adder,
    the young lion and the serpent you will trample under foot.
Those who love me, I will deliver;
    I will protect those who know my name.
When they call to me, I will answer them;
    I will be with them in trouble,
    I will rescue them and honor them.
With long life I will satisfy them,
    and show them my salvation.
[A time of silence may follow for centering prayer.]

CALL TO CONFESSION

God is faithful, leading us into freedom,
but we are conditioned to the slavery of sin.
Comfortable with the way things are,
we lose sight of the way God intends them to be.
We bring our confession before the One
who is more powerful than Pharaoh in Egypt,
mightier than the devil in the wilderness.

PRAYER OF CONFESSION

God, our refuge and fortress, *Luke 4:4, 10*
forgive us when we fail to trust in you.
We fall to temptation;
we are swayed by false words;
we speak false words of our own.
We choose our ease and comfort
over your demanding claims upon us and upon the world.
In turning from you,
we settle for less than the abundant generosity you intend.
Forgive us, we pray.
Do not let us be put to shame, O God.
Hear us as we call to you and show us your salvation.
In Christ's name we pray. Amen.

DECLARATION OF FORGIVENESS

The Lord is generous to all who call on God's name.
Friends, believe the good news:
God does not turn away from us,
but desires to bring us into the glorious freedom
offered in Jesus Christ.
Everyone who calls on the name of the Lord will be saved.
Thanks be to God!

PRAYER OF THE DAY

God Most High, *Ps. 91:1*
thank you for signs of your power and grace,
shown to us even in the wilderness.
Give us courage to stand firm in your Word
in every time of trial and testing, *Luke 4:2, 12*
that we may enter the land of your freedom

and receive the salvation you so generously give;
through Jesus Christ our Lord. **Amen.**

PRAYER FOR ILLUMINATION (OPTIONAL)

SCRIPTURE READING

HOMILY
"That which doesn't kill us makes us stronger." We've all heard that little nugget of wisdom, intended to help us get through difficult times. There is a spiritual depth that is made possible as we respond in faith to trials, trouble, temptation, and testing. Even so, if given a choice, most of us will not intentionally choose a path filled with difficulty. Our prior choices may cause us to stumble onto this path, the choices of others around us may create circumstances that force us onto this path, or we are simply thrown onto the path by disaster or disease, but most of us are slow to deliberately choose the difficult path.

Yet in the season of Lent we are invited to embrace an intentional way of life. For the forty days of Lent (not including Sundays), we follow the example of Jesus who was "led by the Spirit in the wilderness, where for forty days he was tempted by the devil." The Spirit does not just "drop him off" in the wilderness to fend for himself; the Spirit continues to abide with him, enabling him to grow stronger through this season. In today's Scripture, we see that Jesus' faithfulness to God amid testing is essential preparation for his mission. Being chosen and anointed is not sufficient preparation either for our Christian walk. We must be tested, often by being led to places of hunger and despair. Only then do we learn dependence on God, who graciously provides for all of our needs in all of life's seasons.

Last week we looked at the very end of Israel's time in the wilderness. Jesus' sojourn in the wilderness recalls Israel's forty years of wandering—a point underscored by his repeated quotation of Deuteronomy. In the harsh environment of the wilderness, habits formed by slavery in Egypt are discarded and new ways of complete trust in God are formed. Comparing the testing of Jesus with the testing of Israel in the wilderness, we see a close parallel, except that Jesus' response is faithfulness. He renders to God the obedience that Israel does not give.

The devil comes with tempting offers: to turn a stone to bread and thus sate his hunger, to worship the devil and gain influence over the world, and to test God's promises in a freefall faith experiment. These Jesus rejects, preferring instead to trust God's word alone. The story is more about the responses Jesus gives to the temptations than to the temptations themselves. Jesus' responses underscore his faithfulness to God, setting the stage for the whole of his ministry and, ultimately, his sacrifice. His responses come with the full knowledge that obedience to God will bring persecution, misunderstanding, and the cross. Many followers of Jesus wanted him to free Israel, to restore an earthly kingdom marked by honor and glory. To say yes to the world would have required Jesus to say no to God, to the way of God, and to an idea of God's kingdom that those followers simply did not understand. It would have required him to say no to the freedom and love for humanity that are the marks of his death and resurrection.

Jesus is tempted again near the end of his earthly ministry, as he prepares himself for betrayal and ultimate execution. Here Jesus' faithfulness to God's will is fully embraced in his persevering prayers at Gethsemane. By contrast, the disciples, like Israel, fail in the time of great trial and testing. Jesus had warned them, "Pray that you may not enter into temptation" (Luke 22:40). Much more was at stake than practicing spiritual discipline on the Mount of Olives in the face of their sorrow, however. Faithfulness to the divine mission involved persecution, suffering, and death. Hence this was a difficult path not easily embraced. Only by "joining Jesus"—being in total solidarity with him and his mission—could the disciples grow to "walk the talk."

In our own struggles, we may find it easy to resist the temptation to take the easy way out or to glorify ourselves rather than God, or perhaps we find ourselves tested beyond our strength. The good news, however, is that the one who was tempted in the wilderness is also the crucified and resurrected one, in whom God's new life is made available to those who cannot, by their own resources, withstand temptation. The one who was tempted in the wilderness thus strengthens us in our weakness.

Many of us here "give up something" for Lent. Maybe you have been going without your morning coffee or evening dessert for the past three weeks. Maybe you have sworn off social media or unplugged your TV. Or perhaps you are "giving up" some of your free time, committing to a daily prayer regimen or weekly volunteer service. Even if we chose a rather difficult discipline, we know that this trial is minor compared to Jesus' forty days of hunger or the trials of sickness, poverty, and loss suffered each day by people around the globe. The purpose of Lenten discipline is not merely to experience a modicum of Christ's temptation and pain but to cultivate the intentionality and receptiveness to God's grace that enable us to feel the true presence of God in our lives. With this intentionality and openness, we can gain the spiritual depth to be faithful to the mystery of God-with-us even in our unexpected trials and temptations.

Jesus did not ask for trials and temptations; he accepted that they could not be avoided even by doing God's will. Jesus' season of testing was not for a day or two, and it was not a mere luxury that he had chosen to do without. His season of forty days of temptation suggests to us that we may have faithfully to endure seasons of long and protracted difficulty. Jesus' intentionality and receptivity to God's grace show us the way to turn toward God, rather than away from God, during our trials and temptations. If we choose the Lenten struggle to be intentional and receptive to the grace of God, we will encounter a faithful God who leads us not only into the wilderness but also through the wilderness.

PRAYERS OF INTERCESSION
[A period of silence may follow each intercession.]
Almighty, all-merciful God,
lover of justice and giver of peace, Hear our prayer:

For the church of Jesus Christ,
and for all who seek your face.

For leaders and elders,
that they will abide by your commandments.

For the earth that you have made,
trembling for redemption and re-creation.

For those who are tormented
by the demons of illness, addiction, and grief.

Let our lives and our world be transformed by your love;
in the name of Jesus Christ, your chosen one, our Lord. **Amen.**

DISMISSAL
These Lenten days will take us to the cross of Christ.
Go forward, knowing that you do not go this way alone.
May the Word of God strengthen you and the Holy Spirit
    sustain you,
and may the God of the exodus show you the way of true
    justice and peace.

Midweek Service: Week Five

Joel 2:1–2, 12–17

¹Blow the trumpet in Zion;
    sound the alarm on my holy mountain!
Let all the inhabitants of the land tremble,
    for the day of the LORD is coming, it is near—
²a day of darkness and gloom,
    a day of clouds and thick darkness!
Like blackness spread upon the mountains
    a great and powerful army comes;
their like has never been from of old,
    nor will be again after them
    in ages to come.
. . . .

¹²Yet even now, says the LORD,
    return to me with all your heart,
with fasting, with weeping, and with mourning;
    ¹³rend your hearts and not your clothing.
Return to the LORD, your God,
    for he is gracious and merciful,
slow to anger, and abounding in steadfast love,
    and relents from punishing.
¹⁴Who knows whether he will not turn and relent,
    and leave a blessing behind him,
a grain offering and a drink offering
    for the LORD, your God?

¹⁵Blow the trumpet in Zion;
    sanctify a fast;
call a solemn assembly;
    ¹⁶gather the people.
Sanctify the congregation;
    assemble the aged;
gather the children,
    even infants at the breast.

Let the bridegroom leave his room,
    and the bride her canopy.
17Between the vestibule and the altar
    let the priests, the ministers of the LORD, weep.
Let them say, "Spare your people, O LORD,
    and do not make your heritage a mockery,
    a byword among the nations.
Why should it be said among the peoples,
    'Where is their God?'"

ORDER OF WORSHIP

OPENING WORDS / CALL TO WORSHIP

Psalm 50, Selected Verses

The mighty one, God the Lord,
    speaks and summons the earth
    from the rising of the sun to its setting.
Our God comes and does not keep silence,
    before him is a devouring fire,
    and a mighty tempest all around him.
He calls to the heavens above
    and to the earth, that he may judge his people:
"Gather to me my faithful ones,
    who made a covenant with me by sacrifice!"
The heavens declare his righteousness,
    for God himself is judge.
"Hear, O my people, and I will speak,
    I am God, your God.
Not for your sacrifices do I rebuke you;
    your burnt offerings are continually before me.
I will not accept a bull from your house,
    or goats from your folds.
For every wild animal of the forest is mine,
    and all that moves in the field is mine.
If I were hungry, I would not tell you,
    for the world and all that is in it is mine.
Do I eat the flesh of bulls,
    or drink the blood of goats?

Offer to God a sacrifice of thanksgiving,
and pay your vows to the Most High.
Call on me in the day of trouble;
I will deliver you, and you shall glorify me.
Mark this, then, you who forget God.
Those who bring thanksgiving as their sacrifice honor me;
to those who go the right way
I will show the salvation of God."
[A time of silence may follow for centering prayer.]

CALL TO CONFESSION

The prophet Joel cried out: *Joel 2:12–13*
Return to the Lord with all your heart,
with fasting, with weeping, and with mourning;
rend your hearts and not your clothing.
With hearts broken open before God,
let us confess our sins and repent of all unrighteousness.

PRAYER OF CONFESSION

Merciful God,   *Joel 2:12–17*
we confess that we have been a rebellious people.
We have failed to be an obedient church,
failed to love the needy as our neighbors.
We use religion to cover our shame,
fasting in selfishness, not sacrifice,
clothing ourselves in self-righteousness, not repentance.
We have become a mockery of our heritage;
the world looks at us and asks, Where is their God?
Forgive us, O God.
Humble our rebellious hearts
and restore in us the light of salvation,
through Jesus Christ, our Lord. Amen.

DECLARATION OF FORGIVENESS

The Lord receives your contrition
and offers you comfort.
Return to the Lord, your God,   *Joel 2:13*
for he is gracious and merciful,
slow to anger, and abounding in steadfast love.

PRAYER OF THE DAY

God of Righteousness,
you see the secret acts of our devotion
and know the hidden motives of our hearts.
Make our religion genuine,
that our hearts and minds confirm the words we speak
and the disciplines we practice.
Confirm in us a spirit of humility
that without regard to earthly honor
we may live as your faithful children
in the way of Jesus Christ our Lord. **Amen.**

PRAYER FOR ILLUMINATION (OPTIONAL)

SCRIPTURE READING

HOMILY

A trumpet is echoing through the land. It is sounding an alarm, calling to the people, "The day of the Lord is coming!" "Rend your hearts and not your garments!" "Return to the Lord!" "Fast and weep!" These words may sound antiquated to contemporary ears. They echo through the centuries from the lips of the ancient Hebrew prophet and his alien social context, bouncing off the sermons of tent revival preachers, ricocheting from the cries of those who proclaim dire predictions of the end time. How can they possibly have meaning for us?

Though we tend to avoid this kind of alarmism, the fact remains that our world is complex and fraught with conflict. The threat of global warming with its ecological and economic consequences looms large. The First World is warring with the Third World over nonrenewable energy resources. Terrorism is the preferred strategy of competing religious and political ideologies. Poverty with its accompanying issues of hunger and homelessness continues to grow across the globe, as the gap between rich and poor grows ever wider.

In this global context we are invited to hear the prophet's words from a vantage point beyond the cleansing of our individual souls. The Christian community is challenged by the ancient words of the prophet to consider its communal soul as well. It is all too apparent that in the web of life on this earth we are connected globally, economically, politically, and spiritually. We are dependent on one another for our survival. As our Ash Wednesday liturgy reminded us, we are dust and to dust we will return. All creation comes from the hand of the same Creator and from the same particles of energy. The universe is truly one and connected within all its parts.

Joel's word from God in this passage begins with a prophetic cry, "The day of the LORD is coming!" While each Hebrew prophet who invoked this phrase had something specific in mind to challenge the people of his time, this "day" involved God's intervention in history both to save and to judge. In the second chapter of Joel "the day of the LORD" is equated with a great and powerful army spreading like blackness over the mountains. Some scholars have speculated that perhaps this was not the army of a conquering nation, but a plague of locusts destroying the people's crops and their livelihood.

Whichever it may have been, a plague of locusts or a conquering army, could the threat of destruction in the ancient text be analogous to the impending threats on our global community? The effects of global warming, of the violence and greed of our times, of our inability to seek peace with our neighbors are spreading across our land like "blackness spread upon the mountains." Could the twenty-first-century church be called to be a modern-day Joel, crying out, "The day of the LORD is coming" in the face of the global need of God's judgment and salvation?

If the church is to play Joel's prophetic part, it will behoove us to hear the words of challenge and repentance that he gave to his people. "Rend your hearts and not your clothing!" Through "rending" our hearts we are called out of the provincialism and isolationism of our faith communities. We are called to break open our hearts, to allow our hearts to be broken for the good of the whole world, as we see how First-World Christian communities are connected to Third-World Christian communities and how Christians are connected to brothers and sisters of other faiths.

With hearts broken open and vulnerable, we can "return to the LORD!" God's mercy, grace, and steadfast love comprise the healing cauldron where the sins that human beings perpetrate against one another and against creation can be cleansed. God knows we do not need God's punishment, for when left to our own devices we mete out enough anger and punishment upon one another—and on ourselves. We too often try to assuage our feelings of culpability and dis-ease with religious practices, "rending our clothing," so to speak, with gestures of charity or empty piety. In right relationship with God, however, we recognize our implicit and complicit cooperation with the sins of the world without the paralysis of guilt and self-pity. Then our inclinations to "fast and weep" are transformed from lifeless ritual into true and vital action.

"Fasting" beyond the limited discipline of Lent can become our search for simpler lifestyles along with practices that decrease our faith community's ecological footprint. Our tears of repentance can lead us to search for ways to deal with conflict constructively within church communities instead of allowing it to create political and divisive bickering. We cannot hope to call for change in the world without examining our communal souls and seeking the changes of repentance within ourselves.

Bill McKibben, environmentalist and lay minister, called the church to task on the issue of global warming in the February 20, 2007, issue of *The Christian Century*. "The church—which can still posit some goal for human life other than accumulation—must be involved in the search for what comes next." McKibben's words extend to the church a challenge that is larger than involvement in eco-justice issues. The Christian community has been given not only the wake-up call through the prophets but also the promise of resurrection in the Gospels and the apocalyptic prophet's vision in Revelation of a new heaven and a new earth.

Christian faith requires that we face difficult realities with open eyes and open hearts, knowing that injustice begets righteous action, that dust becomes life, and that sin is blown away by grace. The good news of Lent is that the church is called to heed the trumpet call of repentance as we anticipate the glad trumpets of Easter morning announcing God's ultimate defeat of death in Christ Jesus.

PRAYERS OF INTERCESSION

[A brief time of silence may be kept after each intercession.]
Trusting in God's righteousness,
let us pray for the world and for our needs, saying,
Holy God, hear our prayer.

For the church, that in this season of fasting and repentance,
the people of God, with sincere hearts,
may amend their lives and obey the gospel,
Holy God, **hear our prayer.**

For all pastors and teachers,
that they may lead the church by humble example
and give public witness without concern for earthly reward,
Holy God, **hear our prayer.**

For peace among the nations
and integrity within the governments,
Holy God, **hear our prayer.**

For our city *[town]* and for all who live here,
that neighborhoods may be places of hospitality and care,
Holy God, **hear our prayer.**

For the poor and the oppressed
that they may find deliverance from their distress,
and for all who seek to alleviate human suffering,
Holy God, **hear our prayer.**

For those who suffer illness of mind or body
and for those who care for them,
that they may be healed of disease and know the joy of abundant life,
Holy God, **hear our prayer.**

For these concerns and those known only to you, Holy God,
we pray in the name of Jesus Christ our Lord. **Amen.**

DISMISSAL
In the shelter of the Lord,
seek justice and mercy.
Open your hearts in contrition and compassion,
that you may be transformed by the Living God
and the world transformed by God through you.
Go in peace.

Midweek Service: Week Six

Acts 11:1–12

¹Now the apostles and the believers who were in Judea heard that the Gentiles had also accepted the word of God. ²So when Peter went up to Jerusalem, the circumcised believers criticized him, ³saying, "Why did you go to uncircumcised men and eat with them?" ⁴Then Peter began to explain it to them, step by step, saying, ⁵"I was in the city of Joppa praying, and in a trance I saw a vision. There was something like a large sheet coming down from heaven, being lowered by its four corners; and it came close to me. ⁶As I looked at it closely I saw four-footed animals, beasts of prey, reptiles, and birds of the air. ⁷I also heard a voice saying to me, 'Get up, Peter; kill and eat.' ⁸But I replied, 'By no means, Lord; for nothing profane or unclean has ever entered my mouth.' ⁹But a second time the voice answered from heaven, 'What God has made clean, you must not call profane.' ¹⁰This happened three times; then everything was pulled up again to heaven. ¹¹At that very moment three men, sent to me from Caesarea, arrived at the house where we were. ¹²The Spirit told me to go with them and not to make a distinction between them and us."

ORDER OF WORSHIP

OPENING WORDS / CALL TO WORSHIP

Psalm 103, Selected Verses

Bless the Lord, O my soul,
     and all that is within me,
     bless his holy name.
Bless the Lord, O my soul,
     and do not forget all his benefits—
The Lord works vindication
     and justice for all who are oppressed.
He made known his ways to Moses,
     his acts to the people of Israel.

The Lord is merciful and gracious,
  slow to anger and abounding in steadfast love.
For as the heavens are high above the earth,
  so great is his steadfast love toward those who fear him;
as far as the east is from the west,
  so far he removes our transgressions from us.
As a father has compassion for his children,
  so the Lord has compassion for those who fear him.
For he knows how we were made;
  he remembers that we are dust.
As for mortals, their days are like grass;
  they flourish like a flower of the field;
for the wind passes over it, and it is gone,
  and its place knows it no more.
But the steadfast love of the Lord is from everlasting
  to everlasting
  on those who fear him,
  and his righteousness to children's children,
to those who keep his covenant
  and remember to do his commandments.
The Lord has established his throne in the heavens,
  and his kingdom rules over all.
Bless the Lord, all his works,
  in all places of his dominion.
Bless the Lord, O my soul.
[A time of silence may follow for centering prayer.]

CALL TO CONFESSION
  Trusting in the love of God to make all things new,
  let us confess our sin to God and our neighbor.

PRAYER OF CONFESSION
  God of mercy,   *Acts 11:9, 12*
  your command to love one another
    across all differences
  opens us to new horizons,
  yet we often respond with fear and judgment
  that hinders your goal for humanity.
  Forgive our sins, we pray,
  and give us a true repentance

that leads to life for all creation.
We pray in Jesus' name. Amen.

DECLARATION OF FORGIVENESS

God's promises are trustworthy and true;
your sins are forgiven.
Be at peace to serve the Lord,
and may you always be known by your love.

PRAYER OF THE DAY

Surprising God, in the resurrection of Jesus Christ   *Acts 11:1–12*
you make all things new.
Long ago you called your church
to a love beyond all social and cultural differences
and gave them the gift of your Holy Spirit
to open their hearts to enact such love.
Give us that same spirit of openness,
that we too might discern new directions in our day
for your dream to reconcile and heal all creation.
In Jesus' name we pray. **Amen.**

PRAYER FOR ILLUMINATION (OPTIONAL)

SCRIPTURE READING

HOMILY

Today's text from Acts begins with Peter reporting to the church leaders in Jerusalem. It sounds as if he was being called on the carpet for breaking the rules. He had been eating with "the uncircumcised," that is, with Gentiles or non-Jews. A similar charge had been leveled against Jesus for eating with sinners and others deemed unacceptable by the Jewish leaders. So Peter was in good company, but that did not make his confrontation with the Jerusalem leaders easy.

Tensions among religious people still tend to revolve around who is "in" and who is "out." Should we let people who are not official church members be in leadership roles? Can we ordain gay and lesbian individuals? Will people of other religions go to heaven? In Peter's case, the tension was between those who felt followers of Jesus should be or become Jewish and others who were busy expanding the circle until all God's children had a place at the table.

In addition to the physical sign of circumcision, tension between Jewish and Gentile Christians in the early days of the church concerned food. Faithful Jews would not eat pork or shellfish, fish that lacked fins or scales, or foods not prepared according to the specifications of Levitical law. Still today, some of our divisions in the church relate to food—and not just whether you prefer tomato-based or mustard-based barbecue at church picnics. Some Christians believe people of faith should never drink alcohol, even in moderation. Some do not eat meats other than fish during Lent. For first-century Christians, these convictions about eating and drinking governed not just personal preferences but social interactions as a whole. To accept the hospitality of someone who did not adhere to these rules was to risk contaminating oneself with unclean foods.

If Jesus' first followers were prohibited from sharing a meal with non-Jews, could the Gentiles have a place at the table in the budding Jesus movement? That was the question hanging in the balance along with the integrity and expansion of the early church. Fortunately, God had a witness. Peter was the pivotal figure, the rock, whose confession changed the dynamics of Jesus' relationship with his followers and opened the door to discipleship. Remember the promise that the risen Lord made to his disciples, that they would receive the power of the Holy Spirit? The fulfillment of this promise is nowhere more evident than in the boldness of Peter's testimony in Jerusalem. God empowered Peter, an ordinary fisherman, to play a significant role in the mission of the church.

God enables ordinary people to be witnesses to the gospel. This can be frightening, because it voids our excuses that we are not gifted enough, not old enough, not good enough to get the job done. God has always had the audacity to choose ordinary people to do extraordinary things in the service of God's reign. Such a realization should give us hope and strengthen our resolve to join the cloud of witnesses from Abraham, Sarah, and Moses to Esther and Jeremiah, Peter and Paul.

Peter gave testimony to the church leaders about a vision he received while praying on the roof. He saw a sheet being lowered from heaven with a variety of creatures on it, including things like pigs, frogs, vultures, and crabs—animals that Jews were forbidden to eat, even if killed in a humane, kosher manner. Peter was told to "kill and eat." He refused because the food was "profane" and "unclean." Then he heard the crucial line, "What God has made clean, you must not call profane." This cycle repeated three times, and then everything was taken up into heaven.

This vision was followed by the arrival of three men from Caesarea who appeared at the door. Peter was instructed by the Spirit to go with them and not distinguish between "them and us," that is, Jews and Gentiles. When he arrived at Cornelius's house and preached, the Spirit led the Gentiles present to salvation. Peter concluded that God had given them the same gift God had given to Jewish believers. Then he asked the profound question, "Who was I that I could hinder God?"

Think about the astonishing insight contained in that question. If God so loved the world that Jesus came not to condemn the whole world but to save it, who are we to try to limit the mission of God to redeem humanity? Every time we exclude someone from full participation in the redemptive efforts of God, Peter's question should trouble us and the church. What if the church had closed the door to the Gentiles, and Christianity had remained a sect within Judaism? Peter was persuaded that God the creator did not intend to exclude anyone from the community of God's care. His conclusion was revolutionary.

Those in the faith community often use the word "discernment." Peter discerned the connection between his vision and the three visitors who asked him to travel to Caesarea with them. More amazing than Peter's vision and discernment was how the leaders in Jerusalem responded. They listened and were open to the new reality Peter envisioned. They could have said, "You are out of your mind, and this is wrong!" Instead, the Holy Spirit gave them the ability to listen and to change.

The foods and drinks we abstain from—during Lent or throughout the year—typically do not limit our social interactions and relationships as they did in the first century. But let's not fool ourselves into thinking we are so much more open-minded than Peter's compatriots. We have our own litmus tests for "true" Christianity. We may believe that Christian morality specifies marriage between one man and one woman. Or we may believe that those who exclude others based on sexuality are not loving as Jesus loved. Maybe we baptize infants, or maybe we require a reasoned, mature confession of faith to be considered a true believer. We may believe that real Christians vote only for Republicans, or only for Democrats, or maybe even that they should not participate in human political systems at all.

If there is hope for the church today, when there is so much dissension and division in faith communities, then we must pray to have visions that bring us together. The world is watching. Do we have anything to offer that differs from other groups characterized by dissension and division? Can we listen to each other and seek to discover where God's Spirit is leading? We need to be open to the work of God's healing and reconciling Spirit to give everyone a place at Christ's table.

PRAYERS OF INTERCESSION

[A time of silence follows each petition.]
God of steadfast love,
you raise us up when we fall
and place our feet on steady ground.
Strengthened by your faithfulness,
we offer our prayers
in thanksgiving for the grace that is ours in Christ.

We pray for the mission of your church,
that we may proclaim the good news of the age
as we put our trust in you.

We pray for the world,
that your saving love may reach to the ends of the earth
as we serve the common good.

We pray for all who suffer,
that we may heed their cry
as we share in your steadfast mercy.

We pray for your creation,
that we may safeguard its well-being
as we labor together for redemption.

We remember before you those who have died
and pray for those who will die today,
that they may know your peace.

Through Christ, with Christ, in Christ,
in the unity of the Holy Spirit,
all glory and honor are yours, almighty Father,
forever and ever. **Amen.**

DISMISSAL

We, who are baptized into Christ,
now live under God's rule.
Consider, children of the covenant,
how God has welcomed us and loved us all.

Live each day proclaiming the good news
that everyone is accepted,
everyone is part of God's family.
May you go out now to love and be loved by
your sisters and brothers throughout the world.
Amen.

Midweek Service: Week Seven (Holy Week)

Exodus 12:1–14

¹The Lord said to Moses and Aaron in the land of Egypt: ²This month shall mark for you the beginning of months; it shall be the first month of the year for you. ³Tell the whole congregation of Israel that on the tenth of this month they are to take a lamb for each family, a lamb for each household. ⁴If a household is too small for a whole lamb, it shall join its closest neighbor in obtaining one; the lamb shall be divided in proportion to the number of people who eat of it. ⁵Your lamb shall be without blemish, a year-old male; you may take it from the sheep or from the goats. ⁶You shall keep it until the fourteenth day of this month; then the whole assembled congregation of Israel shall slaughter it at twilight. ⁷They shall take some of the blood and put it on the two doorposts and the lintel of the houses in which they eat it. ⁸They shall eat the lamb that same night; they shall eat it roasted over the fire with unleavened bread and bitter herbs. ⁹Do not eat any of it raw or boiled in water, but roasted over the fire, with its head, legs, and inner organs. ¹⁰You shall let none of it remain until the morning; anything that remains until the morning you shall burn. ¹¹This is how you shall eat it: your loins girded, your sandals on your feet, and your staff in your hand; and you shall eat it hurriedly. It is the passover of the Lord. ¹²For I will pass through the land of Egypt that night, and I will strike down every firstborn in the land of Egypt, both human beings and animals; on all the gods of Egypt I will execute judgments: I am the Lord. ¹³The blood shall be a sign for you on the houses where you live: when I see the blood, I will pass over you, and no plague shall destroy you when I strike the land of Egypt.

¹⁴This day shall be a day of remembrance for you. You shall celebrate it as a festival to the Lord; throughout your generations you shall observe it as a perpetual ordinance.

ORDER OF WORSHIP

Psalm 116:1–14, 17–19

I love the LORD, because he has heard
   my voice and my supplications.
Because he inclined his ear to me,
   therefore I will call on him as long as I live.
The snares of death encompassed me;
   the pangs of Sheol laid hold on me;
   I suffered distress and anguish.
Then I called on the name of the LORD:
   "O LORD, I pray, save my life!"
Gracious is the LORD, and righteous;
   our God is merciful.
The LORD protects the simple;
   when I was brought low, he saved me.
Return, O my soul, to your rest,
   for the LORD has dealt bountifully with you.
For you have delivered my soul from death,
   my eyes from tears,
   my feet from stumbling.
I walk before the LORD
   in the land of the living.
I kept my faith, even when I said,
   "I am greatly afflicted";
I said in my consternation,
   "Everyone is a liar."
What shall I return to the LORD
   for all his bounty to me?
I will lift up the cup of salvation
   and call on the name of the LORD,
I will pay my vows to the LORD
   in the presence of all his people.
I will offer to you a thanksgiving sacrifice
   and call on the name of the LORD.
I will pay my vows to the LORD
   in the presence of all his people,

in the courts of the house of the LORD,
in your midst, O Jerusalem.
Praise the LORD!
[A time of silence may follow for centering prayer.]

CALL TO CONFESSION

In all humility
and faith in the grace of God,
let us confess our sin.

PRAYER OF CONFESSION

[Allow a lengthy silence between biddings.]
Holy and gracious God,
our sin is too heavy to bear.
Trusting in your mercy,
we lay before you the truth of who we are.

We confess our failure to love as Christ loved . . .

We confess our covetousness and greed . . .

We confess our weakness before temptation . . .

We confess our frailty before the challenges of this world . . .

Merciful God, forgive us.
Heal us, and make us whole,
for the sake of your Son, our Savior,
Jesus Christ, in whose name we pray. **Amen.**

DECLARATION OF FORGIVENESS

Friends, *Exod. 12:13*
your sin will not bring destruction,
for the Lord passes over you with mercy
to save you and deliver you
into God's own loving arms.

PRAYER OF THE DAY

God of exodus and resurrection,
you have promised to write your law on our hearts.

Help us always to remember and celebrate
your faithful presence with us,
that by the power of your Holy Spirit,
we may show forth the light of Christ,
in whose name we pray. **Amen.**

PRAYER FOR ILLUMINATION (OPTIONAL)

SCRIPTURE READING

HOMILY

It is no coincidence that the Jewish feast of Passover almost always overlaps the Christian Holy Week leading up to Easter. Jesus was in Jerusalem to celebrate Passover with his disciples, and the tensions between Jesus and the Jewish leaders as the community prepared for its most significant festival precipitated his arrest and execution. Jesus' last meal with his disciples, which we observe on Maundy Thursday, was either a Passover meal or held on the eve of the Passover, according to different Gospels. As Jewish faith was centered on a Passover meal, so Christian faith also became centered on a meal, the Lord's Supper. In the emergence of the Christian church from the New Testament onward, connections between the Jewish faith and the Christian faith have been strong; and the Passover has been a major feature of this connectedness.

The Passover is the major feast in the Jewish religion. Its beginnings are linked to God's "passing over" the households of Israel, in slavery in Egypt, that were marked with the blood of a lamb "without blemish" on the two doorposts and lintel of the houses. In households without this sign, "every firstborn in the land of Egypt, both human beings and animals," would be struck down by God. The blood on the doorposts assured safety. The Passover meal, celebrated that night, was prescribed by God, and what later became the Passover ritual became central to the Jewish faith to this day. Passover was a prelude to the exodus through which the people were led out of their servitude in Egypt and began their journey to the promised land of Canaan. God commanded the day of the Passover to be remembered and celebrated "as a festival to the LORD; throughout your generations you shall observe it as a perpetual ordinance."

That Jesus' death occurred at Passover is not just historically logical but also theologically significant. Jesus Christ is the "Lamb of God who takes away the sin of the world." As the people of Israel were charged to "remember" and "celebrate" the Passover event, so Jesus commanded the same of his disciples.

The central convictions of the Christian church about who Jesus Christ is as the fulfillment of Old Testament prophecy and God's promised Messiah led to a different understanding of the place of the Passover in the church, compared to its position in Judaism. For the Jews, Passover is a clear summons to remember God's deliverance of Israel from its slavery in Egypt, a liberation into freedom to live as God's covenant people. The church remembered Israel's deliverance, but it also focused on Jesus Christ and the redemption and liberation now to be found in him.

According to the three Synoptic Gospels, the Last Supper occurred on the first night of Passover and, as such, was a Passover Seder meal. Matthew, Mark, and Luke portray Jesus' Last Supper as the new dispensation of an ancient Jewish practice that, in Christianity, becomes the Eucharist. The association of bread with wine, representing Jesus' blood, has clear precedent in Passover. Today's reading from Exodus 12 stipulates that Israel celebrate Passover with unleavened bread (*matzah*) and the blood of the sacrificial lamb.

It is clear that the Eucharist is the Christian analogue to the Jewish celebration of the Passover, but perhaps the most compelling associations between Exodus 12 and the passion of Jesus lie in John's account of the crucifixion. While the Synoptic Gospels agree that the Last Supper was a Seder, the Gospel of John differs in recording Jesus' crucifixion as taking place during the day before the Passover Seder that evening. With this timing, Jesus' crucifixion would be occurring at the same time families would be slaughtering and preparing their paschal lambs.

John's association of Jesus with the paschal lamb is relatively clear. In Exodus 12, the blood of the lamb, spread on the doorposts, allows for the firstborn Israelites to escape death and leads to the redemption of Israel from a life of bondage to a life of freedom. So also, in Jesus Christ, God saves people now. The common meal in Israel and the church attest to God as the initiator of a redemptive relationship that is eternal. This connection was being made by the time of Paul's writings to the church at Corinth, where the Passover lamb and ritual observances are related to Christ and the life of faith: "Clean out the old yeast so that you may be a new batch, as you really are unleavened. For our paschal lamb, Christ, has been sacrificed. Therefore, let us celebrate the festival, not with the old yeast, the yeast of malice and evil, but with the unleavened bread of sincerity and truth" (1 Cor. 5:7–8). In other passages, Jesus' death bears the image of the Passover lamb—like the lamb, his bones are unbroken (John 19:36), and he is a "ransom" (Matt. 20:28) that redeems believers from sin and death.

There are drawbacks to such interpretations of Jesus as the ultimate Passover sacrifice. The most serious is encouraging the view that Christian claims and rites vacated Jewish claims and rites, which led to anti-Judaism and, eventually, anti-Semitism. Nonetheless, imagining what role the Passover narrative plays in the context of Jesus' passion helps establish continuity between God's prior acts of redemption and the redemption we celebrate in Jesus Christ. The annual celebration of Passover served (and continues to serve) to remind the Jewish people of God's past grace and deliverance and also to fuel their hope in the ongoing faithfulness and redemptive work of God. For Christians, the celebration of the Lord's Supper on Holy Thursday, and every time it is celebrated, has this forward-looking dimension as well, since we "proclaim the Lord's death until he comes" (1 Cor. 11:26).

Our Lenten fast is nearing its end, so it is fitting we shift our focus from fasting to feasting. In the instructions for celebrating Passover, God directs the Hebrews to eat the lamb they have sacrificed—to eat God's food, as it were. Likewise, Jesus invites his disciples to partake of his body and blood. No longer fasting as individuals, we gather together for a holy meal that unites us not only with one another and God's people throughout the centuries, but with Christ himself.

PRAYERS OF INTERCESSION

O Lord, we love you, for you have heard our cries.   *Ps. 116:1–2*
Therefore we will call on you as long as we live.

As you delivered our ancestors from slavery   *Exod. 12:1–14*
and led them to a land of promise and plenty,
liberate all who are captive or oppressed
and bring them to a place of abundant life.

As you saved your people from death   *Exod. 12:1–14*
by the blood of the Passover lamb,
redeem us from sin and death
through Jesus Christ, our Passover.

As Jesus Christ our Savior and Lord
stooped down to wash his disciples' feet,
teach us to love and serve one another
with Christlike compassion and humility.

As Christ the Lord has handed on to us
this feast of grace, his body and blood,
**help us to share with all who hunger
the gifts we have received from you.**

O Lord, we love you, for you have heard our cries.   *Ps. 116:1-2*
**Therefore we will call on you as long as we live;
through Jesus Christ our Savior. Amen.**

DISMISSAL

May God, who led Israel out of slavery into freedom,
may Christ, who led us out of death into life,
and the Holy Spirit, who leads us out of fear into boldness,
abide with you in the holy days ahead,
and forevermore.

❧ HOLY WEEK ☙

Introduction

The Paschal *Triduum*, Latin meaning "three days," encompasses the seventy-two-hour period from the evening of Maundy Thursday to sundown on Easter Sunday. Worship gatherings during this period feature the high drama of Jesus' last hours, from betrayal and execution through his time in the tomb and ultimate resurrection. Liturgical practices vary between Roman Catholic, Anglican, and Reformed traditions, often including changes of (or even removal of) the paraments and veiling or removal of crosses and Communion elements. If the Eucharist is performed on Good Friday or Holy Saturday, the elements are typically "reserved" from Maundy Thursday, not consecrated during these days commemorating Christ's death.

The three services outlined in this section include Maundy Thursday, Good Friday, and Holy Saturday. A variety of liturgical elements are offered, as well as the full array of Sermon Helps, to assist in preparing engaging worship services that suit your congregation's style and schedule and that enhance the Holy Week experience for all who participate.

Holy Thursday

Isaiah 50:4–9a

[4]The Lord God has given me
    the tongue of a teacher,
that I may know how to sustain
    the weary with a word.
Morning by morning he wakens—
    wakens my ear
to listen as those who are taught.
[5]The Lord God has opened my ear,
    and I was not rebellious,
    I did not turn backward.
[6]I gave my back to those who struck me,
    and my cheeks to those who pulled out the beard;
I did not hide my face
    from insult and spitting.

[7]The Lord God helps me;
    therefore I have not been disgraced;
therefore I have set my face like flint,
    and I know that I shall not be put to shame;
    [8]he who vindicates me is near.
Who will contend with me?
    Let us stand up together.
Who are my adversaries?
    Let them confront me.
[9]It is the Lord God who helps me;
    who will declare me guilty?

John 13:1-2, 20-32

[1]Now before the festival of the Passover, Jesus knew that his hour had come to depart from this world and go to the Father. Having loved his own who were in the world, he loved them to the end. [2]The devil had already put it into the heart of Judas son of Simon Iscariot to betray him. . . .

[And Jesus said] [20]"Very truly, I tell you, whoever receives one whom I send receives me; and whoever receives me receives him who sent me."

[21]After saying this Jesus was troubled in spirit, and declared, "Very truly, I tell you, one of you will betray me." [22]The disciples looked at one another, uncertain of whom he was speaking. [23]One of his disciples—the one whom Jesus loved—was reclining next to him; [24]Simon Peter therefore motioned to him to ask Jesus of whom he was speaking. [25]So while reclining next to Jesus, he asked him, "Lord, who is it?" [26]Jesus answered, "It is the one to whom I give this piece of bread when I have dipped it in the dish." So when he had dipped the piece of bread, he gave it to Judas son of Simon Iscariot. [27]After he received the piece of bread, Satan entered into him. Jesus said to him, "Do quickly what you are going to do." [28]Now no one at the table knew why he said this to him. [29]Some thought that, because Judas had the common purse, Jesus was telling him, "Buy what we need for the festival"; or, that he should give something to the poor. [30]So, after receiving the piece of bread, he immediately went out. And it was night.

[31]When he had gone out, Jesus said, "Now the Son of Man has been glorified, and God has been glorified in him. [32]If God has been glorified in him, God will also glorify him in himself and will glorify him at once."

ORDER OF WORSHIP

OPENING WORDS / CALL TO WORSHIP
[Members of the congregation bring forward a towel,
a bowl of water, a loaf of bread, and a cup of wine.]
In the growing darkness we gather.
Our Lenten journey has brought us here.
Jesus, our Teacher and Lord, sets before us: *John 13:13*
a towel,
a bowl,
bread,
a cup.

He gives us an example
and a commandment ever-new: *John 13:34–35*
to love one another as he has loved us.
This is how everyone will know
we are his disciples,
when we love each other.

HYMN, SPIRITUAL, OR PSALM

CALL TO CONFESSION
[Water is poured into the font.]
Our hearts are a battleground
between faithfulness and betrayal.
We are weak, but he is steadfast.
Trusting in the unwavering love of Jesus Christ,
who has delivered us from sin and death,
let us confess our sin.

PRAYER OF CONFESSION
Lord Jesus Christ, *John 13:21–30*
how well you know our hearts,
and still you love us—
you have loved us to the end.

We have denied you,
and we have denied our calling
to serve one another.

We have betrayed you,
and we have betrayed your commandment
to love one another.

Pour out your Spirit of grace upon us.
Teach us to love and serve you faithfully
and to love and serve one another
by the example you have set for us;
in your holy name we pray. Amen.

DECLARATION OF FORGIVENESS

Now the Lord Jesus Christ has been glorified, *John 13:31*
and God has been glorified in him.
Now the promise is fulfilled,
and love's redeeming work is done:[1]
In Jesus Christ we are forgiven.
Thanks be to God!

PRAYER OF THE DAY

God of love,
during Holy Week,
we give you thanks for this night
Jesus shared with his disciples.
Between the public parade
and the public charade
is this intimate hour.
Though even now we do not fully understand,
we long to follow his example:
to serve as he served,
to love as he loved.
Jesus promised
that if we know these things and do them,
we will be blessed.
Help us, then, to know and to do
all that Jesus taught.
Though we betray and deny,
we still come seeking a blessing,
for this much we do know:
we cannot live unless you bless us. **Amen.**

HYMN, SPIRITUAL, OR PSALM

PRAYER FOR ILLUMINATION

Gracious God, feed us with your holy Word.
There is much we do not understand,
but we seek you nonetheless,
and in seeking, we will find. **Amen.**

---

1. Charles Wesley, "Christ the Lord Is Risen Today!" *Glory to God* (Louisville, KY: Westminster John Knox Press, 2013), 245.

SCRIPTURE READINGS

SERMON

HYMN, SPIRITUAL, OR PSALM

LITURGY OF FOOT WASHING

John 13:3–10a, 12–17

³Jesus, knowing that the Father had given all things into his hands, and that he had come from God and was going to God, ⁴got up from the table, took off his outer robe, and tied a towel around himself. ⁵Then he poured water into a basin and began to wash the disciples' feet and to wipe them with the towel that was tied around him. ⁶He came to Simon Peter, who said to him, "Lord, are you going to wash my feet?" ⁷Jesus answered, "You do not know now what I am doing, but later you will understand." ⁸Peter said to him, "You will never wash my feet." Jesus answered, "Unless I wash you, you have no share with me." ⁹Simon Peter said to him, "Lord, not my feet only but also my hands and my head!" ¹⁰Jesus said to him, "One who has bathed does not need to wash, except for the feet, but is entirely clean." . . .

¹²After he had washed their feet, had put on his robe, and had returned to the table, he said to them, "Do you know what I have done to you? ¹³You call me Teacher and Lord—and you are right, for that is what I am. ¹⁴So if I, your Lord and Teacher, have washed your feet, you also ought to wash one another's feet. ¹⁵For I have set you an example, that you also should do as I have done to you. ¹⁶Very truly, I tell you, servants are not greater than their master, nor are messengers greater than the one who sent them. ¹⁷If you know these things, you are blessed if you do them."

LITANY OF FOOT WASHING

Loving God,
as Jesus took a basin and poured the water long ago,   *John 13:5*
we bring these basins of water before you.
Bless this water for washing,
and bless the feet of your servants, too.
Wash away the stains and strains of this life, we pray,
that we may walk anew in the ways of Christ.
In true humility, we bend our lives in service to you.

Help us all, by your example, to grow in understanding: *John 13:7*
how we are meant to serve
rather than be served,
for love's sake.
In Christ we pray. **Amen.**

PRAYERS OF INTERCESSION
God of tenderness and compassion,
on the night before he died,
Jesus set a table for his disciples.
Those who would soon deny, betray, and scatter.
All gathered together.
They took off their sandals
and sat down in the presence of their Teacher and Lord,
who washed their feet, one by one.

We pray for people whose feet are tired and dusty from hard labor;
for those whose backs are bent by care and worry;
those laid low by illness or guilt or grief.
Wash away, we pray,
the tiredness of our bodies and souls.
Hold gently in your healing hands
the broken places in our lives and relationships.
Be our company in isolation,
our source of hope in despair,
and the way forward at every dead end.

God of all good gifts,
thank you for setting a table of welcome for everyone;
for making room whether we are faithful or faithless or failures.
We pray that all who are hungry will find enough to eat
and clean water to drink
as we share and live more responsibly.
Teach us to sit down with enemies,
sharing common meals and common hopes.
Make us true servants of yours for the sake of the world.
Teach us to love as you love for the sake of the world.
In Christ's name we pray. **Amen.**

THE EUCHARIST

INVITATION TO THE TABLE

Friends, this is the Table of the Lord.

From the night of his arrest through succeeding generations,
Jesus' disciples have continued to come to the Table for this holy meal.

As he did that night in Jerusalem,
so ever since in all times and places,
Christ meets us here.

We are included in this feast,
whether we are filled with faith or emptied by doubt;
whether we are first among saints, last among scoundrels,
or somewhere in between.

In bread broken and cup poured out,
we remember the full extent of Christ's love for us
and give thanks.

Come, let us join the whole communion of saints
as we keep the feast!

THE GREAT PRAYER OF THANKSGIVING

The Lord be with you.
And also with you.
Lift up your hearts.
We lift them to the Lord.
Let us give thanks to the Lord our God.
It is right to give our thanks and praise.

You sent your Son Jesus for the healing of the world
that we might learn to follow his life of humility
and share in the joy of his glorious resurrection.
And so we praise you as we say:
Holy, holy, holy Lord,
God of power and might,
Heaven and earth are full of your glory.
Hosanna in the highest.
Blessed is the one who comes in the name of the Lord.
Hosanna in the highest.

On the night before he died for us
Jesus gathered his friends for a meal.
He took bread, gave you thanks, broke it,
gave it to them and said,
take, eat, this is my body
which is given for you;
do this in remembrance of me.

After supper he took the cup;
when he had given thanks,
he gave it to them and said,
this cup is the new covenant in my blood
poured out for the forgiveness of sins;
do this in remembrance of me.
Christ has died,
Christ has risen,
Christ will come in glory.

Gracious God,
pour out your Holy Spirit upon us
and upon this bread and wine,
that the bread we break
and the cup we bless
may be for us the communion of the body and blood of Christ.
Unite us with Christ in his suffering
that we may also know his glory,
and strengthen us to reveal your justice,
until all are made whole again
in your kingdom without end.
Amen.

PRAYER AFTER COMMUNION

O Lord our God,
we rise from this table
knowing a love beyond our deserving.
Thank you for giving us a place at your table;
for serving us the bread of life;
for offering to us,
even to us,
the cup of salvation.

In humility and hope,
we go now from this night
to your promised day.
In Christ we pray. **Amen.**

LORD'S PRAYER

HYMN, SPIRITUAL, OR PSALM

DISMISSAL

Jesus has set an example for us:
to serve others as he has served us,
and to love one another as he has loved us.
Go and do likewise,
so everyone can tell
that we are his disciples.
And may the Lord bless you in times of trial
and in times of rejoicing.
Amen.

SERMON HELPS

Isaiah 50:4–9a

THEOLOGICAL PERSPECTIVE

Holy Week now moves into the Triduum, the three holiest days of Maundy Thursday, Good Friday, and Holy Saturday, with the glory of Easter still over the horizon. We continue to read the servant texts christologically as the liturgical context demands, but with caution. In that light, today's reading from Isaiah points squarely to the vicarious suffering of Jesus on our behalf (though not necessarily punishment in our place, v. 6). As in the picture of Jesus' betrayal in today's Gospel from John, Jesus (or the representative covenant figure) is portrayed as embracing the coming suffering with faith and perhaps some foreknowledge of ultimate vindication (vv. 7–9).

This suffering is preceded, however, by a lovely passage about teaching and learning that may give a deeper perspective for our time. The passage describes teaching not merely as a vocation, but as a direct gift from God, from whom the prophet or Jesus receives the tongue of a teacher. The purpose is "to sustain the weary with a word." Liberation theology has taught us to see in such texts God's fundamental option for the poor, and it lies here at the very heart of what it means to be a teacher: it is not an act for personal gain or glory, but of loving service to the neighbor. It is not enough merely to have a gift in the abstract, however. One needs content—something to teach. And so there is the lovely passage about the teacher also being a student as morning by morning he or she is awakened by God to listen like a student.

The application of this text to Jesus as a teacher who speaks words God has given him is not surprising. The conjunction with submitting to violence (v. 6) is more challenging, especially since it follows directly from what has just been said about the gift and vocation of being a teacher who is also a student (vv. 4, 5). The original reference (v. 6) may have been to submitting to a human pedagogy laced with violence of the kind described, such as being smitten on the back. The traditional Christian reading of the text in today's liturgical context, of course, has seen this as a prophetic prefiguring of Jesus being mocked and scourged by the Roman authorities prior to Pilate allowing him to be crucified. Here we already face the ongoing struggle of Christian theology to account for how such horrible acts of violence, culminating in the cross itself, can have ultimate salvific significance.

One contemporary approach that honors this text is to see Jesus as fulfilling the vocation of suffering Israel precisely as a teacher of nonviolent resistance. From the Sermon on the Mount right through the great theological and moral lessons of the paschal mystery itself, we see Jesus, and God in Jesus, refusing the expectations that violence should be corrected by more violence. This is a Messiah who rejects the image of liberating military commander and is, instead, a teacher/student who willingly submits to the violent reaction raised to his teaching and person. This is a God whose power is chiefly shown in not being used, in restraint, in mercy or steadfast love, in forbearance, even in weakness.

It is not new to see these themes in the figure and teaching of Jesus. Despite the terrible involvement of the later church in war and the politics of war, there have always been countervailing trends, including the ban on clergy or monastics bearing arms, even the stories of Francis and Ignatius Loyola discovering the difference between being a soldier for a king and being a soldier for Christ. Teachers of nonviolence through the ages have found inspiration and example in Jesus' teaching and death, from the classic peace churches to Henry David Thoreau to the Fellowship of Reconciliation. In the twentieth century, of course, two teachers of nonviolence stand out: Mohandas Gandhi, a Hindu who found inspiration in Jesus to resist British colonial oppression of India, and Martin Luther King Jr., who rediscovered Jesus in Gandhi's teaching and made nonviolent resistance the core of the

American civil rights movement.[2] The portrait of Jesus as a great teacher of nonviolence has become largely indelible, thanks to these two giants of the movement.

But nonviolence is not passive submission to abuse and repression, though some critics have painted it in this light, especially those espousing revolutionary violence. It is rather a means of resistance against injustice that its practitioners believe has pragmatic as well as moral value, a strategy with a better chance of ultimate success than acts that simply feed an unending cycle of violence, because it relies on vindication by God (vv. 7–9). It is not a call to the oppressed to continue submitting to their victimization, but most especially at the foot of the cross, a deep assertion that there should be no more victims, a primal protest against all abuse and victimization. This has led some theologians to point out that resisting being hurt or protecting one's loved ones from harm, preferably in a nonviolent manner, can also be a true form of martyrdom or witness.[3] The cross is seen in the light of the teacher/student (vv. 4, 5) not as the ultimate celebration and justification of violence and abuse, but as the end of any and all excuses for violence and victimization.[4] In the suffering of Israel and the cross of Jesus, God reveals the nonviolent love at the heart of the divine nature.

ROBERT DAVIS HUGHES III

PASTORAL PERSPECTIVE

"Do you have homework?" Each evening, everyone in my household knew that I would have to ask my girls this question eventually. The homework took them hours sometimes, and sometimes they would have to wake up early in the morning to finish it all. Often, I could not help with the math, having forgotten everything I had ever learned about it, and I felt more than a little useless. Why do they give these kids so much homework? I sometimes wondered resentfully, feeling a little as if the heavy assignments were mine, as if I were the one in school.

A teacher can be a hard taskmaster, but Isaiah 50:4 gives us a different view of a teacher. A teacher is not someone who loads us with more than we

---

2. See Erik H. Erikson, *Gandhi's Truth: The Origins of Militant Nonviolence* (New York: Norton, 1969); Martin Luther King Jr., *Strength to Love* (New York: Harper & Row, 1963).

3. Elizabeth Johnson, *Friends of God and Prophets: A Feminist Theological Reading of the Communion of Saints* (New York: Continuum, 1998), 156.

4. See esp. Walter Wink, *Jesus and Nonviolence: A Third Way* (Minneapolis: Fortress, 2003); Cynthia S.W. Crysdale, *Embracing Travail: Retrieving the Cross Today* (New York: Continuum, 1999), James W. Douglass, *The Nonviolent Coming of God* (Maryknoll, NY: Orbis Books, 1991), and many works by John Howard Yoder.

can carry but someone who actually helps us lighten our load. A teacher is someone who "sustains the weary with a word."

There are few jobs more important than that of a teacher. I remember every one of mine in school, but I also remember many others: scout leaders, choir directors, older children, more experienced clergy. There is so much to know, so many ways in which to be wise, and none of us can really say we are "self taught." We have all had many teachers, and we are the product of all of them.

Jesus' followers called him Teacher. So did everybody else, in fact, because that is what he was, an itinerant rabbi. He was executed for his teaching, although it is not clear whether that was because of its content or because of its effect on people. Did the Romans really care whether or not Jesus claimed to be the Son of God? Probably not; they were not particularly interested in the Jewish religion. However, they would have cared mightily if enough people *thought* he was and if they drew revolutionary inspiration from that belief.

One thing about good teaching is that it is indelible. You can never will yourself *not to know* what you know. We may forget—and we hate how forgetful we become as we age—but we cannot "un-know" things. It may take a while to sink in, but good teaching becomes part of the learner. We grow because of it, and we build on it. We see this process in the unfolding story of the disciples of Jesus: frightened, puzzled, and confused, they are not an impressive bunch at first. However, what Jesus has given them endures in them. Long after the events we remember this week, they go on, from strength to strength, becoming the courageous leaders whose memory we revere still. They little resemble the students they once were. Specifically, they develop the courage to live their lives and even *give* their lives for the survival of the Way, and inspire others to do as well.

This kind of growth can happen only when the teacher brings herself or himself into the encounter. I have said that I remember all my teachers, and that is true; but I also remember that not all of them brought themselves to their encounter with us, and—young as we were—we knew it when they did not. We know that the story of the events of this week was the first story taught by Christians to newer Christians and to would-be Christians, and this must be the reason: the awe with which they greeted the lengths of love to which Jesus would go for his people. He held nothing back from his encounter with us, and every last thing he had was taken—up to and including his life.

Holy Week itself is a teacher. Like any good teacher, it embodies what it teaches. It enables us to enter the story ourselves. We may know a lot about the story. We can probably tell it ourselves. We may even be able to recite parts of it from memory, we have heard it so many times. However, knowing about something is not the same thing as living it, and Holy Week gives us the chance to live it. We walk the story again, its sorrow and pain. We even walk its tedium. We fail to walk it well, often: our minds wander, our spirits fail, we fall asleep instead of remaining present to its demand. We are just like Jesus' disciples.

"Let's do the passion in real time," somebody said, and we did so. Groups of people studied the texts that the earliest Christians told, the story of the execution of Jesus, and together they built a liturgy that would take the same number of hours, from Maundy Thursday to the afternoon of Good Friday. We would leave the church for a garden we would call Gethsemane. There Jesus would be arrested. We would journey through the dark streets to another place; it would be the courtyard of the home of the high priests. Peter would deny Jesus there. In and out of the roles we came and went; sometimes Jesus was a man, sometimes a woman. Different people would play different parts. There would be poetry and song. We would carry a heavy cross up Ninth Avenue, stopping at places that would call to mind the varieties of human experience and human need: a homeless shelter, a soup kitchen, the Port Authority, the police station.

Up all night, after a Holy Week already long and hard. What were we thinking? We realized, as the hours passed, that this was exactly right. The weariness of it was the most important part. It was important to know just how long and hard it was.

A hard taskmaster? An exacting teacher? Certainly Holy Week is challenging, even exhausting: extra worship services, extra study, extra preparation, extra self-examination and self-denial. Does it not sustain? Does it not teach us with a word? Is not that word "love"?

BARBARA CAWTHORNE CRAFTON

EXEGETICAL PERSPECTIVE

Although these verses do not include the word "servant," they are normally characterized as the third Servant Song. An individual speaks. He could be the author of the poetry, but since the identity of the author of these verses remains obscure, it is probably best to identify the speaker as the Servant. The song itself seems a bit disjointed. Verses 4–5a focus on verbal imagery and the relationship of the Servant to God. Then, in verses 5b–9, attention shifts to the interactions between the Servant and those who have attacked him. Nonetheless, in the second section, the Servant reaffirms that the Deity "helps" him, a claim that he makes twice (vv. 7, 9). Vocabulary associated with the human head integrates these two sections (ear [v. 4], cheeks [v. 6]).

The song begins with the Servant making a claim about his tongue. Unfortunately, the Hebrew text is obscure. The RSV translates the first line "The Lord God has given me the tongue of those who are taught," whereas the NRSV translates it, "The Lord God has given me the tongue of a teacher." In the former case (the more literal translation), the Servant appears to be a student; in the latter case, he functions as a teacher. Since the end of verse 4 describes the Servant as one who is taught, the RSV translation, which also views the Servant as one who is taught, is to be preferred.

Hearing and speaking—and in that order—dominate the imagery of verses 4–5a. Every morning, God awakens the "ear" of the Servant so that he can hear something valuable. That which the Servant hears is, no doubt, the "word," a word to help those who are weary. In order for that word to be communicated, the Servant is given a "tongue" by means of which to voice the word. Even though the prophet Jeremiah was also given "words" from the Lord, the emphasis on "teaching" in Isaiah 50:4 offers a different way to think about the way in which God communicates with the Servant. Rather than a herald of the divine council, the Servant is a student of the Lord on a daily basis. And, as was clear in the first Servant Song, the teaching of the Servant extends to the coastlands (Isa. 42:4).

This first section (verses 4–5a) defines the role of the Servant and also his mode of activity. He is supposed to "sustain the weary." Here the Servant exercises a pastoral role. Moreover, it is a role the Servant shares with God. Earlier this same author wrote that God "gives power to the faint" (Isa. 40:29; the word translated "faint" is the same word translated here as "weary"). In Isaiah 49, the author makes clear that God can provide such comfort to the weary through the activity of his Servant. The healing power of the Deity is conveyed through the agency of the Servant.

Further, the Servant is supposed to provide such sustenance through speech. The power of the divine word looms larger here. Both at the beginning and at the end of that literature known as Second Isaiah, the poet reflects about the word of God. In Isaiah 40:8, the author writes, "the word of our God will stand forever." And in the final verses attributed to Second Isaiah, one reads, "My word . . . shall not return to me empty, but it shall accomplish that which I purpose, and succeed in the thing for which I sent it" (Isa. 55:11). The word of the Lord endures and it is preternaturally powerful. This third Servant Song builds on this theology of the divine word and reports that the Servant will have immediate and regular access to the words of the Lord for the purpose of providing comfort to those who are in need of divine succor.

To sustain the weary with a word remains central to life-sustaining religious practice. Sermons and pastoral counseling offer concrete ways for the provision of such powerful words today.

In the second section of the Servant Song (vv. 5b–9a) the first-person personal pronoun becomes particularly prominent ("I," "me," "my"). Clearly the Servant is concerned about what has happened to him. Further, the quiet world of listening and speaking has been transformed into one in which hitting and the pulling of whiskers is a hallmark. What has happened? Unfortunately, there is no easy answer to this question. One might surmise that the Servant has tried to undertake his pastoral office. However, instead of being welcomed, he has been brutalized by those with whom he has interacted. Instead of hearing his words, they have attacked him. The vocabulary used to describe these attacks is particularly telling. His "back," "cheeks," "beard," and "face" have been assaulted. He was surrounded. And, amazingly, he let the attack continue, presumably since he thought that to have done something else would have constituted "rebellion" against the will of the Deity.

In verse 7, the poet overtly alludes to the world of the Psalter. In the individual laments, a psalmist will routinely express the conviction that the Deity will help a person in trouble (e.g., Pss. 13:5; 31:14). The Servant shares that hope and offers a striking image to symbolize it. He has set his "face like flint." (The poetic diction continues to focus on various parts of the human head.) Flint is a tough mineral, used in antiquity for domestic implements and weapons. It could also be used to start fires, when it was struck with a piece of metal. Whether it worked or not, flint's primary quality was its obduracy. Hence, a face like flint would symbolize resoluteness with a sharp edge. Twice, in the final three verses, the Servant affirms that God "helps" him. With God on his side, no adversary can contend successfully against him. This conviction plays itself out in a judgment about the Servant's adversaries. They are like a piece of textile that will be consumed by a moth. This image of impermanence stands in implicit contrast with the tough rock of the Servant and the perduring word of the Deity. The Servant suffers as he attempts his pastoral role, but he remains confident that he will be vindicated.

DAVID L. PETERSEN

HOMILETICAL PERSPECTIVE

The calls come, late in the night, to every pastor's house. "We're at the hospital," a mother whispers. "Something terrible has just happened," a brother cries. "Can you come right away?" a stranger's voice implores. We go, of course, leave the warmth of home and go, aware yet again that we will arrive with empty hands and sorrowful hearts and with no answers whatsoever for another family in the midst of trial, in the midst of suffering, in the midst of fear.

We will join the family in their vigil, find hot coffee or ice-cold water, offer an embrace and a calm presence, we hope. There are a few words we have found useful in the past. We recite prayers that we hope will bring solace. We read from a couple of psalms or recall them by memory. This night at least, we will not dare to offer reasons. Reasons that from one hour to the next a family's story will be forever changed, reasons that some terror has visited nearby? We will have none.

However, we do know what we will not say. We will not say that this time of suffering is deserved. We will not suggest that the shooting, the car accident, the act of random violence, will serve some greater purpose, yet to be revealed. Not only would such a claim abuse the pastoral relationship into which we have been invited. We do not believe it to be true. We do not believe that suffering comes to sustain us, that suffering is some bizarre and unwelcome gift from a whimsical God.

Unless it is Holy Week. Unless we are reading the texts of Christ's passion. Unless we are standing at the foot of the cross and trying to create a theological explanation for the terror of unjust crucifixion. Faced with the harrowing story of a suffering Savior, Christian theology has sought to do what Christian practice would never attempt. We have developed a theory of justified suffering, an atonement theology that gives thanks to God for the necessary pain, humiliation, and finally, death endured by Jesus.

We turn to these very words in the third Servant Song of Isaiah and hear in the midst of the brave anguish of the prophet a whisper of Christ's own voice, insisting that vindication is near for the one who endures. At such a moment, it is necessary to remember that atonement theology understands such a sacrifice to be a singular event in human history. The one who endures such pain for every human sin, such theology declares, frees all who follow in his name from the requirement to bear such a debt. The payment has been made on our behalf. That is the real gift of this Holy Week.

The real danger in this text, the real danger in atonement theology for those who have sought to follow Jesus in every way, is that—as has happened far too often in the history of the church—Christ's struggle turns the ongoing reality of human suffering into meritorious activity. The most painful aspects of the human experience, from slavery to genocide to misogyny and racist violence, have been included by some as necessary suffering, just as Jesus suffered. The seemingly smaller struggles known in nearly every human life, from physical pain to tragedies of the heart, will similarly be named, as a necessary part of submission to the powers in our lives. Even torture will lead in the end to redemption, some will preach this week. If it was so for Christ, it will surely be so for us as well. Since Christ suffered, and my suffering is insignificant compared to his, the present trials are but a foretaste of the glory that awaits us.

So it is that too many clergy, faced with the privilege and responsibility of standing in pulpits this week, have upheld, and even sponsored, real harm in the lives of many. Imagining ourselves to proclaim a gospel truth, we have instead preached submission to the evil powers of this world, mistaking them for God's purpose in human history.

We need not read this text in such a way. The key to finding the good news in this Scripture, and the Gospel passion that in the Christian narrative generally follows it, is to make clear the distinction between the shameful treatment that too many human lives will at some point endure and the notion that those lives are somehow deserving of such shame.

The Servant in Isaiah 50 has been ridiculed and abused, but there is no redeeming goodness in such treatment. It is undeserved. Throughout this indecent behavior, the Servant trusts in God. In that trust, the Servant is vindicated. When the Lord God sides with the one who is oppressed, there is no earthly power that can prevail.

What of the suffering that has been endured? It brings shame upon itself and upon the ones who have acted with violence, with disdain, with hatred. The oppressed one, be that Isaiah or Israel or Jesus himself, is able to be resolute and faithful because of the absolute certainty that God is not the cause of the hurt. God does not abandon the one who is hurting.

The models of suffering that we have witnessed show this to be true, in every generation. So we are back to the hospital bed, the accident site, the place of grief late in the night. We are back with the family who grieves, who fears, who wonders where God could possibly be in such a time. "Right here," we are able to affirm. "God is right here, at our side, weeping as we weep, hurting as we hurt." We are certain of God's presence, even in the hardest of times, because of the constant witness in the biblical record that God has ever been at the side of those who are hurting. Never are God's own abandoned. Somehow, because of God's grace alone, we will be able to stand in faith, even on the very hardest of days.

WILLIAM GOETTLER

John 13:1–2, 20–32

THEOLOGICAL PERSPECTIVE

In John's portrayal of the Last Supper, Jesus both washed the feet of the disciples and announced to them that he would be betrayed. In spite of the facts that the events leading toward the glorification of Jesus had begun, that the disciples had been commissioned to carry out the word, and that the powers of darkness had begun to be defeated, all was not well. Among the disciples, the nascent church's leadership were not altogether clear about where this was all leading. Ambiguity existed within and among them about what Jesus was doing. Peter objected to Jesus' self-humbling action. Did the foot washing represent a Levitical practice of ritual purification at the time of Passover, a kind of commissioning for a new mission, an exemplary act of service of master to followers, or a "sacramental" act? The question is still debated.

What is clear is that the disciples were not unified, faultless, or certain about what all Jesus' words or acts meant after being exposed to them. Doubts still were present in the most loyal disciples. Still, Jesus assured them that those who receive a witness to him through such followers receive what they have to offer from the Lord (13:20). This assurance has been a comfort to missionaries, evangelists, clergy, and witnessing laity over the centuries.

There was also a deeper fissure among the movement's leadership that Jesus had chosen, although the references to parts of it seem to be stated very subtly. On one side was Judas, the symbol of all that would betray Christ and the movement. He accepted the material nourishment Jesus had offered him. Further, he may have lifted his foot to be washed, signaling a readiness to receive this blessing. Jesus' comment that he "lifted his heel" (v. 18) may imply that he had already turned his back on Jesus and was walking away. The two meanings of verse 18 may both be so, suggesting that he received but rejected the meaning of the gift, for he already had plans to leave the movement and to plot Jesus' death. He had also been suspiciously said to advocate giving money to the poor, while he really wanted it for himself or for some movement other than Jesus' that he was dedicated to (12:6). In this connection, he is said to be the son of Simon Iscariot for no apparent reason—unless 13:26 suggests that he was partial to the group of nationalist rebels, the *sicarii*, who advocated violence as a way of "saving" Israel from Roman rule.

On the other side was the one "whom Jesus loved," who remains unnamed in the text. By tradition, of course, he is understood to be the one to whom Jesus gave the care of his mother at the foot of the cross, the one who founded the tradition that authored this Gospel and the other Johannine books, and the son of Zebedee. He is portrayed as the exemplary disciple, the model Christian, who often clarified Jesus' identity and intent to Peter and James but who had the modesty not to name himself before the public. Peter tried to get him to find out from Jesus who the betrayer was, but he got no direct response. Still the inquiry was a signal that there was distrust in the group, and perhaps a self-doubt among the disciples. No wonder Jesus "was troubled in spirit" (v. 21).

In any case, our text says that when Judas received the morsel given by Jesus, a sign that identified the betrayer, even though the other disciples did not recognize it as one, Satan entered him. This has been taken by parts of the tradition as an indication that those who want to appear to be communing with Christ, but have intentions that are contrary to all that is implied in the Last Supper, are open to a diabolical spiritual resolve that is damning. That is "Satan"—the historic personalized word for an objective force that can subjectively distort reason, misguide the will, and misdirect the affections. It represents the shadow of unbelief to the point where it engenders the temptation, accusation, and the slandering of authentic belief, due to the placing of belief in a false center of loyalty. Thus a wrong way, an untruth, and a consequence of death—not "the way, and the truth, and the life" (14:6)—remain the ruling principles of this world. Objective evil remains in the world and can infect those who are thought to be close to the Lord.

Jesus instructed Judas to do what he was going to do quickly. Again the disciples did not understand what was going on or why Jesus had said this. They failed to realize the evil in their own midst. Instead, they attributed Judas's departure as he went out—significantly, into the darkness—as due to his alleged care for the poor or his buying more provisions for the festival. Jesus knew what Judas was up to and recognized that this departure would set in motion the final chapter in his earthly life and the beginning of his heavenly reign. Thus Jesus issued the revealing meaning of it all: his glorification as the eschatological Son of Man was at hand, and in the process God was to be glorified. Further, if God was glorified in Christ, Jesus too would be glorified in God—all at the same time.

This ends our reading, but it may be helpful to note three points about the chapters that follow. First, the earthly sign of this glorification would be the manifestation of love. Jesus issues the commandment that his disciples must love one another and points out that the world will see this as the authenticating mark of fidelity. Second, the disciples still do not fully get the point that Jesus is united with God. Peter, Thomas, and Philip want to know where Jesus is going and what empirical evidence there is for this. Third, Jesus offers his longest discourse to the disciples—but that is another text.

MAX L. STACKHOUSE

PASTORAL PERSPECTIVE

The stakes get higher and higher as we make our way with Jesus through Holy Week. The final stories of Jesus' last days before his crucifixion and death are intense. Today's passage is a story of personal betrayal. The modern listener is quite likely to have experienced betrayal in one form or another. Whether one has been betrayed, or has in fact betrayed another, can influence how one responds to this text.

Jesus and his disciples are reclining around the table when Jesus becomes troubled in spirit. His thoughts move from the importance of humble acts of love, embodied in the washing of feet, to the sting of betrayal. "Very truly, I tell you, one of you will betray me" (v. 21). The disciples are stunned. One of *us* will betray Jesus? Surely not one of *us!* We are his disciples, the ones whom he has called, the ones who have said yes, the ones who have been with him day in and day out. If someone is going to betray Jesus, it is going to be one of *them*, not one of *us*. They look around the table, seeking a sign. Is someone smirking? Does someone have a guilty look upon his (or her) face? Who is averting her (or his) eyes?

The suspense is killing them. Jesus has not shared the identity of the betrayer. Finally, the "disciple whom Jesus loved" pries it out of him. Jesus tells them that the betrayer is the one who will eat the bread that he dips. Amazingly, Judas accepts the bread from Jesus and then immediately leaves to do the dirty work of betrayal. Also amazing is the fact that the other disciples still do not understand what Jesus has said and what is happening at that very hour. They hear Jesus' words. They see Judas accept the morsel and depart. They just cannot wrap their minds around the thought that Judas is off to betray Jesus. Surely he must be off handling administrative details related to the coming festival. If not that, then perhaps he is off helping the poor. This is the kind of behavior they expect from Judas. The disciples are living these events day by day. We, who live on the other side of the crucifixion and resurrection, have always known Judas Iscariot as the one who betrayed Jesus. The disciples, on the other hand, do not know this at the time.

Betrayal always comes as a shock. If you could see betrayal coming, you might be able to arm yourself or defend yourself. The very essence of betrayal comes with the surprise. The sting of betrayal hurts precisely because we cannot imagine this friend or family member or coworker treating us like that.

Modern readers of this story would be consoled a bit if all the disciples had known that Judas was the betrayer. "Of course it was Judas, remember the time when he . . ." "Obviously it is Judas. He never really fit in. He is not like the rest of us." "Judas was just a bad apple."

We like to believe that people who are capable of this kind of betrayal are such horrible human beings that everyone would know and be on guard. This is simply not the case. Only Jesus knew the heart and mind of Judas. Everyone else, apparently, thought he was just a regular guy. When a crime is committed today, folks who live near the perpetrator are often shocked by what they learn. When the reporters talk to the neighbors, you hear the same story over and over again. "He seemed like a real nice guy. I never would have thought he could do that. He lived right next door. Scary."

Many people in our congregations will know the sting of betrayal first-hand. It comes in the form of a gambling addiction or an extramarital affair. Maybe the betrayer says, "I never loved you in the first place." Perhaps it is the relative who pawns family heirlooms to buy drugs. Maybe it is the financial advisor who takes your retirement money and runs. Perhaps the betrayer shared with others what you had offered in confidence. The betrayer may be the company where you worked for years as a loyal employee, only to find yourself in the unemployment line. Maybe the betrayer stole your childhood. Maybe the betrayer is the lover who sent you to the emergency room with a bloody face.

To be betrayed is to be vulnerable to a unique kind of pain. It can take many years to recover from the sting of betrayal. In our pews, there may be folks whose hearts are still raw and in need of healing and wholeness. The betrayal of Jesus may touch upon this pain and present opportunities for pastoral care. The other painful reality in proclaiming this text is the realization that if the disciples could not see betrayal coming from Judas, maybe those who betray are not the demons we imagine them to be. Those who would betray are a lot more like you and me. It is easy to look down our noses at Judas and imagine us among the other eleven disciples. As painful as it is, we must admit that we also are capable of betraying those we love, including our Lord.

In an era when prayers of confession are considered by some to be passé or depressing, we must hold fast to the Christian understanding of sin and acknowledge the pervasiveness of sin in our lives. "All have sinned and fall short of the glory of God," the apostle Paul proclaims in the book of Romans (3:23). The good news of the gospel is that by God's grace we are forgiven.

The Good Friday cross is good news for all of us, who, like Judas, have betrayed both our friends and our God. The resurrection of Jesus is good news for those who seek wholeness and healing from the sting of betrayal.

NANCY A. MIKOSKI

EXEGETICAL PERSPECTIVE

John 13 presents the cosmic conflict between darkness and light in a narration of the Last Supper. Satan enters into Judas (v. 27). The story of Judas's betrayal is reshaped by the author of the Fourth Gospel to highlight the role of Satan and Jesus' ultimate control over the action. In the course of what seems to be an ordinary human meal, the decisive act in the cosmic conflict between God and evil is set in motion. The story ends in verse 30, "So, after receiving the piece of bread, he immediately went out. And it was night." Judas goes out into the night, aligned with the forces of darkness. This is not a reference to the time of day but an intimation of what is coming. Evil, in this case betrayal, takes place under cover of darkness, not in the light. The unit concludes with a Johannine saying about the glorification of the Son of Man.

Jesus' demeanor has been changing as his final week advances, but Thursday is a different day and a different place. The ironic "Now my soul is troubled" of 12:27 bears only superficial likeness to the genuine distress Jesus expresses in chapter 13 when declaring that one of the disciples will betray him. All of Jesus' words of suffering stand under the shadow of the cross, but this particular affliction occurs in the context of a meal, where fellowship is sacred and social bonds are reinforced. Betrayal takes place within the innermost circle. Judas is a friend who becomes a traitor. Nothing prepares us for betrayal by friends—especially not in the heart of our most sacred time, Passover for Jesus, Holy Week for us. Like the troubled passage of chapter 12, the betrayal provides another locus for the glorification of God and, this time, of the Son of Man.

John's account of the Last Supper features the unknown Beloved Disciple. Historically this has been thought to be a modest oblique reference to the author, assumed to be the apostle John. More recently, other identities have been proposed for this figure: John (author or not), Lazarus, and Mary Magdalene; but there is nothing in the text that points definitively to an identity. Perhaps the Beloved Disciple is a composite symbol whose actions and discipleship mirror ways for the Johannine community to follow Jesus.

As is common in John, the meal becomes an occasion for extended discourse. Here Jesus inaugurates a series of final talks he will give in John's Gospel. These Farewell Discourses are Jesus' last will and testament to disciples and listeners in the Gospel. Of this particular form there are many examples in the Bible: Moses (Deut. 33), Paul (Acts 20:17–38), Stephen (Acts 7:2–60). These discourses function in the life of the ongoing community just as the "I Have a Dream" speech of Dr. Martin Luther King Jr. has. We can see the process as it evolves, in the reception of "The Last Lecture" by Professor Randy Pausch, who at 48 was dying of cancer; this received eight million viewings on YouTube by the end of 2008.

John's Gospel shows Jesus preparing his community for the death that is about to happen, but John develops this distinctive material of Jesus' last speeches more to reinforce an understanding of that death for the Johannine community. Material for these discourses comes from sayings of Jesus spoken earlier in the Gospel. We have discussed the lifting up on the cross as exaltation. The Son of Man will be lifted up on the cross, but to the eyes of faith, he will be lifted, exalted into God's glory (12:32). The path through the darkness of what is to follow will lead to the divine presence. Without diminishing its pain, John transforms the hour into an hour of celebration and victory (12:31–33).

John 13:31–32 is a typically Johannine statement in which the strands of meaning are interwoven into a dense cord. After Judas departs, Jesus begins, "Now the Son of Man has been glorified." This "now," referring to the complex of events that Judas's departure has initiated, is the same "now" as in 12:27. So it is best to take the "now" in 13:31 as also referring to the whole event that has arrived. In this event God will be glorified "in" the Son of Man, because Jesus will be bringing his mission to completion, and God and Jesus engage in acts of mutual glorification. Later Jesus will invoke this reciprocal glorification in 17:1, 4, citing the completion of the work God has given him. On the cross he will declare: "It is finished" (19:30). The prayer in 17:5 sheds further light on what is being said here: the Father glorifies the Son "with himself" (NRSV "in your own presence"), that is, with the glory that is the divine presence.

Simply put, the Son will seem to enter darkness, but this is the pathway through which God will bring the Son home and surround him with glory. That glory is nothing other than God's own being. The lectionary ends the reading here, with an abrupt dissection of the discourse. The somewhat convoluted statement in verses 31–32 indicates that Jesus knows he has reached the end of the journey and will soon be rewarded with the divine presence. The reward is not things or places but the person of God. Oneness with God, not absorption into God, is the goal and the reward, as it has also been the characteristic of Jesus' whole life. That is why John can also say that already in his life we saw God's glory (1:14). Jesus' suffering *is* his glory.

The continuing discourse in verses 33–35, however, suggests an organic connection between Jesus' glorification of God and the disciples' exercise of love for one another. The lectionary notwithstanding, the glorification of God does not cease with the withdrawal of Jesus from the earth.

DEIRDRE J. GOOD

HOMILETICAL PERSPECTIVE

This passage represents one of the ways in which Holy Week will not allow us to dodge a confrontation with the power of evil in humanity.

Not long ago an ancient manuscript that purported to be the Gospel according to Judas was discovered and caused considerable discussion. We have often wondered about Judas and his role in the final week of Jesus' earthly life. Why in the world did he betray Jesus? What would motivate a disciple who had been with Jesus since early in his ministry to turn him in to the authorities? The mysterious manuscript is purported to have told the story in a very different way than do our canonical Gospels. It does not picture Judas as a betrayer but as a colleague. Judas and Jesus were soul mates, and Jesus asked Judas to betray him to the religious officials. It was Judas's love of his friend Jesus that motivated his dastardly act!

The smoke that arose from the heated discussion ignited by the so-called Gospel of Judas has now mostly settled. However, nearly every Holy Week many of us search again to understand Judas's role in the passion story. The Gospel of Judas is just the newest of many theories that have been proposed for his cowardly deed, and we are still in the dark. Preceding the recent uproar concerning Judas, there had already been various theories advanced as to why Judas betrayed Jesus.

—The accounts of Judas in the Gospels seem content with the theory that he turned Jesus in for the money (Mark 14:10–11).
—Some have sought to understand Judas by means of his full name, Judas Iscariot. Iscariot, they claim, represents a rebellious Jewish group known as the *sicarii,* those who carried swords in order to be ready for the Messiah's rebellion against Roman authorities. Judas hoped to force Jesus to initiate a revolt against the foreign oppressors.
—While we commonly know Judas as "the betrayer," the Greek word in Mark 14:21 simply means "the one who hands over."
—Others have been content to explain Judas's act as predestined by God as a means to have Jesus crucified for human salvation.

John's portrayal of Judas is similar to the ones we find in the other Gospels. John's Gospel, however, suggests that Judas is present when Jesus washes the disciples' feet (13:1–11), and before he leaves, Jesus gives him a morsel of bread (a symbol of hospitality—13:26–27). John does not mention the money the religious establishment gave Judas to turn his master in. The power of Satan alone might have motivated Judas to do his vicious deed. Of course, we will never know what Judas's goal was. John's insistence that Satan is the power behind Judas's act emphasizes the fact that Jesus' mission could only be accomplished by a cosmic power and that Jesus knew all along what his fate was to be.

For the Fourth Evangelist, Judas is controlled by the power of evil in the world represented by the theme of darkness in contrast to light. So, upon his departure from the table, "he immediately went out. And it was night." Hence, for John, Judas represents the evil side of the good-evil dualism. (See John 1:5.)

We will eventually celebrate Christ's victory over death, but only after we have walked in the darkness of his betrayal and crucifixion. Our contemporary world does not need a lesson in the reality of evil. It is all too evident for us. Watch the evening news! There is a steady stream of murders, thefts, and angry outbursts. We are confronted with the actions of those who will stop at nothing to achieve their goals. It is, then, all the more important that we focus on the meaning of the betrayal and crucifixion. Holy Week is premised on the assumption that we need always to have in mind that our struggle is with mighty forces that led to the cross. Whether we should think of the force of evil as a cosmic figure (Satan or the Devil) or as the accumulation of the evil that roots in humanity finally does not matter. However you may conceive of this force, we cannot deny its reality.

The Academy Award–winning movie *Crash* makes much the same point on the individual level. The movie takes a frightening look at our failures to live together without the stigma of prejudice—prejudice of all kinds. As the plot of the movie progresses, however, we gradually begin to think that at least one character in the story seems free of any such prejudice. However, in the movie's tragic conclusion, that same character demonstrates the prejudice against which he has been struggling through the whole story. We are left stunned! And we cannot escape the conclusion that no one is free of evil.

Most of us have probably found ourselves acting (or thinking) in ways that are the opposite of what we hold to be good. Maybe it is our secret desire for vengeance against another. Maybe it is the temptation to act in a way that benefits us, even though it hurts others. Maybe it is simply trying to avoid another person who is desperately lonely and troubled. None of us can claim to be free of all forms of evil.

In recent years we have been invited to label the behavior of others and of whole nations as evil. President George W. Bush spoke of the "axis of evil." After he had used the label a number of times for other nations, a representative of one of those nations followed him to the podium at the United Nations' General Assembly. From the podium, he spoke of the odor of Satan still lingering where our president had stood! Whatever you think of national leaders, the truth is that no one nation or people can claim to be pure and free of evil.

As we move toward the conclusion of another Holy Week, not one of us can claim to be free of evil, but in Christ we can find a grace that is stronger than that evil.

ROBERT KYSAR

Good Friday

Isaiah 52:13–53:12

[13]See, my servant shall prosper;
 he shall be exalted and lifted up,
 and shall be very high.
[14]Just as there were many who were astonished at him
 —so marred was his appearance, beyond human semblance,
 and his form beyond that of mortals—
[15]so he shall startle many nations;
 kings shall shut their mouths because of him;
for that which had not been told them they shall see,
 and that which they had not heard they shall contemplate.
[53:1]Who has believed what we have heard?
 And to whom has the arm of the Lord been revealed?
[2]For he grew up before him like a young plant,
 and like a root out of dry ground;
he had no form or majesty that we should look at him,
 nothing in his appearance that we should desire him.
[3]He was despised and rejected by others;
 a man of suffering and acquainted with infirmity;
and as one from whom others hide their faces
 he was despised, and we held him of no account.

[4]Surely he has borne our infirmities
 and carried our diseases;
yet we accounted him stricken,
 struck down by God, and afflicted.
[5]But he was wounded for our transgressions,
 crushed for our iniquities;
upon him was the punishment that made us whole,
 and by his bruises we are healed.
[6]All we like sheep have gone astray;
 we have all turned to our own way,
and the Lord has laid on him
 the iniquity of us all.

⁷He was oppressed, and he was afflicted,
 yet he did not open his mouth;
like a lamb that is led to the slaughter,
 and like a sheep that before its shearers is silent,
 so he did not open his mouth.
⁸By a perversion of justice he was taken away.
 Who could have imagined his future?
For he was cut off from the land of the living,
 stricken for the transgression of my people.
⁹They made his grave with the wicked
 and his tomb with the rich,
although he had done no violence,
 and there was no deceit in his mouth.

¹⁰Yet it was the will of the Lord to crush him with pain.
 When you make his life an offering for sin,
 he shall see his offspring, and shall prolong his days;
through him the will of the Lord shall prosper.
 ¹¹Out of his anguish he shall see light;
he shall find satisfaction through his knowledge.
 The righteous one, my servant, shall make many righteous,
 and he shall bear their iniquities.
¹²Therefore I will allot him a portion with the great,
 and he shall divide the spoil with the strong;
because he poured out himself to death,
 and was numbered with the transgressors;
yet he bore the sin of many,
 and made intercession for the transgressors.

John 18:28–19:30

²⁸Then they took Jesus from Caiaphas to Pilate's headquarters. It was early in the morning. They themselves did not enter the headquarters, so as to avoid ritual defilement and to be able to eat the Passover. ²⁹So Pilate went out to them and said, "What accusation do you bring against this man?" ³⁰They answered, "If this man were not a criminal, we would not have handed him over to you." ³¹Pilate said to them, "Take him yourselves and judge him according to your law." The Jews replied, "We are not permitted to put any-one to death." ³²(This was to fulfill what Jesus had said when he indicated the kind of death he was to die.)

³³Then Pilate entered the headquarters again, summoned Jesus, and asked him, "Are you the King of the Jews?" ³⁴Jesus answered, "Do you ask this on your own, or did others tell you about me?" ³⁵Pilate replied, "I am not a Jew, am I? Your own nation and the chief priests have handed you over to me. What have you done?" ³⁶Jesus answered, "My kingdom is not from this world. If my kingdom were from this world, my followers would be fighting to keep me from being handed over to the Jews. But as it is, my kingdom is not from here." ³⁷Pilate asked him, "So you are a king?" Jesus answered, "You say that I am a king. For this I was born, and for this I came into the world, to testify to the truth. Everyone who belongs to the truth listens to my voice." ³⁸Pilate asked him, "What is truth?"

After he had said this, he went out to the Jews again and told them, "I find no case against him. ³⁹But you have a custom that I release someone for you at the Passover. Do you want me to release for you the King of the Jews?" ⁴⁰They shouted in reply, "Not this man, but Barabbas!" Now Barabbas was a bandit.

¹⁹:¹Then Pilate took Jesus and had him flogged. ²And the soldiers wove a crown of thorns and put it on his head, and they dressed him in a purple robe. ³They kept coming up to him, saying, "Hail, King of the Jews!" and striking him on the face. ⁴Pilate went out again and said to them, "Look, I am bringing him out to you to let you know that I find no case against him." ⁵So Jesus came out, wearing the crown of thorns and the purple robe. Pilate said to them, "Here is the man!" ⁶When the chief priests and the police saw him, they shouted, "Crucify him! Crucify him!" Pilate said to them, "Take him yourselves and crucify him; I find no case against him." ⁷The Jews answered him, "We have a law, and according to that law he ought to die because he has claimed to be the Son of God."

⁸Now when Pilate heard this, he was more afraid than ever. ⁹He entered his headquarters again and asked Jesus, "Where are you from?" But Jesus gave him no answer. ¹⁰Pilate therefore said to him, "Do you refuse to speak to me? Do you not know that I have power to release you, and power to crucify you?" ¹¹Jesus answered him, "You would have no power over me unless it had been given you from above; therefore the one who handed me over to you is guilty of a greater sin." ¹²From then on Pilate tried to release him, but the Jews cried out, "If you release this man, you are no friend of the emperor. Everyone who claims to be a king sets himself against the emperor."

¹³When Pilate heard these words, he brought Jesus outside and sat on the judge's bench at a place called The Stone Pavement, or in Hebrew Gabbatha. ¹⁴Now it was the day of Preparation for the Passover; and it was about

noon. He said to the Jews, "Here is your King!" [15]They cried out, "Away with him! Away with him! Crucify him!" Pilate asked them, "Shall I crucify your King?" The chief priests answered, "We have no king but the emperor." [16]Then he handed him over to them to be crucified.

So they took Jesus; [17]and carrying the cross by himself, he went out to what is called The Place of the Skull, which in Hebrew is called Golgotha. [18]There they crucified him, and with him two others, one on either side, with Jesus between them. [19]Pilate also had an inscription written and put on the cross. It read, "Jesus of Nazareth, the King of the Jews." [20]Many of the Jews read this inscription, because the place where Jesus was crucified was near the city; and it was written in Hebrew, in Latin, and in Greek. [21]Then the chief priests of the Jews said to Pilate, "Do not write, 'The King of the Jews,' but, 'This man said, I am King of the Jews.'" [22]Pilate answered, "What I have written I have written." [23]When the soldiers had crucified Jesus, they took his clothes and divided them into four parts, one for each soldier. They also took his tunic; now the tunic was seamless, woven in one piece from the top. [24]So they said to one another, "Let us not tear it, but cast lots for it to see who will get it." This was to fulfill what the scripture says,

"They divided my clothes among themselves,
    and for my clothing they cast lots."
[25]And that is what the soldiers did.

Meanwhile, standing near the cross of Jesus were his mother, and his mother's sister, Mary the wife of Clopas, and Mary Magdalene. [26]When Jesus saw his mother and the disciple whom he loved standing beside her, he said to his mother, "Woman, here is your son." [27]Then he said to the disciple, "Here is your mother." And from that hour the disciple took her into his own home.

[28]After this, when Jesus knew that all was now finished, he said (in order to fulfill the scripture), "I am thirsty." [29]A jar full of sour wine was standing there. So they put a sponge full of the wine on a branch of hyssop and held it to his mouth. [30]When Jesus had received the wine, he said, "It is finished." Then he bowed his head and gave up his spirit.

[These texts are offered to supplement, but not necessarily replace, the ancient and ecumenical liturgies of Good Friday, particularly the Solemn Intercession and the Solemn Reproaches of the Cross, which are found in the service books of many denominations.]

ORDER OF WORSHIP

OPENING WORDS / CALL TO WORSHIP

Today God makes common cause with our human suffering.
**We read the Scriptures, sing the hymns, feel the feelings
of the day Christ died.**
Suffering is not rational. It has no answer.
But in the cross God meets us in our suffering.
From this day forward we know that
there is nowhere we can go
where God is not with us.

HYMN, SPIRITUAL, OR PSALM

CALL TO CONFESSION

The promise of our faith is that
if we call on the name of the Lord,
our God will remember our sin no more.
Therefore, let us confess our wrongdoing.

PRAYER OF CONFESSION

*[This brief litany is modeled after the Solemn Reproaches of the Cross, a
Good Friday tradition that can be traced to the Middle Ages. Here the
Solemn Reproaches are streamlined and simplified for contemporary
worship.]*
The cross that held the Savior of the world.
**Holy God,
holy and mighty,
holy immortal one,
have mercy on us.**

The cross that held the Savior of the world.
**Holy God,
holy and mighty,
holy immortal one,
have mercy on us.**

The cross that held the Savior of the world.
**Holy God,
holy and mighty,**

**holy immortal one,
have mercy on us.**

My people, my people,
why have you forsaken me?
Answer me!
I delivered you from captivity
through the water of baptism;
but you handed me over to my captors,
giving me up to die;
and you have made a cross for your Savior.
Lord, have mercy.

I fed you in the wilderness
with the bread of life from heaven;
but you are consumed with desire,
biting and devouring one another;
and you have made a cross for your Savior.
Lord, have mercy.

I claimed you as my family,
as branches of my vine;
but you cut off my chosen ones,
spilling innocent blood;
and you have made a cross for your Savior.
Lord, have mercy.

I spoke to you my Word,
the promise of my love for all;
but you silence my prophets,
refusing to hear my voice;
and you have made a cross for your Savior.
Lord, have mercy.

I came to be your light,
to overcome the darkness;
but you remain in the shadows,
hiding your light from the world;
and you have made a cross for your Savior.
Lord, have mercy.

I gave you the keys to my realm
and welcomed you inside;
but you turn away strangers,
closing the doors that I open;
and you have made a cross for your Savior.
Lord, have mercy.

I offered you my peace
and clothed you with compassion;
but you divide my garments,
tearing apart what I design;
and you have made a cross for your Savior.
Lord, have mercy.

I sent my Holy Spirit
to empower you with grace;
but you trust your own devices,
squandering my good gifts;
and you have made a cross for your Savior.
Lord, have mercy.

I came to dwell among you
as the Word made flesh;
but you ignore neighbors in need,
failing to recognize my face;
and you have made a cross for your Savior.
Lord, have mercy.

DECLARATION OF FORGIVENESS

Take heart, for our Lord Jesus Christ, the son of God,
understands our human experience,
felt the depth of our pain   *John 19:28–30*
and sympathizes with our weakness.
He deals gently with the ignorant and the wayward
and is the source of our eternal salvation.

PRAYER OF THE DAY

We stand near the cross, O God—   *John 19:25–27*
disturbed, distraught, discouraged.

Yet we gather here as disciples,
those whom Jesus loves.
In the face of such suffering,
show us the face of our Savior.
In the shadow of such evil,
show us the light of your grace
On this day of great solemnity,
let us stand as witnesses
to your great love for all the world,
revealed in the outstretched arms
of Jesus Christ our Lord. **Amen.**

HYMN, SPIRITUAL, OR PSALM

PRAYER FOR ILLUMINATION

"I came to testify to the truth," the Lord said. *John 18:37–38*
"What is truth?" we reply.
Open our hearts to know your truth, Lord.
Speak your truth to us now. **Amen.**

SCRIPTURE READINGS

SERMON

HYMN, SPIRITUAL, OR PSALM

PRAYERS OF INTERCESSION

[A time of silence follows each petition.]
Redeeming God,
we cry out to you
for the suffering of the world.

We pray for the church, both near and far,
that we may always be on the side of the oppressed and
    not the oppressors.

We pray for the gift of faith,
that we may put our trust in you,
even in times of suffering.

And so we pray for those who suffer,
that they may feel your presence with them.

We pray for those who care for those who struggle
and for those who are dying,
that, through us, you may strengthen them
　　in their service.

We pray for those who mourn,
that they will feel your comfort
as they kneel at the foot of the cross.

We pray for all who wrestle with their faith,
struggling to know if you are with them,
that your face will not be hidden from them.

We pray for all the families and all the nations of the earth,
that they shall remember and turn toward you,
and find peace.

We pray in the name of our great High Priest,
Jesus Christ,
your Son and our Lord. **Amen.**

SENDING

*[Traditionally, the blessing is omitted on Good Friday, since the service
continues at the Easter Vigil or on Easter Sunday. Service may close with
the Stripping of the Altar, as paraments, the processional cross, Bible, and
other altarware are carried out of the sanctuary in silence. All may depart
in silence when Stripping of the Altar is complete.]*

SERMON HELPS

Isaiah 52:13–53:12

THEOLOGICAL PERSPECTIVE

So great is the significance of this passage for Christian theology that it has led many interpreters to dub Isaiah a "fifth evangelist." Indeed, it is probably difficult for anyone acquainted with the New Testament not to hear this fourth Servant Song as a description of the suffering and exaltation of Jesus Christ. The difficulty of determining any original historical referent for the Servant in this text has only added to its intrigue.

As Joseph Blenkinsopp points out, a number of the theological ideas of the passage are already nascent in older or contemporaneous biblical texts, such as the suffering of prophetic figures, God's servants as intercessors for the people, and the power of the righteous to influence the fate of the unrighteous.[1] The revelatory nature of the Servant's work—the way it makes the world see and hear (52:15)—also reverses the people's earlier failure to see or hear in Isaiah 6:9 and other verses.

The real theological innovation of the passage is that the suffering of God's innocent Servant can be a *substitute* for that of the truly guilty. That surprising and counterintuitive theme pervades Isaiah 53, but the author expresses it particularly graphically with the image of the *asham* sacrifice in 53:10. That sacrifice is specifically to make atonement with God for sin (Lev. 5:6, etc.); typically it is a sheep, and nowhere else in the Old Testament is the term used in any way comparable to Isaiah 53. Thus, this passage is the key proof text for the image of Jesus as the Lamb of God who by his sacrifice takes away the sin of the world (John 1:29, 36; 1 Pet. 1:18–19; Rev. 5:6; 7:14). The doctrine of Christ's death as a substitutionary, atoning sacrifice was developed most famously by Anselm of Canterbury in *Cur Deus Homo (Why God Became Man).* Some theologians have expressed discomfort with substitutionary atonement, as if it made God a "cosmic child abuser," and the idea that "it was the will of the LORD to crush [his Servant] with pain" (53:10) is indeed a potentially troubling one. However, from a Trinitarian perspective, Christ's suffering death is better understood as a gracious choice of God to take on the punishment for human sin. In his *Commentary on John,* Origen of Alexandria[2] combined the references to Christ as sacrificial Lamb with

---

1. Joseph Blenkinsopp, *Isaiah 40–55,* Anchor Bible 19A (New York: Doubleday, 2002), 119.
2. Origen, *Commentary on the Gospel according to John Books 1–10,* trans. Ronald E. Heine, vol. 80 in *The Fathers of the Church: A New Translation* (Washington, DC: The Catholic University of America Press, 1989), 242–44.

Hebrews 8:1 and John 10:18 to portray Christ as both the sacrifice *and* the high priest who offered it.

The idea of suffering as redemptive can be problematic in other ways, however. First Peter 2:18–25 held up the Suffering Servant as a model for slaves' submission to their masters. In the wake of the Holocaust, both Jewish and Christian theologians have called into question the idea that suffering can be redemptive. Indeed, there are times when suffering is simply evil and must be resisted rather than embraced. The suggestion that other people's suffering is redemptive is particularly dangerous; it risks making the observer complicit in the evil. True imitation of Christ means choosing holiness for oneself despite any cost in suffering. Christ's death for our sins does not mean saying thanks and sitting on the sidelines: "If any want to become my followers," Jesus said, "let them . . . take up their cross and follow me" (Mark 8:34).

It is possible that Jesus himself invoked this text to explain his mission; in Mark 10:45 he says he came "to give his life as a ransom for many." However in Luke 22:35–37 he uses Isaiah 53:9 to portray himself as a political radical (cf. Matt. 10:34).

When the authors of the New Testament looked to the Scriptures for explanations of the death of the Messiah, Isaiah 52:13–53:12 was one of the most important passages they used. Paul was the first we know of who did this, invoking 53:9–11 to explain atonement in Romans 4:22–25 by identifying Jesus as the one "who was handed over to death for our trespasses and was raised for our justification" (cf. 2 Cor. 5:21; 1 Cor. 15:3–4). Paul also took Isaiah's reference to the incredible news about the Servant (52:14–53:1) to emphasize the importance of spreading the gospel (Rom. 10:14–17; cf. Rom. 15:18–21, which cites the Septuagint translation of Isa. 52:15).

The evangelists also read the passage in new and interesting ways. John found in Isaiah 53:1 an explanation for the disciples' failure to believe despite all the signs that Jesus had performed in their presence (John 12:36–38). The failure of the Servant's contemporaries to understand who he was until after his suffering death is a major theme of the passage, and might press readers to consider the ways in which they too overlook the gifts of those whom society deems deformed or unattractive. As Augustine wrote, "A root is not beautiful, but contains within itself the potentiality for beauty"—that is, it grows into a tree, which Augustine meant to symbolize the church.[3]

---

3. St. Augustine, *The Works of Saint Augustine: A Translation for the Twenty-First Century*, part 3: Sermons, vol. 2: Sermons 20–50, trans. Edmund Hill, ed. John E. Rotelle (Brooklyn, NY: New York City Press, 1990), 244.

Matthew understood Jesus' healings as the fulfillment of Isaiah 53:4's reference to "bearing our infirmities and carrying our diseases" (Matt. 8:14–17). Thus the present-day believers might see this as a warrant for their own ministries of health and healing.

One of the most famous New Testament references to the passage is Acts 8:26–38, in which an Ethiopian eunuch reads Isaiah 53:7–8 and is converted, asking Philip to baptize him. It may not be immediately clear why these verses spoke to the eunuch, but I suggest that he saw himself in the Servant's lack of offspring (Gk. *genea*, "generation," 8:33 NRSV). Extrapolating this point much more broadly, the Song's images of suffering, as applied to Jesus, emphasize Christ's solidarity with those who suffer in many ways.

CHRISTOPHER B. HAYS

PASTORAL PERSPECTIVE

While it is customary to preach from the Gospel reading on Good Friday, one cannot find a better outline of the passion narratives than this fourth Servant Song of Isaiah. Through the use of this wrenchingly beautiful poem in Isaiah, we may begin to undermine those charges of anti-Judaism with which we have for many years been particularly besieged during Holy Week. Such has often been the pressure that one felt compelled to make a hundred disclaimers before publicly reading one of the Gospel narratives. Be careful, for the use of this text provides an implicit, not an explicit, benefit.

Here is a pastoral opportunity not to be overlooked. The stories of Jesus' crucifixion are embedded with descriptions of this Servant: "He was despised and rejected by others; a man of suffering. . . . He was oppressed, and he was afflicted, yet he did not open his mouth. . . . They made his grave with the wicked and his tomb with the rich; although he had done no violence, and there was no deceit in his mouth." The references are pointed. Yes, we can argue that the Gospel writers had the Servant Songs beside them as they composed their narratives. What they had beside them were their Scriptures—their holy Scriptures that became our Scriptures also. After all, these were Jews, writing about the extraordinary life, death, and resurrection of a Jew. What could have been more natural—or faithful and inspired—than to use their own Scriptures to help them describe those awe-full, degrading, and miraculous events of Good Friday and Easter?

This Servant Song is redolent also with what we might call New Testament theology—or at least the theology and interpretation that undergird the New Testament understanding of Jesus' crucifixion and resurrection. The first verse of the text, before describing the suffering, the vicarious atonement, the death and burial of the Servant, says that this Servant will prosper and be lifted up, exalted. These words call to mind Paul's letter to the Philippian Christians when he ends his own "servant song" about the suffering and self-emptying of Jesus: "Therefore God also highly exalted him and gave him the name that is above every name" (Phil. 2:9).

Then there is Paul's letter to Corinth, with his meditation on wisdom and power. In that letter he declares that "God chose what is foolish in the world to shame the wise; God chose what is weak in the world to shame the strong; God chose what is low and despised in the world . . . to reduce to nothing things that are, so that no one might boast in the presence of God" (1 Cor. 1:27–29). The Servant in Isaiah "shall startle many nations; kings shall shut their mouths because of him" (Isa. 52:15).

Finally there is the pivot of the entire passage, which comes twice. It is the claim that keeps this Servant from simply being one more victim in a world of victims: "[for] we accounted him stricken, struck down by God and afflicted" (53:4), or again, "Yet it was the will of the Lord to crush him with pain" (53:10). This point is emphasized by Paul Hanson when he writes:

> The servant was not a pawn in the hands of an arbitrary god but one who committed himself freely to a deliberate course of action. Not a victim of circumstances, not a pathetic casualty in the ruthless atrocities that have always been part of human existence, but one who willingly and obediently followed the vision of God's order of righteousness in defiance of all worldly wisdom and human cowardice. Such was the Servant who chose to make his life an instrument of God's healing.[4]

While it may have been the will of the Lord to bruise him (the old translation), it was the willingness of the Servant to pour himself out to death that makes this startling—to kings as well as to us. This makes Good Friday a day to startle the powers that be with the claims of reality that we find in this fourth Servant Song. This same reality became Jesus the Messiah, the one we say was born of a woman as is every child, and yet was born of God's spirit as is no other child.[5]

He is the one who grew to maturity and healed the sick, preached the kingdom of God through repentance and forgiveness, calmed the storm, and cast out demons as fierce as Legion. However, when the time came for him to be handed over, to be delivered up, Jesus did not raise the sword in

---

4. Paul D. Hanson, *Isaiah 40–66* (Louisville, KY: John Knox Press, 1995), 160
5. *A Declaration of Faith* (Presbyterian Church in the United States, 1977), 6.

his defense or call upon legions of angels. Rather, as he hung dying on the cross, he said with simplicity, "Father, forgive them; for they do not know what they are doing" (Luke 23:34). Bystanders cursed him, mocked him, and spat upon him. So God declared that at the name of Jesus, every knee should bow and every tongue "confess that Jesus is Lord [and Caesar is not], to the glory of God the Father" (Phil. 2:11).

Here is the good news of Good Friday. Here is God in the flesh. Here is the counternarrative to the world's tired old narrative that might makes right and that those who live by the sword will really live. Not so, says the Lord of Hosts; not so, says YHWH; not so, says Jesus; but Jesus says it, not in prophetic word, but in prophetic deed. The mouths of kings have been shut in wonder (and often in rage) ever since.

O. BENJAMIN SPARKS

EXEGETICAL PERSPECTIVE

These fifteen lines, known as the fourth Servant Song, are among the most compelling and controversial in the Hebrew Bible. Christians have long understood these verses to predict the coming of Jesus the Messiah and, as a result, the passage is read on Good Friday as a reference to Jesus' suffering and crucifixion. While this understanding of this passage makes sense in the context of the passion narratives, it is our purpose to gain the perspective of the author and culture from which the Isaiah passage comes. In so doing, we enrich our understanding of not only Isaiah 52:13–53:12 but also its relation to Good Friday.

We begin by noting that the Suffering Servant of our passage is associated with the appearance of the Servant ('ebed) in other parts of Second Isaiah. Scholars generally agree that the book of Isaiah can be divided into two, possibly three, distinct parts that represent different historical periods. First Isaiah (chaps. 1–39) is understood to come predominately from the original prophet and can be dated to the last half of the eighth century BCE.

Isaiah 40–66 constitutes Second Isaiah, which was likely produced in the late exilic and early postexilic period (ca. 550–500 BCE). Some scholars identify chaps. 56–66 as Third Isaiah. It is the context of the exile and early postexilic period that helps to explain the content and focus of our Good Friday passage. As literature formed in the crucible of exile and its attendant traumas and disappointments, Second Isaiah struggles to understand the tragedies in the recent past.

The period subsequent to the Babylonian invasion and destruction of Jerusalem and its temple (ca. 586 BCE) was the most traumatic period in Israelite history and a time of intense self-reflection, both personal and communal. In sorting out what had happened, many among the remnant of Judah immediately questioned why the catastrophe had occurred. Survivors had witnessed unspeakable horror, made worse because the events surrounding Jerusalem's destruction seemed to abrogate God's covenant with the Davidic dynasty and with God's own children. Among answers to the painful questions raised by Jerusalem's downfall, some blamed the lack of righteousness among her citizens. Others raised questions about God's faithfulness, while others, like our text, sought to see in the suffering of Jerusalem and her people some redeeming quality.

The identity of the Suffering Servant in our passage is unclear and irresoluble. In Jewish interpretation some take "him" (the noun 'ebed is grammatically masculine) to represent all Jews, while others see in the Servant a righteous minority within Judah. In contrast, some in Jewish tradition have made the case that the Servant is an individual, who has been identified alternately as Jeremiah, Moses, and the Messiah. In reality, the text never identifies the Servant, and Christian tradition saw in him an adumbration of Jesus' own suffering.

In the initial speech, God emphasizes the Servant's reversal of fate. In 52:13 God announces the exultation of the Servant that will follow his humiliation. The announcement uses three distinct terms, exalted (yarum), lifted (nissa'), and high (gavah). The repetition reinforces the elevation of the Servant and highlights the utter change in his fortunes. Clearly, for Christian readers, the threefold exultation resonates with the doctrine of the Trinity, and the irony of the Servant's exultation coming on the heels of humiliation would be familiar. Jews in the exilic and postexilic period would have hoped for just such a reversal of their own fortunes. In verse 15 we are told that the Servant's elevation will come as a shock to the rest of the world. Clearly, in the exilic and postexilic experience of ancient Jews, any such elevation would have been as surprising to them as to foreigners.

In 53:1–11a we read an amazed observer's reflections on the Servant. The observer declares unbelievable the events he has witnessed. In verse 3 he notes that the Servant was "despised, rejected" and "a man of suffering." The perspective articulated in verses 4–6 is perhaps the most remarkable part of our passage. The author suggests that the Servant's suffering serves a positive purpose. To the modern and Christian ear, this notion hardly seems unusual; but within the biblical idiom, it is new. The author makes this claim in several ways, but verse 5 is the most moving: "But he was wounded for our transgressions, crushed for our iniquities; upon him was the punishment that made us whole, and by his bruises we are healed."

Again, to the modern ear, verses 4–6 seem obviously to suggest the notion of vicarious suffering of the Servant and consequent restoration for a community. This notion would be entirely new to the Hebrew Bible, and we might be meant to understand that rather than suffering alone, the Servant innocently suffers along with his community. While the latter idea is more in keeping with ancient Israelite understanding of corporate guilt and punishment, clearly Christian tradition understands the Servant's suffering to be vicarious.

In verse 7, "like a lamb that is led to the slaughter" resonates closely with Jeremiah 11:19 and has encouraged some to identify the Servant with that prophet. More to the point, in verses 7–10 the text makes frequent and varied references to death. The Hebrew Bible often uses such references as hyperbolic ways of describing distress (e.g., Psalm 18:5–6; Jonah 2:2). Because the Servant is delivered from his fate at the end of the episode, the notion that he has actually died would be unique in the Hebrew Bible.

As the fourth Servant Song concludes, we learn that the Servant's merit lies in exposing himself to death, bearing the guilt of many, and making intercession for sinners. Clearly, to the degree that one understands this Servant Song in the context in which it was written, it provides a moving account of tragedy and redemption of a Servant, group, or community that was as good as dead. The continuing frustration of subjugation and oppression over the next five hundred years would make Jewish Christians turn anew to Isaiah 52:13–53:11 to understand a new and equally remarkable resurrection that was to be the final victory in a long history of death and catastrophe.

LARRY L. LYKE

HOMILETICAL PERSPECTIVE

The focus of today's text is the last Servant Song of the Hebrew Scripture, a passage that evokes emotion, personal connection, and memory. Preached and studied as a text for Good Friday, it conveys the power of the one who suffers in a palpable way.

In the very first verse, the reader is invited to know that what is at once despised is also "lifted up and exalted" by God. The poem moves on to describe in detail the disfigured form of the Servant. The text suggests ugliness in human form, what we might refer to in contemporary language as deformation. Perhaps a good point of reflection on the text is to think about what is difficult to look at in our society. What do we consider disfigured or ugly? What things make us turn away from the sight of them?

Good Friday is a day to consider the people on the earth who suffer. Examples of what it means to be despised by human beings can be found in the newspaper, in our history texts, and in the routines of daily life. Today the preacher is asked to bring home the horrors of the suffering that some human beings cause others. This not only allows the community of faith to stay connected to suffering; it also allows them to remember that events of horror continue to happen. This is a hard text for people who do not suffer, or who do not own up to the suffering in the world.

In preparation for preaching this text, it will be helpful to form a working definition of the term "servant," both as it refers to the people of Israel and to followers of the Christian faith tradition. In the text at hand, the Servant is the one who bears responsibility for the many, guiding the faithful to God's redemption. The preacher might consider those in the community or larger society whose vocations involve maintaining order and safety. People in public service jobs such as nurses, librarians, and social workers come to mind, as do teachers, firefighters, and those serving in the National Guard. By reflecting on the ways such people respond to those in need, the preacher may be able to help connect the faithful to the supreme sacrifice of Good Friday, even without death.

Out of context, the term "suffering servant" may have no sense of redemption for those who hear it. In this text, however, the Suffering Servant guides the faithful to God's redemption. This story of the Servant is a story of victory for people who work hard to know what it means to be redeemed of God, even when that involves suffering. This calls up many contemporary images. While considering the Suffering Servant of God, the one who redeems us, the preacher might also consider those whose work cuts them off from people in the faith community. Young soldiers fight in wars that many people do not understand. They experience suffering in the line of duty. There is no end to those who are despised and rejected.

In Isaiah, the people of Israel bear the grief and sorrow of the nations. In the Gospels, Jesus' suffering and death become the sacrifice made by God's own for God's people. On Good Friday, Christians see in Jesus the Suffering Servant, taken "like a lamb . . . to the slaughter" (53:7) as the one chosen by God to bear the transgressions of many. The Servant is oppressed and afflicted, yet the Servant does not open his mouth. The Servant has done no violence but is stricken for the transgressions of the people. This is a harsh punishment. Is it really required of those who work for God's promise? The Isaiah text raises grave questions about the place of suffering in human life.

Clearly we lament the death of Jesus Christ as those left behind. Is it equally clear that we persist in making separations between people, so that there are still those who are outcast and despised? Why do we ask the innocent to go on suffering affliction? How can the preacher make the connection between the Isaiah text and our continued willingness to sacrifice a few for the comfort of the many? In our own time, it seems sadly true that the nations have not ceased to ask for such sacrifices. When will we put an end to suffering?

Working to make this text live in the sermon and in the congregation will involve asking such hard questions, while at the same time reminding God's people that the Servant in the Isaiah text comes to understand God's purpose. Though he is crushed with pain (53:10), he also sees the light (53:11), discerning the meaning of the suffering.

God's work—the theological work of "bearing away" the sins of many—is done by a people and by Jesus, both of whom bear a legacy of being outcast and despised. Yet the text also promises that the Servant shall prosper (52:13). What, then, is the relationship between the Servant's suffering and his prospering? If the text connects the suffering of the Servant with his prospering, what does this suggest about our own suffering?

The cycle of suffering remains part of human experience, and the role of the Servant is still with us. Even as preachers make connections between the text and those who live lives of service, it is fair to ask how many more Good Fridays we will enact before we accept God's redeeming grace. How, as Christians, might we act on the hope of new life? What connections can we make to those who suffer, without insisting that their suffering continue? What concrete possibilities for healing and renewal might we act upon, so that the redemption of Good Friday is made real? For even on this day we hold the vision of a kingdom where people serve one another—woman to man, person to person—offering one another the gift of peace in a place where pain and suffering are no more.

CLAUDIA HIGHBAUGH

John 18:28–19:30

THEOLOGICAL PERSPECTIVE

If one were to gaze upon and adore the crucified Jesus of the Romanesque era (eleventh/twelfth century), one would see Christ on the cross with a majestic air—head upright with no crown of thorns, eyes open and gazing mercifully upon the world he is renewing and redeeming. He may be draped in a royal garment with a purple sash around his waist. There are faint signs of blood on his hands and feet. Such a portrayal is in large part a representation of the Johannine Jesus, who is in control of his fate, even to the point of choosing when he dies, declaring, "It is finished." John unifies the crucified

Jesus with the resurrected Jesus. The crucified Jesus we behold (John 19:5) is our Lord and God. The suffering Jesus is the glorified Jesus.

This is in some contrast to later depictions of the crucified Jesus. In the famous Isenheim Altarpiece in Colmar, France, the tryptich by Matthias Grünewald (early sixteenth century) shows the suffering Jesus hanging his head with eyes closed, his sorely wounded body slumped, green and yellow with death. Here the suffering Jesus is identified with all suffering humans; one has to look at the other side of the altar to see the fully resurrected Jesus, whole and healthy with the remembrance of scars. Good Friday is thus portrayed as a shameful day, the product of humanity's sinfulness and the need for Christ's sacrifice and atonement.

While there is clear biblical basis for this atoning theme in the death of Christ, John clearly sees the crucified God as a victorious Lord for us. One does not look upon the cross without anticipating the resurrection. The one accused by his own people, judged and executed by the Roman Empire, judges us graciously and with forgiveness. To know and believe in him—that is, to be in a relationship of faith with him—is to know the truth (John 18:37). He creates this renewed, believing community from the cross as he charges John to care for his own mother, Mary. He dies, the Passover lamb without blemish, at the very hour when the lambs are being slaughtered; his limbs, like those of the Passover lambs (Num. 9:12), are not broken. He will now feed the community in baptismal renewal with water and in the Lord's Supper with bread and wine, that is, his body and blood. This is symbolized by the blood and water that pour from his side when his body is pierced by the soldier.[6]

There is little doubt, as reported both by Jewish and pagan historians, that Jesus was crucified as a political criminal by the Romans (John 19:16–19). While some of the Jewish leaders of the time accused him, it was the Romans who killed him. It is very important that we not generalize from a first-century account in John that demonstrates tensions between the early Christian community—who were Jews—and the synagogue. In fact, Good Friday is a day to observe the ancient custom to pray in the "bidding prayer" for our relationships with Jews, as well as persons of all other religions, so that God may keep us from the interreligious strife that has plagued believers through the ages.

When we adore the crucified and resurrected one on Good Friday, we "look on the one whom [we] have pierced" (John 19:37). We are the ones

---

6. For a detailed discussion of many of the points on this pericope noted here, see Raymond E. Brown, *The Gospel according to John XIII–XXI: A New Translation with Introduction and Commentary*, The Anchor Bible (Garden City, NY: Doubleday & Co., Inc., 1970), 785ff.

who are in need of renewal and life through the death and resurrection of the one whom God glorified. As human beings we are all linked with the biblical narrative that roots our sin and death in betrayal in a garden: from the first bloodshed between brothers to our destruction of one another and now even the earth itself. The new Adam, Jesus, is himself betrayed in a garden, but he is also raised again in a garden. Easter is celebrated in the Northern Hemisphere in the springtime, the season in which nature is renewed, but it important to note that this pericope ends in chapter 19 with the burial of Jesus in a garden.[7]

Whenever we confess the Apostles' Creed, the ancient baptismal creed, we confess that Jesus suffered under Pontius Pilate, was crucified, and died. His suffering and death were not illusory but real, like our own deaths. When we are baptized, we are baptized into his death, but, just as Christ was raised by the power of God, so also we are baptized into his resurrection. As we remember our baptisms in the Three Days from Holy Thursday to Easter, we have our faith renewed. It is ancient tradition to do baptisms or reaffirm our baptisms at Easter. In our baptismal faith we can confess with the psalmist in the face of death, "I shall not die, but I shall live" (Ps. 118:17). We can also witness about our dear fragile earth that is to us like a garden, "Earth shall not die, but shall live."

PHILIP D. KREY

PASTORAL PERSPECTIVE

Everybody sings "O Come, All Ye Faithful." Only the faithful sing "O Sacred Head, Now Wounded." This week, for better and worse, we are pretty much on our own. That is the cultural difference between Christmas and Holy Week—but why do the faithful, and to be honest, the wondering and questing and not-really-sure-at-all, come to a Good Friday service?

If you have a great choir, it could be for the Bach. Those days are mostly gone for most of us—no *St. John Passion* on the calendar this Friday, even in churches that keep the *Messiah* and Lessons and Carols traditions going in Advent. No, it is not the music—not that the music is not wonderful and important. It is something else, something more elusive and indescribable. There is a distinct yearning on Good Friday like no other. If you can speak to what this is, you and they will be blessed.

John Dominic Crossan and Marcus Borg rightly pointed out that in many traditions "Palm Sunday" has become "Passion Sunday" for the simple

---

7. For an excellent discussion of the themes of Good Friday, see Gail Ramshaw, *The Three-Day Feast: Maundy Thursday, Good Friday, Easter*, Worship Matters (Minneapolis: Augsburg Fortress, 2004), 40–51.

reason that no one is coming to church during Holy Week.[8] So the only way the gathered people will hear the story of the passion before the story of the resurrection is if it supplants Palm Sunday. More the pity, as those familiar with Holy Week traditions realize—the abrupt shift from "Hosanna" to "Crucify him" fifteen minutes later is very hard to process and understand, even if most Passion Sunday sermons focus precisely on this difficulty. Perhaps we should give a pass to those who pledge to come on Friday and let them wave their palm branches a little longer before folding and twisting them into crosses.

Maybe, just maybe, some will come at noon, and others at night, this Friday. Why? What are they coming for, and how does the preacher help them find it? By looking with them, not for them. They have two questions: Why did Jesus die/have to die? What does this death mean for my life? Not the easiest questions, but we are not needed for the easy ones. There are times when the role of the preacher is to get out of the way and let the texts and the occasion speak for themselves. Good Friday is not one of those times.

So, pastor, why *did* Jesus die/have to die? Help me understand how my emerging theology of God's love and grace meshes with the sacrificial atonement bloodiness inescapably lurking behind the texts for this day. Is this the best plan God could come up with? Is this the tradition's way of fitting what happened with what it hoped for? I understand the brutality of the Roman Empire, the fragility of life for those in the underclasses in ancient Mediterranean societies, and the collaborative instinct of the ruling religious elite in Judah in the first century. Could God not overwhelm this as God overwhelmed Pharaoh? If not, *why* not?

While you are at it, pastor, you might want to explain how I am supposed to make some sense of "the old rugged cross" for my present overwhelming circumstances. Even wearing a cross around my neck does not seem to help me understand its meaning. If Jesus "died for my sins" and I believe that "Jesus Christ is Lord," why do I still feel so trapped in my skin, so souled out every day? How does the work of the cross impact the reality of my increasingly lousy and desperate life?

Such are the real questions that those who are questioning enough to come to church on Good Friday bring with them. They are not the only questions, and all the questions do not feel so negative or so difficult to answer; but if you try to answer these two questions in your sermon—(1) why did Jesus die/have to die? and (2) what does his death mean for my

8. Marcus J. Borg and John Dominic Crossan, *The Last Week* (San Francisco: HarperSan-Francisco, 2007).

life?—then you should not be surprised if folks with different questions are seriously interested in your answers to these two. Like most preachers, you have thought long and hard about your answers to these critical questions, which inevitably blend the biblical, theological, spiritual, and pastoral. In other words, you are prepared to address exactly the sort of topic set before you today.

Pastorally, the second question (what does Jesus' death mean for my life?) may be more important than the first, however interrelated they are. A sound pastoral approach, then, would be to start with the second question and let it lead you to the first (why did Jesus die/have to die?). Death, any death, often unconsciously brings anxiety about our own deaths into our feelings, thoughts, and questions. The closer to home a death is, the more concern and anxiety it will generate. By extension, the closer a person feels to Jesus, the more profoundly that person will experience Jesus' death and want guidance in understanding what his death means for his or her life.

Continuing in this line of thought, is it not possible that the second question and the first question finally blend? Not just, why did Jesus die/have to die? but, why do I die/have to die? The virgule (/), then, is an illusion. "Die" and "have to die" are the same from the moment of birth, for all who are born, including Jesus. What is needed, pastorally and theologically, is a radically incarnational understanding of the cross, an understanding that relates the cross to the whole of Jesus' life from annunciation to crucifixion. In providing this, the preacher helps the congregation relate the whole of their lives to the whole of the life of Christ, so that the death of Christ is not just about their deaths, but profoundly also about their lives.

WILLIAM F. BROSEND

EXEGETICAL PERSPECTIVE

John highlights the religious-political dynamics surrounding the execution of Jesus. Jesus is presented as one accused of challenging the Roman emperor by claiming to be "king." Jesus is repeatedly referred to as "king" (*basileus*). He even talks about his "kingdom" (*basileia*). The Roman soldiers mock Jesus, calling him "King of the Jews" (19:3). In John's telling, Jewish religious leaders reject Jesus' kingship because of their allegiance to the emperor. They have "no king but the emperor" (19:12–15). While much of Christian theology claims that Jesus *died* for humanity's sins, John makes it clear that Jesus was *killed* for political reasons.

Jesus before Pilate (18:28–19:16a). There is no formal Jewish trial in John, only a brief questioning (18:12–27). In contrast to the Synoptics, the absence of a Jewish trial here weakens the view that Jesus was executed for religious offenses. Accusations that Jesus claimed to destroy the temple are missing, as is the question of Jesus' claim to be the messiah and subsequent charge of blasphemy.

The title "king" is repeatedly associated with Jesus in John's account of Jesus before Pilate, heightening the political aspect of his arrest. While it is debatable what the political reality may have actually been, the author uses Pilate's thrice-repeated claim, "I find no case against him" (18:38; 19:4, 6) as a way of suggesting that Jesus' claims of kingship were not considered serious political claims. By flogging Jesus, dressing him in a purple robe with a crown of thorns, and repeatedly presenting him to the Jewish authorities as "your King," Pilate mocks Jesus. The mockery, however, is not merely aimed at Jesus; it is also aimed at the Jewish people. It is Rome's way of ridiculing the Jewish quest for political independence.

In John, Pilate and the Jewish authorities are presented as having mutual contempt for each other while at the same time being beholden to each other (18:29–31; 19:7, 12). The depiction of the two indicates that in John they, not Jesus, are the ones on trial. Pilate is portrayed as weak and pandering to Jewish authorities, and Jewish authorities demonstrate their disloyalty to God and Jewish liberation by repeatedly claiming Caesar as their king. As a declaration of Pilate's impotence and a condemnation of Jewish betrayal, Jesus declares to Pilate, "You would have no power over me unless it had been given you from above; therefore the one who handed me over to you is guilty of a greater sin" (19:11).

The Crucifixion (19:16b–30). Cicero called crucifixion the most extreme form of punishment. It was often used by the Romans against political agitators and non-Romans of the lower class, particularly slaves. John's portrayal of Pilate as being forced by Jewish authorities to crucify Jesus distorts historical power dynamics. Pilate, not Jewish authorities, was in charge. Pilate is not, however, portrayed in John as innocent. When the chief priests complain regarding the inscription, "Jesus of Nazareth, the King of the Jews," Pilate's response indicates that the inscription is not to honor Jesus but to mock and ridicule Jesus and the Jewish people.

As a king, Jesus does not experience much of the shame portrayed in the Synoptics. Jesus carries his own cross in John. There is no mockery by the crowd or abandonment by his followers. He dies with his mother and beloved disciple with him. He remains in control of his death to the very end. He determines when his mission is "finished" and when it is time for him to lay down his life (10:17–18).

Postcrucifixion (19:31–42). To expedite death, the legs of the crucified were often broken to prevent them from pushing up to get breath, leading to swift suffocation. Once again, Jesus maintains control over when and how he dies. The water from Jesus' side might be an allusion to an earlier reference by Jesus to the Spirit being "rivers of living water" that flow out of the believer's "belly" (*koilia*; 7:38). Joseph and Nicodemus represent "secret" believers who are no longer afraid to come forward because of fear of persecution (9:18–22; 12:42; 16:1–2; 20:19). The large amount of spices (19:39) was most likely a sign of the great honor due to "king" Jesus.

John emphasizes the kingship of Jesus and criticizes religious and political authorities, not only for failing to recognize his kingship, but also for undermining his kingship. Despite the claims of Caiaphas and other religious authorities, the salvation of oppressed people is not the result of an allegiance to imperial kingdoms. Deliverance of oppressed people is the result of an allegiance to the kingdom of God. Good Friday commemorates Jesus' crucifixion and death as "king of the Jews." On this day, let us examine our own religious-political allegiances to make sure we are not claiming that we have "no king but the emperor."

GUY D. NAVE JR.

HOMILETICAL PERSPECTIVE

Good Friday is a day for all Christians to approach with trembling, but none more than those called to preach. The texts of Jesus' passion are so familiar that we wonder how to help people hear them afresh. Is there some original point of entry into the story? How might Pilate interpret his unsettling interview with the accused blasphemer, followed by the crowd's frenzied demand for the release of Barabbas, rather than the man they had hailed with hosannas just the week before? What would Jesus' mother have to tell us, if she could speak about the unspeakable from her vantage point, huddled with Mary the wife of Clopas, and Mary Magdalene, and the disciple whom Jesus loved, on the site of the execution? Or Joseph of Arimathea and Nicodemus, newly courageous in their discipleship, as they seek official permission to take the body down from the cross and lovingly prepare it for burial?

Our challenge in approaching this text is not that there is so little to say but that there is so much. Not only do the perspectives of the lesser-known characters invite our exploration, but also the major questions of the text. "Put away the sword," Jesus commands. What does his order imply for our human propensities to respond to violence with violence? "My kingdom is not of this world," Jesus announces—but does this give us license to neglect the needs of "this world" in focusing on an otherworldly salvation? "What is truth?" Pilate asks, but we hear no further answer: because Jesus himself *is* the truth. What does it mean for us that truth is found in a *person* rather than a set of propositions?

The questions are enormous and important. Even so, none of them eclipses the power of the simple chronicle of events as told in the passion narrative. Without any philosophical or theological or homiletical assistance from us, this chronicle has the power to astonish and transform lives.

Yet there are still reasons for the preacher to approach any retelling of the story with trembling. Chances are good that the person called to deliver a Good Friday homily is someone who dreads reencountering the stark account of betrayal and brutality; someone who cringes at the sound of flogging, the sight of deliberately inflicted wounds; someone who shies away from confronting the agony of the walk to Golgotha, the unimaginable pain of the nails tempered only by the body's own self-preserving reflex of physiological shock. True, the preacher can choose to dwell on the facts of Roman execution in literally excruciating detail; indeed, filmmakers have discovered great box-office success in so dwelling. For some people, graphic renderings of the passion may strengthen the life of faith, intensifying awareness of the extreme sacrifice made for our sakes. But others find such images overwhelming. Our minds, like our bodies, have a shock reaction with which they shut down and refuse to assimilate any more details.

For these latter among us, John's rendering of the passion comes as something of a comfort: it portrays a Jesus who is supremely confident, in control of even the most sordid events leading to his end. The tone is set with his proclamation in 12:23: "The hour has come for the Son of Man to be glorified." Jesus approaches the last meal with his disciples, knowing "that his hour had come to depart from this world" (13:1). Judas does not slip away from the meal to accomplish his betrayal; Jesus deliberately sends him (13:27). After the meal, John reports a lengthy farewell discourse, but no prayers of agony in the garden. When the soldiers come for the arrest, Jesus is not identified by Judas's kiss but steps forward, magisterially announcing, "I am he"—whereupon they draw back and fall to the ground (18:6). Jesus is not silent before Pilate, but speaks to him of a superior "kingdom . . . not from this world" (18:36). Jesus carries his own cross to Golgotha (19:17) and does not even stumble under its weight. He looks down upon his mother and the beloved disciple from the cross, assuring their future care for one another in the hour when he might seem to be the one in deeper need of caring (19:26–27). John records no cry of dereliction but rather a climactic declaration: "It is finished" (19:30), a verdict of accomplishment and completion.

John's picture of Jesus is comforting. While the world hurls forth the worst it has to offer, Jesus remains unfazed and triumphant. We need this picture, because without it, the other images of brutality could be simply brutalizing. Without it, we might prefer not to enter into the story, finding its weight too hard to bear. Without it, there is little that is "good" about Good Friday at all.

Yet how do we know if John's glorious images are salutary for us and not merely escapist? We might rephrase the question. Does John's portrait tempt us to neglect the humanity of Jesus, like the early gnostic communities, or does it offer us a richer view of what humanity is capable of becoming under the transformative impact of the Holy Spirit? Does it make us less or more likely to be present to others in the world in the depth of their personal and political horrors? Does John's passion narrative cultivate in us an equanimity and assurance that strengthens our ability to confront evil and not be defeated by it?

As with so many faith matters, we ultimately judge by the fruits—whether they are bitter as gall or sweet as the promise of resurrected life.

MARY LOUISE BRINGLE

Holy Saturday

Job 14:1–14

[1]"A mortal, born of woman, few of days and full of trouble,
　　[2]comes up like a flower and withers,
　　flees like a shadow and does not last.
[3]Do you fix your eyes on such a one?
　　Do you bring me into judgment with you?
[4]Who can bring a clean thing out of an unclean?
　　No one can.
[5]Since their days are determined,
　　and the number of their months is known to you,
　　and you have appointed the bounds that they cannot pass,
[6]look away from them, and desist,
　　that they may enjoy, like laborers, their days.

[7]"For there is hope for a tree,
　　if it is cut down, that it will sprout again,
　　and that its shoots will not cease.
[8]Though its root grows old in the earth,
　　and its stump dies in the ground,
[9]yet at the scent of water it will bud
　　and put forth branches like a young plant.
[10]But mortals die, and are laid low;
　　humans expire, and where are they?
[11]As waters fail from a lake,
　　and a river wastes away and dries up,
[12]so mortals lie down and do not rise again;
　　until the heavens are no more, they will not awake
　　or be roused out of their sleep.
[13]O that you would hide me in Sheol,
　　that you would conceal me until your wrath is past,
　　that you would appoint me a set time, and remember me!
[14]If mortals die, will they live again?
　　All the days of my service I would wait
　　until my release should come."

John 19:38–42

[38]After these things, Joseph of Arimathea, who was a disciple of Jesus, though a secret one because of his fear of the Jews, asked Pilate to let him take away the body of Jesus. Pilate gave him permission; so he came and removed his body. [39]Nicodemus, who had at first come to Jesus by night, also came, bringing a mixture of myrrh and aloes, weighing about a hundred pounds. [40]They took the body of Jesus and wrapped it with the spices in linen cloths, according to the burial custom of the Jews. [41]Now there was a garden in the place where he was crucified, and in the garden there was a new tomb in which no one had ever been laid. [42]And so, because it was the Jewish day of Preparation, and the tomb was nearby, they laid Jesus there.

ORDER OF WORSHIP

OPENING WORDS / CALL TO WORSHIP
Our Lord has died.
The tomb is sealed.
We gather today to mourn, to remember,
to grieve the thought of a world without Christ.

HYMN, SPIRITUAL, OR PSALM

CALL TO CONFESSION
With Job we pray, O Lord,   *Job 14:13*
"that you would conceal me until your wrath is past,
   that you would appoint me a set time, and remember me."
Let us confess our sin to the Lord.

PRAYER OF CONFESSION
We have kept our faith in secret.
We have distanced ourselves from your flock.
For all the times we have denied you, Lord:
Forgive us, we pray.

We have broken our promises of faithful service.
We have preferred confident lies to uncertain silence.
For all the times we have betrayed you, Lord:
Forgive us, we pray.

We have averted our eyes from your suffering.
We have chosen not to see your brothers and sisters in need.
For all the times we have turned away:
Forgive us, we pray.

Hear our cries, O Lord.
Forgive us!
Forgive us!
Forgive us!

DECLARATION OF FORGIVENESS
Surely Jesus Christ has borne our sin.
By his wounds we are healed.

PRAYER FOR ILLUMINATION
As the tomb is sealed shut,
our hearts are broken open.
Speak into our open hearts, Lord,
that we may hear your words of comfort. **Amen.**

SCRIPTURE READINGS

SERMON

HYMN, SPIRITUAL, OR PSALM

PRAYERS OF INTERCESSION
In the days of his flesh,
Jesus offered his prayers
with loud cries and tears
to the one who was able
to save him from death.

On this day, we pray in Jesus' name:
O Lord, do not be far away;
O God, come quickly to help us.

Remember your church . . .
Keep us faithful to the gospel,

proclaiming the good news of salvation
even in the face of danger and death.
O Lord, do not be far away;
O God, come quickly to help us.

Remember your world . . .
Rescue this perishing planet,
condemned by human cruelty;
do not let it be destroyed forever.
O Lord, do not be far away;
O God, come quickly to help us.

Remember all nations . . .
Break the sword and snap the spear;
trample the high walls and thorny fences
that separate neighbors and nations.
O Lord, do not be far away;
O God, come quickly to help us.

Remember those who face death . . .
Restore the lives of those who suffer,
give hope to those who are despairing,
and welcome the dying into your arms.
O Lord, do not be far away;
O God, come quickly to help us.

We ask these things in the name of Jesus,
who suffered and died for our sakes. **Amen.**

HYMN, SPIRITUAL, OR PSALM

DISMISSAL

Mortals die, and are laid low;   *Job 14:10, 12–13*
mortals lie down and do not rise again.
Remember us, O Lord. Remember us.
Amen.

SERMON HELPS

Job 14:1–14

THEOLOGICAL PERSPECTIVE

In the earliest accounts of Holy Week observances, there were no liturgies for Holy Saturday, save the private observance of the daily office. Nonetheless, patristic theologians such as Basil of Caesarea (ca. 330–79), Gregory of Nyssa (ca. 330–ca. 395), Gregory of Nazianzus (ca. 329–89), and Amphilochius of Iconium (ca. 340–95) composed reflections on the death of Christ, which in turn influenced Western and Eastern liturgies for Holy Saturday that developed in the eighth century as an offshoot of the Easter Vigil.

Two interpretations of the death of Christ predominated in these reflections. One was that the death of Christ resembled the Sabbath of God at the end of the seven days of creation (Gen. 2:2–3), as well as the regular observance of the Sabbath on Saturday. In *On the Three-Day Interval between Our Lord's Death and Resurrection,* Gregory of Nyssa wrote: "Behold the blessed Sabbath of the first creation of the world, and in that Sabbath recognize this Sabbath," for "on this day the only-begotten God truly rested from all his works, keeping Sabbath in the flesh by means of his death." Another was that after his death Christ descended into hell to free captive souls through the power of his resurrection (1 Pet. 3:19). In his fifth oration of *For Holy Saturday,* Amphilochius preached: "Today we celebrate the feast of our Savior's burial," for Christ, who is "with the dead below, is loosing the bonds of death and filling Hades with light and awakening the sleepers while we, upon earth, have the resurrection in mind and rejoice."[1] Taken together, these two interpretations reflect the complex emotions often felt at Holy Saturday liturgies—feelings of longing and grief, on one hand, and of expectation and joy, on the other.

This interpretive history and emotional tension display affinity with the passage assigned for this service from Job's response to his friend Zophar (12:1–14:22). Zophar has tried to convince Job that God's hidden wisdom provides an underlying order that can explain the cause of Job's suffering

---

1. Gregory of Nyssa, *On the Three-Day Interval between Our Lord's Death and Resurrection* in *Easter in the Early Church: An Anthology of Jewish and Early Christian Texts,* J. Quigley, SJ, and J. T. Lienhard, SJ, trans., R. Cantalamessa, ed. (Collegeville, MN: Liturgical Press, 1993), n. 72, 77; Amphilochius of Iconium, *Oration 5: For Holy Saturday, 1* in *Easter in the Early Church,* n. 73, 77.

(11:7–12). Job accepts the language of hidden wisdom but turns it back on his friend—it is precisely on account of the hiddenness of God's wisdom that Zophar and Job's other friends have nothing of substance to say. They offer him "proverbs of ashes" and "defenses of clay" (13:12).

Only God can respond to Job, and therefore Job brings his case directly to God, with all the vulnerability this entails (13:13–19). Job poses a series of questions: Given that mortal life is "few of days and full of trouble" (14:1), does God even notice the plight of suffering humanity? And even if God does notice, does God have the power to bring redemption to humans, given their mortality? Unlike "trees," which die and rise following the rhythm of the seasons, "mortals lie down and do not rise again" and are not "roused out of their sleep" (v. 12). Indeed, Job takes refuge in the thought that death will mark the end of his suffering (v. 13).

Towards the end of the passage, however, Job appears to wish the impossible—"if mortals die, will they live again?" (v. 14). Is it possible that God would remember Job, as "God [had] remembered Rachel" in her barrenness (Gen. 30:22) and Israel in its oppression (Exod. 2:24)? Such a thought requires Job to develop a different frame for his case against God from that originally constructed. Job had assumed that a just God must reward the righteous and punish evildoers within a temporal context, which enabled him to criticize God's treatment of him. Now Job imagines a cosmic context in which God might be free to act in a way that is reminiscent of God's original act of creation. This changed context does not explain why God permits innocent suffering to occur in the first place, but it does provide a larger theater for the enactment of God's redemption. Given that Job's vindication occurs in history, with the return to his former prosperity (42:10–17), this possibility is only hinted at in the passage. But these reflections point toward the development in Old Testament theology of the belief in the resurrection.

In the history of interpretation, Job is often viewed as a type, or foreshadowing, of the trials of Christ and the church. "Because Christ and the church, that is the head and the body, is one person," Gregory the Great (ca. 540–604) wrote in his commentary on Job (*Magna Moralia*), "we have often said that blessed Job figuratively stands sometimes for the head and sometimes the body." Alluding to the passage above, Gregory argued that, "as the seasons pass we see trees lose their green leaves and stop producing fruit; and suddenly, look, a kind of resurrection comes as we see leaves burst forth as if from withered wood, pieces of fruit growing, and the whole tree clothed with a beauty again." This passage from Job, then, provides believers "hope for our resurrection from reflecting on the glory of our Head."[2] And yet, because he viewed Job's suffering as completely resolved through Christ's resurrection without remainder, Gregory's interpretation, like others of this vein, lacks the emotional complexity and theological tension rooted in the passage and in Holy Saturday liturgies.

A better interpretation that honors this complexity and tension is that the only true friend of Job is Jesus Christ, who also suffered innocently. As Jürgen Moltmann has argued, Job makes clear that "the person who is torn by suffering stands alone," for no "explanation" and "no consolation of higher wisdom" can "assuage" his "pain." Job therefore claims a "dignity" that "neither men nor gods can rob him of," and "no theology can fall below Job's level" in seeking to respond to those who suffer similarly. Such a theology must be able to live with innocent suffering as an open question that cannot be answered, even in light of the resurrection. Indeed, the only resolution possible comes in the form of another question: "Does Job have any real theological friend except the crucified Jesus on Golgotha?"[3]

WILLIAM JOSEPH DANAHER JR.

PASTORAL PERSPECTIVE

"Few of days and full of trouble," that's human life, Job sighs. Surely this has been true for Job. Once he was prosperous with a large family. But in one swoop of destruction, all his children die, his livestock and livelihood are stolen, and his health is ruined. His so-called friends rush in, but instead of comforting him, they defend God and try to convince Job that he must have done something wrong to bring on such devastation. Sorry, not only for himself, but for all human beings who share death as their fate, Job turns to address God. We can hear resignation in his voice when he asks God, "Do you fix your eyes on such a one?" (v. 3). As wispy as flowers, and as sure to wither, we cannot amount to much and are not even worthy of God's attention. And then we hear Job's bitterness. "Look away . . . and desist," he spits (v. 6), as if addressing the playground bully. Since God has already planned all our days, and even our deaths, Job inquires, why can't God just leave us alone to live out whatever life we have been given?

According to Job, our fate is hopeless. We all die, he points out. And when we do, we stay dead. When human beings breathe our last, we lie down and never get up. Never. Even the trees have more hope. Chopped down, their

2. Gregory the Great, *Magna Moralia*, 35.14.24 and 14.55.69, in John Moorhead, *Gregory the Great* (New York: Routledge, 2005), 137, 61.
3. Jürgen Moltmann, *The Trinity and the Kingdom: The Doctrine of God* (Minneapolis: Fortress Press, 1993), 47–48.

roots can still spread out underneath the ground. With only a few drops of water, a fresh sprout forms new buds. But human beings, we dry up like riverbeds never to be filled again.

The passage turns, however, on the last verse. After Job severely states his convictions about the finality of human death, he asks a question. "If mortals die, will they live again?" (v. 14). His question mark whispers ever so faintly that something else might be possible. Something, some doubt or sense of wonder, cracks the window open and lets in a little fresh air. Job confesses what we all have to admit, that he really does not know what happens after death. After throwing up his hands and turning his back, pushing God away like an offended child to lick his wounds, he once again turns back toward God with a fervent, even heartrending request. "Remember me," he pleads, and then with a patience that replaces his resignation, "I would wait until my release should come" (vv. 13–14).

We think of waiting as an Advent theme, but waiting also sits at the center of Holy Saturday. I would submit, however, that the quality of the waiting is different. In spite of the Advent warnings about the tumultuous second coming, the waiting of Advent brims with expectation, of bustling preparation for hope to ring and joy to arrive. The waiting of Advent is like having warm bread in the oven.

By contrast, the air of Holy Saturday smells more like stale smoke, as though something essential was burned the day before. If we were to live in the fullness of Holy Saturday, perhaps the only thing we would hear would be silence. Indeed, tradition has it that this is the quietest day of the Christian year. But the silence of this day does not feel like a restorative peacefulness. It sounds more like the buzz of a lonely streetlight on a dark deserted road in the middle of nowhere. Added to the overwhelming sadness left over from Good Friday, there is a lingering sense of shock, and even of danger. Nothing feels safe or dependable anymore. The waiting of Job and the waiting of Holy Saturday are like waiting for a teenage son or daughter who has missed a midnight curfew to come home, or waiting for the surgeon to emerge from the hospital operating room, or waiting for the phone to ring with a report of the biopsy results, or waiting for the dust of an earthquake to settle so that you can find out if anyone is trapped under the rubble. Like Job's question, Holy Saturday is a day of suspense. We hang between two worlds—the world of darkness, death, and despair, and the world of resurrection light and the hope of new and eternal life.

For Job, death has already arrived. It has stripped him of his loved ones, his livelihood, and his own health. And it seems, for a while, that all his hope has died too. It is the same for the followers of Jesus who have witnessed

Good Friday. But just when it looks as if there is nothing left to recover from the devastation, something new takes a shallow breath. Job asks a question. Jesus' disciples look for and find each other. Car headlights pull into the driveway, the surgeon strides into the waiting room, the phone rings, and the air clears. Everyone exhales, even as we take in the apparent damage. We know we have been changed, that life will never be as it was before. But as soon as our hearts leave our throats, we realize that they are still beating. We begin to consider what this means for our future. Even if only in the faintest shafts of light, it dawns on us that perhaps God has not abandoned us. Not at all.

"Remember me," Job reminds God just a breath after he has pleaded with God to leave him alone. Someone kindles the fire of the Easter Vigil, and the disciples are comforted in the warmth of each other's arms. Having paused the appropriate number of days, Mary Magdalene and the other sleepless women meet. While it is still dark, they prepare all they will need to anoint and wrap the lifeless body of Jesus. They prepare to visit the tomb where he is buried. Job's question echoes as they step into the night. "If mortals die, can they live again?" If Jesus died, can he live again? If Jesus died, can *we* live again? And if we can, what will our lives become?

CHRISTINA BRAUDAWAY-BAUMAN

EXEGETICAL PERSPECTIVE

In contrast to the narrative frame (chaps. 1–2; 42:7–17), the poetic dialogues of Job are often bypassed. After all, why should one continue past Job's curse of his birthday and his wish not to be born in chapter 3? Yet a careful study of today's reading can perhaps pave the way for a closer study of Job that provides an important voice on the reflection of undeserved suffering and the tragic certainty of death.

Today's reading is the final section of Job's longest speech up to this point in the book (chaps. 12–14). It concludes the first phase of dialogue between Job and each of his friends. Here Job continues his direct accusation against God that he begins earlier in 13:20. Job's complaint against God in chapter 14 forms a frame with Job's opening lament in chapter 3 and shows the failure of the "wise" counsel of Job's friends to change Job's assertion of the unjust and undeserved nature of his sufferings. Yet toward the end of the first cycle of speeches, Job's outlook shifts from a wish to die (3:11; 6:9–10; 7:15) in order to escape his misery, to a daring challenge to meet and argue his case before God (13:2, 13–28), and finally to a tantalizing musing at the prospect that death might not signal the end of hope (14:7–9; 13–17).

The birth and death of human beings frames chapter 14 (vv. 1, 22), and in between, various observations from nature are employed in classic wisdom style to underscore the brevity of life and the futility of hoping for an escape from death. The basic structure of chapter 14 is characterized by the movement from despair due to the finitude and finality of human existence to the possibility of hope that is dashed by a return to despair: verses 1–6 (despair); verses 7–9 (hope); verses 10–12 (despair); verses 13–17 (hope); verses 18–22 (despair). This structure serves to negate the hope passages and thus creates a somber, sober voice that nevertheless must not be muted by imposing a concept of an afterlife with eternal blessings or punishment. This concept is foreign to the worldview of Job and to the rest of the Old Testament, with the exception of one or two late texts, and begins to emerge in the period between the Old and New Testaments.

Ephemerality of Human Existence (vv. 1–6). In the opening section, the analogies of the withering flower and fleeting shadow underscore the ephemeral nature of human existence. Since humans will die anyway in a life "full of trouble," with no possibility for hope (vv. 4, 5), Job concludes that it is illogical for God to add to the misery of human existence (v. 1–2) and thus pleads with God to leave humanity alone so that the remaining years of life can be enjoyed (v. 6).

A Whiff of Water (vv. 7–12). Yet, following the vivid portrayal of death as an unsurpassable barrier, Job raises the possibility of hope by pointing to the example of a tree. If a tree is cut down or is old and rotten, just the mere "scent of water" will revive the tree to sprout new branches with the vitality of a young tree. At first glance, the rejuvenation of this old and rotten tree might raise the prospect of hope, but Job returns to the hopelessness of humanity in verses 7–10. The hope afforded to an old tree is denied to even a healthy and vigorous mortal (v. 10; NRSV's "mortal" obscures the meaning of the Heb. *geber* in vv. 10, 14 as a healthy or strong man) who will dwindle and waste away into nothingness (v. 10) in manner analogous to the gradual drying up of a lake or river (v. 11). And to underscore the finality of humanity's destruction, Job switches to the analogy of sleeping, portraying death as a state of slumber that will not be disrupted, even at the end of time (v. 12). Thus the words of hope in verses 7–10 only heighten the harsh and tragic reality of certain death. Humans are denied the hope that even trees have!

Safety in Sheol? (vv. 13–17). With the certainty of suffering and death, Job returns to the possibility of hope, here during humanity's existence in the realm of the dead (NRSV "Sheol"), a place where Job wishes he would be hidden and safe until God's anger abates. The only remaining source of hope lies in the hands of God. Job calls God to "remember" him, perhaps as God did in the past with Noah and the Israelites in Egypt. The solution now lies in God's initiative to "call" for Job and to "long" for Job as God's handiwork (vv. 15–17).

No Hope for Humanity (vv. 18–22). Lest the reader stake out a secure basis for hope, Job makes a final return to despair by accusing God of destroying the "hope of humanity" articulated in verses 13–17. Job compares the debilitating decline of humanity with the gradual crumbling and erosion of mountains. Job places the blame of the grim human condition squarely in the hands of God (vv. 19–20), who will always overpower humans to the point of constant suffering and lamenting that continues even in the state of death (v. 22).

At this point, Job concludes his speech, the longest and most substantial address to God in the book. Despite the accusation against God as the cause of humanity's hopelessness, Job maintains an attitude of waiting "until my release should come" (v. 14). This attitude is especially appropriate for the observance of Holy Saturday. Reflections from today's readings provide a rationale for creating a time of somber and sober reflection on the death of Jesus with an attitude of waiting for God to act.

DANNY MATHEWS

HOMILETICAL PERSPECTIVE

In Terrence Malick's *Thin Red Line,* the filmmaker intersperses haunting voice-overs with scenes that depict the awfulness of the final battles for control of the South Pacific island of Guadalcanal late in World War II. The voice-overs are philosophical and somewhat—but not entirely—detached from the frenzy of the battle scenes. The voice of a young soldier ponders the imponderable "thin red line" between life, war, and death:

> This great evil. Where's it come from? How'd it steal into the world? What seed, what root did it grow from? Who's doing this? Who's killing us? Robbing us of life and light. Mocking us with the sight of what we might have known. Does our ruin benefit the Earth? Does it help the grass to grow or the sun to shine? Is this darkness in you, too? Have you passed through this night?[4]

---

4. *A Thin Red Line* (Fox 2000 Pictures, Terrence Malick, director, 1998).

Is Job the voice-over of an ancient Hebrew writer who pondered the otherwise imponderable question of suffering and God's apparent absence—or worse, God's direct involvement in this suffering?

The *Thin Red Line* and the words of Job are a perfect fit for this thin red line of a day. Holy Saturday is that day where we frankly are not quite sure what to do with ourselves. If we have successfully kept hidden from the eyes and memory of our faith the glistening day that is only a daybreak away, then we will find preaching and worship to be a worthy challenge in the deep shadows of Holy Saturday.

Many of us know deep grieving to be a dry and lifeless time. Our tears ebb, the mind grows listless and dull, the spirit recedes beyond reach. We are in a state of spiritual and emotional limbo. Our losses take on an air of unreality, but so does life and its prospects. This is our time in death's shadowed valley. This is St. John of the Cross's dark night of the soul.[5] For those who have the nerve to face it, this is the day we enter deeply into Job's despair and find there an analog for our own—and the world's—despairing, suffering, hopelessness, and sense of being forsaken. Today Job invites us to join him on the ash heap where we may, for a time, sit and scrape our sores together. Holy Saturday is our dark day of the soul, and Job is a fitting companion.

What is eroding Job's hope? While creation seems to be in a continual state of rebirth, Job fears that death is an end from which there is no exit. Job's words—in this day's lection and nearly everywhere else—are depressing. And who could blame Job for being depressed? Human dereliction and despair can close off the sense of hope and possibility, an open-ended future that one can know in less oppressive times. While we are dwelling in the valley, the gloom of the valley may nearly convince us that all the world is a valley, shadowed and deathly. Today is a day for dwelling among shadows and death while not yet allowing our hope to be destroyed.

Today is also a day for deepening our skills of solidarity. We may know how Job's story ends, and we know how tomorrow begins, but there are billions of Jobs in the world who need our attention, who need us not to look away or return to "life as usual" too quickly, who need us to wait patiently with them while they sort through the tatters of their existence. There is room for challenging the faithful to more active forms of compassion in sermons developed for this day.

Most of all, today is a time of waiting because in the spiritual netherworld of suffering, we have little choice but to wait. Job is the ultimate waiter, the

---

5. For a new translation and introduction by Mirabi Starr see Saint John of the Cross, *Dark Night of the Soul* (New York: Riverhead Books, 2002).

one who must exist within a long, slow, excruciating existential pause while waiting for God to reveal either God's self or God's intentions for causing Job's terrible agony. This is the time of complete dereliction. Lamentations and the psalms of lament were surely familiar literary companions for the author of Job. We can hear in his words echoes of our commemoration of the crucifixion a day earlier, where in Psalm 22 the psalmist cries desolately: "My God, my God, why have you forsaken me?"

Like the psalmist, Job reminds us that times of suffering inevitably bring with them questions of a spiritual nature. It seems inevitable in the face of suffering to ask the larger questions of existence and meaning. Suffering and grief can lead to concerns of divine passivity. Job asks: "Who can bring a clean thing out of an unclean?" and then nearly shouts his own rhetorical response: "NO ONE CAN!" (v. 4). In our pitiable states, we can wonder with Job if we are beyond redemption, which is another way of saying beyond God. Does our suffering place us beyond God's reach? Yet here is a time for allowing our belief and our unbelief to coexist without judgment—as so often seems to be the case in Job's utterances—without attempting to fix what seems to be broken, without rushing to replace what seems to be missing.

Taking our lead from Job, let us not allow our experience of this day to confound us into losing our tongue. Job lapses into silence at times, but more often Job gives full voice to his frustration and pain. C. S. Lewis said somewhat famously, if not also cruelly, that pain is God's "megaphone to rouse a deaf world."[6] More helpfully, Job starts instead with the megaphone turned the other way and uses it to try to rouse a seemingly disinterested God. It's a thin red line, but Job wishes to remain on this side of it. Instead of waiting for a voice-over, we preachers do well to cry out on this day, giving homiletic voice to despair, lest hope die for lack of courageous and sympathetic proclamation.

GREGORY LEDBETTER

John 19:38–42

THEOLOGICAL PERSPECTIVE

The Gospel of John orients the entirety of the life and ministry of Jesus to his death on the cross. This death is not a tragedy that befalls him, raising the question as to whether God has forsaken him, as in Mark and Matthew, but

6. C. S. Lewis, *The Problem of Pain* (New York: The Macmillan Co., 1944), 81.

is rather the destiny that Jesus consistently and consciously chooses for himself, in obedience to the will of his Father who sent him. The divine power that Jesus claims for himself keeps anyone from taking his life from him, but this same power allows Jesus to lay his life down when he so wills. "No one takes it from me, but I lay it down of my own accord" (John 10:18).

Jesus never wavers in his obedience to this command of the Father and does not ask the Father to take the cup from him, as in the other Gospels, but rather calmly says, "And what should I say—'Father, save me from this hour?' No, it is for this reason that I have come to this hour" (John 12:27). Jesus reminds Peter of this obedience when Peter tries to fight for him in the garden: "Am I not to drink the cup that the Father has given me?" (John 18:11). The willingness of Jesus to lay down his life on the cross therefore makes his death into the moment of his greatest glorification and the focal point of his saving power. "And I, when I am lifted up from the earth, will draw all people to myself" (John 12:32).

Thus, when Jesus dies, he does not cry out with a loud voice, "My God, my God, why have you forsaken me?" and then give a loud cry and breathe his last (Mark 15:34, 37), but rather, knowing that his death completes the work the Father gave him to do, quietly says, "It is finished," bows his head, and gives up his spirit (John 19:30).

John also goes to greater lengths than do the other Gospels to show that Jesus is truly dead. The soldiers come to break his legs so that he will die before the Sabbath begins but discover that he is already dead. To make sure, they pierce his side with a spear, and water and blood at once come out, showing if nothing else that Jesus is truly dead, adding the insistence that these things are witnessed firsthand (John 19:34–35). All of this seems to indicate that, for John, what is of significance for the world is not only the dying of Jesus but also the being dead of Jesus, his complete and utter lifelessness, that is attested by the Jews, Roman soldiers, and the unnamed firsthand witness.

The paradoxical saving power of the one who is himself dead is attested in John by the appearance of Joseph of Arimathea and Nicodemus at the foot of the cross when they come to bury Jesus. Joseph is said to be a disciple of Jesus, "though a secret one because of his fear of the Jews" (John 19:38). Mark and Luke add that Joseph is also a member of the council that condemned Jesus, indicating that he is a powerful person in the Jewish community in Jerusalem, from which Jesus did not appear to win any followers.

Similarly, John describes Nicodemus as a Pharisee and a leader of the Jews in Jerusalem (John 3:1). Nicodemus first comes to Jesus at night, indicating that he also is a disciple, though a secret one because of his fear of his fellow Jews. The question then arises as to how these two men, who hide their allegiance to Jesus during his life out of fear of persecution, come to have the courage publicly to ally themselves with Jesus after he is condemned by the Jews and executed by the Romans. The answer that John seems to suggest is that the saving power of Jesus is even more effective after Jesus is dead than it was during his life—as Jesus told Nicodemus himself in their first meeting at night: "And just as Moses lifted up the serpent in the wilderness, so must the Son of Man be lifted up, that whoever believes in him may have eternal life" (John 3:14). Thus the death of Jesus shows its power by drawing unto him two prominent Jews who saw firsthand that both the Romans and their own people would seek to kill anyone who followed Jesus, thinking in so doing that they were "offering worship to God" (John 16:2).

This narrative thus raises the question posed by Bultmann as to whether the resurrection narrative should even be considered as an original part of the Gospel of John. After all, the decision of Joseph and Nicodemus to make a public profession of their faith and discipleship takes place when Jesus is indisputably dead, not after he is attested to be raised from the dead. All that Joseph and Nicodemus can see is that Jesus is dead, and they already know that both their own people and the Romans will seek to kill anyone who professes faith in him. They do not wait until they can see that their venture of faith will be guaranteed to succeed in light of the resurrection of Jesus but rather believe his message that the eternal life he came to offer is most powerfully effective when he is raised up on the cross, in spite of the fact that this guarantees that their own lives will likely be lost for the sake of his name.

After all, if Jesus is loved by God and shows the complete extent of his love for the world precisely when he lays down his life of his own accord, how could it be otherwise than that his followers would show their love for him and for one another by laying down their lives for the sake of his name?

RANDALL C. ZACHMAN

PASTORAL PERSPECTIVE

The times when the four Gospels agree on tidbits of data are few, and the description of the burial of Jesus is one of them. The agreements are incomplete, however. The Synoptic Gospels agree that the tomb was "hewn from rock." Matthew, Luke, and John state that the tomb was "new," or "one in which no one had ever been laid." All the Gospels agree that the body was "wrapped" or "wound" in linen cloth but use different verbs and nouns—just enough to keep the Shroud of Turin a slim possibility, but not nearly enough to support its historicity.

John adds that Nicodemus came also and anointed the corpse with one hundred pounds of spices (Mary Magdalene comes alone in John 20:1). The only real point of complete agreement is that Joseph of Arimathea (a village we know nothing about, historically or archaeologically, with any certainty) took responsibility for the burial. Joseph offered Jesus the tomb he had prepared for himself.

We know as little about Joseph as we do about the village he came from. We surmise he was wealthy, and Mark 15:43 tells us he was "a respected member of the council, who was also himself waiting expectantly for the kingdom of God," whose devotion to Jesus was such that he "went boldly" to Pilate asking for the body. Given Joseph's status in the community, asking for the corpse of an executed criminal was indeed bold, but not so much in the face of Pilate as before the community as a whole. By honoring the body of Jesus, Joseph risked bringing dishonor upon himself. Courage, surely, was not the only motivating virtue or emotion. Grief, respect, and, if faint, hope, were all mixed in. Was Joseph much different from any who grieve the loss of one they love?

Joseph offered Jesus the tomb he had prepared for himself. Where is that tomb? If you come to Jerusalem, you have to pick between two tombs, the Church of the Holy Sepulchre, established in the early fourth century, and the "garden tomb" identified a century or so ago. They are less than a mile from each other, but could not be more different—Holy Sepulchre crowded and crumbling with competing communions, the garden tomb surrounded by a bus station on three sides and an ominous "Skull"-ish-looking rock formation on the fourth. I have no idea how pilgrims who visit both sites on the same day make any sense of the competing histories and ecclesial ideologies.

Does it matter which is the "real" tomb? No. The surprising thing to Holy Land pilgrims may be that there are only two to choose from. There is a larger distinction for the preacher to consider, between a "geography of spirituality" and a "geography of faith." Competing holy sites, like differing pieties, hymnody, and liturgy, are more about spirituality than faith. The Lutheran may sing a different tune or stand in a different posture from that of her Pentecostal sister, but they share the same Lord. We express, form, and grow the one true faith in a variety of modes. What matters is not that we know where the tomb is, but that we know there was a tomb. Today is about that knowing, as discomforting as it may be.

Joseph offered Jesus the tomb he had prepared for himself. For many gathered on Holy Saturday, the issue is profoundly similar: what do I need to bury so that I may be prepared for the new day promised me in Jesus' name? There is a powerful pastoral reality to Holy Saturday, the reality of absence, in the mystery and contradiction of the tomb. Few traditions have liturgies for Holy Saturday; even fewer have well-attended services. Easter egg hunts abound. Good liturgy not so much. In my own tradition the liturgy for Holy Saturday requires one page, and half of it is instructions. One instruction, the first one, jumps off the page. *There is no celebration of the Eucharist on this day.*[7] Holy Saturday is the only day on which the sacrament is specifically not offered, the "reserve sacrament" remaining from Maundy Thursday consumed on Good Friday.

On Saturday there is nothing left but death and tomb. Who comes to worship that? The faithful. They may be there only to complete all corners of the Triduum, the great three days of Holy Week; but however few, if you are preaching to them, your challenge is to find a way to bless them and their devotion. The temptation to be avoided above all others is the temptation to resolve the tension and gloss over the emptiness of this particular, peculiar day. On this Saturday there is nothing left but death and tomb. Do not roll away the stone. Today is not supposed to be easy, the story so hard to tell that John seems to give it backwards, mentioning the tomb as an afterthought: "Now there was a garden in the place where he was crucified, and in the garden there was a new tomb in which no one had ever been laid. And so, because it was the Jewish day of Preparation, and the tomb was nearby, they laid Jesus there" (vv. 41–42).

Joseph offered Jesus the tomb he had prepared for himself and invites us to ask what we may need to bury on Holy Saturday. There is nothing easy about death and tomb and stone. There is nothing easy about this day. There is only waiting.

O God, Creator of heaven and earth: Grant that, as the crucified body of your dear Son was laid in the tomb and rested on this holy Sabbath, so we may await with him the coming of the third day, and rise with him to newness of life; who lives and reigns with you and the Holy Spirit, one God, for ever and ever. Amen.[8]

WILLIAM F. BROSEND

7. *The Book of Common Prayer* (New York: The Church Hymnal Corp., 1986), 283.
8. Ibid.

The Burial of Jesus

	John 19	Matthew 27	Mark 15	Luke 23
1. *Time:* Day of Preparation	vv. 42, 14	vv. 57, 62	v. 42	vv. 54, 56b
2. *Place:* tomb	vv. 41–42	v. 60	v. 46	v. 53
3. *Agent(s):* Joseph and Nicodemus	vv. 38–39	vv. 57, 59–60	vv. 43, 46	vv. 50–51
4. *Authority:* Pilate's consent	v. 38	v. 58	vv. 44–45	v. 52
5. *Implements:* various	vv. 39–40	v. 59	v. 46	v. 53
6. *Observers*	None	vv. 56, 61	v. 47	vv. 49, 55
7. *Other Details:* burial customs	vv. 38, 40	vv. 60, 62–66	16:4, vv. 44; cf. v. 5	vv. 46, 56

As in the Synoptic Gospels, John's description of the burial creates smooth transition between the death of Jesus and the empty tomb. In narrative detail the Fourth Gospel is among the simplest. Less is said about Joseph of Arimathea than in the Synoptics. Though a woman will be first to report the tomb's emptiness (20:1–3), the women do not witness the body's interment in John. That item's omission might suggest that the Fourth Evangelist and his community were less concerned than others in fending off accusations that the tomb was found empty for reasons simpler than Jesus' resurrection: that the women went to the wrong grave, for instance, or that the body was stolen (esp. Matt. 27:62–66).

Nevertheless, John develops other details. Most obvious is reference to Joseph's "fear of the Jews" (19:38), a recurring theme in this Gospel (7:13; 9:22; 20:19). As Luke clearly knows (23:50), Joseph himself is Jewish, as are the Galileans in John 7:1–13 and Jesus' own disciples in 20:19–23. The term "the Jews" is John's shorthand for authoritative Pharisees and Sadducees who oppose Jesus because he has acted and spoken as though "equal with God" (5:15–18). Those Jews in John who believe in Jesus fear the consequences of openly expressing their faith (7:10–13; 9:18–23; 16:1–4a). While

John does not describe him as an influential person, Joseph of Arimathea is among those fearful disciples of Jesus who have kept their allegiance a secret (12:42–43). Here (19:39) Joseph is joined by Nicodemus, whom we meet only in John: a Pharisaic Jewish authority who earlier had paid a night visit to Jesus and had professed him "a teacher . . . come from God," as suggested by the signs Jesus had done (3:1–2).

The position of Joseph and Nicodemus in this Gospel is obscure. On the one hand, they have been drawn together and to Jesus by his death (see 12:31–33), giving the teacher's body an appropriate burial (19:40b, 42). On the other hand, Nicodemus had been left "in the dark" by Jesus (3:3–10; 19:39: "by night"), while only now does Joseph appear, covertly conducting his negotiation with Pilate (19:38). The penumbra occupied by the figures—notable in a Gospel that associates faith with "coming to the light" and unbelief with "love of the dark" (3:17–21)—is captured in their embalming technique, which is equally ambiguous. Although a Roman pound (*litra*) weighed less than that used by modern Americans (11.5 versus 16 ounces), 1,600 ounces of blended myrrh and aloes is excessive preservative for the remains of a single person. It could be that they are offering Jesus a burial fit for the king that he is (1:49; 12:13, 15; 18:33, 37, 39; 19:3, 14–15, 19). On the other hand, by his own testimony, Jesus' kingship is not of this world (18:36). A hundred pounds of burial mixture could suggest lack of comprehension or belief that Jesus and his disciples will be raised from death (2:19, 22; 5:21; 6:39–40, 44, 54; 21:14).

While agreeing with Luke (23:53) that Jesus' remains were put in a tomb where no other body had ever been buried, John alone notes that the grave was new, or fresh (*kainon*, 19:41). Though left undeveloped, this detail chimes with some others in this Gospel. The commandment Jesus gives his disciples on the eve of his death is equally new (*kainēn*: 13:34). The hour of the Son's glorification by the Father has been described as the falling of a grain of wheat into the earth, a death that bears much fruit (12:23–24). Fruit is found in gardens; John alone locates Jesus' fresh grave in a garden (19:41; cf. 20:15). In any case Jesus' grave will not be like that of Lazarus, who was called out of one tomb only to enter another (11:43; 12:9–10).

C. CLIFTON BLACK

HOMILETICAL PERSPECTIVE

Holy Saturday (in Latin, *Sabbatum Sanctum*), the "day of the entombed Christ," is the Lord's day of rest, for on that day Christ's body lay in his tomb. This is a day where grief is given space to settle into the hearts of the disciples as they lay Jesus' bones to rest. Hence the tone of the sermon, like that of John's text, is one of reflective sadness and controlled grief. It is controlled because this is a day suspended between two worlds, between darkness and light, between death and resurrection. Thus this sermon that takes place between the hours of Good Friday and Easter Day gives voice to the finality of death, even as we wait for the inauguration of a new era made possible on the day of Christ's resurrection.

Because Holy Saturday provides its own theme and focus, let us look at a few things to avoid before we look at some ideas to consider for the sermon.

First, avoid preaching hope. On this particular occasion, the church is given permission to mourn. There is a somberness that comes with waiting at the tomb. Ours is not a culture that grieves with ease. We resist death, trying to prevent it at all costs. When death does occur, we do not know what to do or how to respond so that we may skip over it too quickly.

Do not let the sermon follow this reluctance. Christ is dead. John's text gives no hint of hope and does not try to hide from the reality of Jesus' death with a false sentimentality. The sermon needs to stay close to the tomb, just as John's witness does.

Second, avoid trying to solve the problem of death. If we follow the text from John, the disciples go about their work of preparing Jesus' body with a sad seriousness. The text does not luxuriate in asking why Jesus is dead. Holy Saturday is the silence between notes. Resist the temptation to find resolution in this hour between death and resurrection. This is not a day to find answers. It is a day to take seriously the reality of Christ's human mortality, without trying to answer the problem of his death.

Third, avoid saying too much in the sermon. Ideally, Holy Saturday should be the quietest service of the church year. Though the sermon is a time to speak, it is not a time to be chatty or garrulous. The occasion is sober, and the sermon needs to reflect and honor this mood. As when a friend dies, it is better to sit in silence than to say too much. The general rule for preaching on Holy Saturday is that less is more. Hence, the sermon for Holy Saturday may ruminate and embrace silence, giving the hearer permission to contemplate a world fallen under the spell of death's finality.

With these few suggestions about what to avoid in mind, let us consider a few ideas that may help a sermon take shape.

First, let the sermon give voice to the world's sadness. Preaching, like other forms of leadership, is about naming reality. This is a day to name the reality of death. This is not a time to hide from grief, but to gaze into its face. Take one of the characters, such as Joseph of Arimathea or Nicodemus (or even Pilate), and follow him, allowing the congregation to overhear as he moves through the story.

Everyone, at one point or another, will go to the tomb—and the feelings associated with it are as real as they are universal. Holy Saturday offers the preacher an opportunity to name a grief that touches all. Jesus is dead, and those who do the work of last rites do so in the belief that the story is finished. John's testimony to Jesus' burial is sharply factual and does not give into emotional melodrama, yet there is a deep sadness behind these words that is felt. The same should be true of the sermon.

Second, it may be wise to reflect on the significance of the ritual of Jesus' burial. This will allow the congregation to contemplate their own customs. Many of us, even in churches, have lost any sense of proper rites for the dead. There is a methodical nature to John's description of the preparation of Jesus' body for the tomb. Joseph and Nicodemus give Jesus an honorable burial, according to Jewish custom, and they seem to spare no expense. They bring for his embalming a vast quantity of spices that would befit a king (cf. 2 Chron. 16:14). This good work must be done before the Sabbath begins.

What are the rituals and customs of your congregation when someone dies? Is there a way to reflect on those who have died in the past year, reflecting on the preparation for grief you have done with your congregation? What might we learn about how to do this in our own churches from the way Jesus was buried?

Third, allow the form and language of the sermon to reflect the aesthetic mood of the service. Holy Saturday is intended to be one of the most contemplative services in the church cycle. The aesthetic of this service is typically marked by a stark and Spartan mood. There are no flowers, banners, or even musical instruments. The text is not hurried and should be read slowly, with long pauses along the way.

The same mood should be reflected in the tone and tenor of the sermon. On this day, as on no other, we are invited into the profound silence of God, whose Son Jesus lies buried in a tomb. This is the reality we can perceive from this side of Easter.

TRYGVE DAVID JOHNSON

Acknowledgments

M aterials in this volume were drawn from *Feasting on the Word: Preaching the Revised Common Lectionary*, edited by David L. Bartlett and Barbara Brown Taylor, and *Feasting on the Word Worship Companion*, edited by Kimberly Bracken Long.

Midweek homily credits:
Week 1: Nick Carter and Thomas W. Currie
Week 2: Kimberly M. Van Driel, Patrick J. Willson, and
    Sharon H. Ringe
Week 3: Darryl M. Trimiew and Daniel M. Debevoise
Week 4: Jeffery L. Tribble Sr., Lori Brandt Hale, and
    Kimberly M. Van Driel
Week 5: Jane Anne Ferguson
Week 6: Joseph S. Harvard
Week 7: Donald K. McKim, Larry L. Lyke, and
    William Joseph Danaher Jr.

Prayers and liturgical material were written by Kimberly Clayton, David Gambrell, Daniel Geslin, Kimberly Bracken Long, L. Edward Phillips, Melinda Quivik, and Carol L. Wade, with Jennifer Carlier, Marissa Galvan-Valle, Kathryn Schneider Halliburton, L'Anni Hill, Jessica Miller Kelley, Elizabeth C. Knowlton, Franklin Lewis, Elizabeth H. Shannon, and Margaret LaMotte Torrence.

Children's sermons were written by Carol Wehrheim and Jessica Miller Kelley.

Scripture Index